Studies in Educational Leadership

Volume 24

Series Editors

Kenneth A. Leithwood, Toronto, ON, Canada
Qing Gu, School of Education, University of Nottingham, Nottingham, UK

Leadership we know makes all the difference in success or failures of organizations. This series will bring together in a highly readable way the most recent insights in successful leadership. Emphasis will be placed on research focused on pre-collegiate educational organisations. Volumes should address issues related to leadership at all levels of the educational system and be written in a style accessible to scholars, educational practitioners and policy makers throughout the world. The volumes - monographs and edited volumes - should represent work from different parts in the world.

Please contact Astrid Noordermeer at Astrid.Noordermeer@springer.com if you wish to discuss a book proposal.

More information about this series at http://www.springer.com/series/6543

Rose M. Ylimaki • Lynnette A. Brunderman
Editors

Evidence-Based School Development in Changing Demographic Contexts

 Springer

Editors
Rose M. Ylimaki
Department of Educational Leadership
Northern Arizona University
Flagstaff, AZ, USA

Lynnette A. Brunderman
Education Policy Studies and Practice
Department
University of Arizona
Tucson, AZ, USA

ISSN 1572-3909   ISSN 2543-0130   (electronic)
Studies in Educational Leadership
ISBN 978-3-030-76839-3   ISBN 978-3-030-76837-9   (eBook)
https://doi.org/10.1007/978-3-030-76837-9

This Springer imprint is published by the registered company Springer Nature Switzerland AG
The registered company address is: Gewerbestrasse 11, 6330 Cham, Switzerland

For the late Jeffrey Bennett, our colleague, dear friend, and co-founder of AZiLDR, whose scholarship and commitment to building leadership capacity in school development lives on in this volume.

Foreword

This book takes on the longstanding and "wicked" problem of school improvement. At the core of this problem is the interaction between students (their understandings, capacities, aspirations and dispositions) and their experiences in schools. These experiences are shaped - but not determined - by their teachers, peers, families, classroom and school structures and wider communities. In the face of the enormous potential diversity on both sides of this interaction is society's expectation that, somehow, all students will achieve (among other unpredictable things) a common core of outcomes. Logically speaking, this is an entirely irrational expectation and the extent to which it is realized stands as something of a taken-for-granted miracle.

Achieving this miracle becomes more likely, we are to believe, when teachers and school leaders do things certain ways, when district leaders provide certain forms of support, when policy makers establish certain systems of sanctions, rewards and the like. All the while, these certain ways of doing things, forms of support and systems of sanctions and rewards are variously ignored (often for good reasons) or under constant refinement, debate, critique and re-formation. Achieving the miracle, one might easily conclude, stands no chance absent an innate disposition on the part of children to learn from social interaction.

So, that is one perspective on why the school improvement problem is "wicked"; it can sometimes be reduced in complexity and made easier to understand. Occasionally someone even hits a home run. But is never going to be "solved" in the typical meaning of the term. Just because the problem is wicked, however, does not mean we have the choice of not working on it. Taking on this problem, the best way we know how, is a requirement not an option, for all of us working in and around schools.

This book provides a well-informed, historically grounded account of the current state of school improvement know-how and illustrates it with an impressive series of attempts carried out in the significantly different international contexts including the US, Sweden, Australia and Germany. The challenges associated with school improvement in culturally diverse contexts and with traditionally underserved students are foundational concerns throughout the book. Central to these concerns is the tension between the (often neo-liberal) evidence-based improvement policies designed for large-scale implementation across widely different contexts and the legacy of reform represented by Dewey's (progressive) approach to democratic education, the humanistic values it reflects and its emphasis on an image of the educated person as a self-directed problem solver.

While the book describes multiple, nationally diverse approaches to school improvement, the illustration that most closely reflects principles explicitly guiding the book is provided by the lead authors' own work with schools in Arizona, the Arizona Initiative for Leadership Development and Research (AZiLDR) project. Leadership teams, culturally responsive forms of pedagogy and formative data collection guiding improvement processes were central features during the three cycles of project implementation which closely resembled a Learning by Design process.

The book's extended account of this project, including its extension into two projects in South Carolina, offers important insights into processes that enhanced the relevant capacities of school and district leaders. This account also shows how robust research can be used effectively, illustrates the uses of local evidence to guide school improvement decision making and demonstrates one approach to nurturing the development of culturally responsive pedagogy in classrooms.

Chapters describing improvement efforts in non-US countries provide especially powerful insights about the importance of both individual and distributed forms of school leadership and how such leadership can be developed. The book also offers important insights about the nature of productive school-university partnerships.

Emeritus Professor, University of Toronto   Kenneth Leithwood
Toronto, Canada

Acknowledgements

The work that has inspired this book has been encouraged by many individuals and agencies from the field. From the Arizona Board of Regents, who provided initial funding, and the Arizona Department of Education, who allowed us to provide services to schools through school improvement funding, to the many school principals with their teams of teachers and district representatives, we offer our thanks for the support. Specifically, we thank Olof Johansson who inspired the concept of working with schools on improvement efforts during the research and practice conference hosted at Umeå University for the International School Principalship Project. We thank Ron Marx and Bob Hendricks for the organizational support from the University of Arizona as this work was initiated. We also thank our colleagues from both the University of Arizona and the University of South Carolina who struggled with us to complete grant applications to continue funding the work. And we must also thank our colleagues from our sister state universities, Arizona State University and Northern Arizona University, for their work with us on the initial stages of the project as well as their continuing support and encouragement, often serving as a sounding board.

Finally, we would be remiss if we did not thank the individuals who worked hard during the project to make sure that the institutes and regional meetings were successful. Our deepest thanks are extended to Maria Menconi, for without her expertise, we would not have survived. Also, we thank all of the presenters who facilitated different sessions throughout the project, those individuals who served as regional directors, the district personnel who supported the efforts, and the graduate assistants who also attended and did much of the work in the background. It is with sincere gratitude that we recognize the efforts of so many who believe in continuous school improvement and were willing to try something different in support of that goal.

Contents

Part I
Changing Context for School Development and Description of the Model

This part features an analysis of the contemporary situation for school development amidst evolving policy demands for improved academic outcomes and equality, recent neoliberal policy pressures for open-market competition, and the need to educate increasingly culturally diverse, students throughout the world. We refer to these tensions and challenges as the Zone of Uncertainty for educators and policy-makers. More specifically, we review and consider popular school development models designed to meet policy demands for strong evidence about what works to improve or turnaround failing or persistently underperforming schools. Here we consider U.S. research grant demands for What Works and the institution of the What Works Clearinghouse for generalizable research-based models with strong evidence from experimental or randomized controlled trials. As we see in subsequent chapters, literature on school turnaround models from the U.S. and similar models in the U.K. have informed school improvement work in other national contexts, such as Germany. Our review of the literature from popular school turnaround models indicated a number of strengths and limitations as well as the need for a new approach with a balanced view of evidence grounded in education and culturally diverse values in schools and communities throughout the world. The context then frames a new approach to school development in Arizona, the Arizona Initiative for Leadership Development and Research (AZiLDR).

Chapter 1
School Development Approaches Over Time: Strengths, Limitations, and the Need for a New Approach

Rose M. Ylimaki and Lynnette A. Brunderman

Abstract Across the globe, we observe policy trends towards evidence-based school development, "scientific" research, and increasingly centralized curriculum, all occurring amidst growing digitalization and demographic changes resulting in increasingly pluralistic schools and communities. As a result of these policy pressures, many universities and other educational organizations have proposed various evidence-based school development models or projects aimed at continuous improvement. In this chapter, we contest evidence produced from quasi-experimental research designs with other empirically tested evidence. We critique several established school development programs across the U.S. Finally, we propose that in order to have school capacity for continuous development, we need a school development process that is contextually-based and able to consider, reflect upon and use data from evidence-based programs and other sources as appropriate for school-identified problems, and that schools must be able to evaluate their own programs and processes in their particular contexts, with particular populations. For this, we need school development grounded in understandings of education and leadership as well as evidence. For our purposes, we define school development as a continuous growth process for school teams supporting education amidst tensions between policy expectations for use of research-driven evidence and the needs of students in increasingly diverse contexts.

Keywords Global policy trends · Cultural diversity · Democratic and humanistic values · School development

R. M. Ylimaki (✉)
Northern Arizona University, Flagstaff, AZ, USA
e-mail: rose.ylimaki@nau.edu

L. A. Brunderman
University of Arizona, Tucson, AZ, USA
e-mail: lbrunder@arizona.com

© The Author(s) 2022
R. M. Ylimaki, L. A. Brunderman (eds.), *Evidence-Based School Development
in Changing Demographic Contexts*, Studies in Educational Leadership 24,
https://doi.org/10.1007/978-3-030-76837-9_1

The book is about leadership capacity for continuous school development and improved student outcomes for culturally diverse youth in traditionally underserved communities amidst the contemporary evidence-based policy context. Across the globe, we can observe policy trends toward evidence-based school development, instrumentalism, evaluation, "scientific" research, and increasingly national or centralized curriculum, all of which is occurring amidst growing digitalization with a knowledge economy as well as global and internal demographic changes toward increasingly pluralistic schools and communities. As a result of policy pressures on schools and related pressures on higher education to demonstrate impact of research, many universities and other educational organizations across the U.S. and elsewhere have proposed various evidence-based school development models or projects aimed at continuous improvement. While many of these projects or models have been empirically tested and are working toward a so-called gold standard of strong evidence, few have strong evidence from experimental design promoted in What Works Clearinghouse and a number of research grants. Approaches grounded in standards, assessments and other central regulations seek to manage school practice, but Bryk et al. (2015) and others argue that these solutions are often oversold, under-implemented, and soon replaced with little learned in the process. Closely related, other evidence-based practices for school development involve creating potentially effective and replicable programs, evaluating them (ideally according to What Works Clearinghouse in randomized controlled experiments) and providing incentives for schools to use those that are found to be effective. Rather, Bryk et al. (2015, p. 468–469) notes that while clinical trials are worth doing in education, they are a very slow and expensive process, and such studies are not likely to be the primary resource for improving schools anytime soon. Bryk et al. go on to argue that randomized trials may just report effect sizes, indicating that a program can work, but it may not show how to make it work reliably over diverse contexts and populations. Moreover, from our perspective, clinical trials do not take into account leadership capacity, teachers' pedagogical capacity, or increasingly diverse student needs and interests. In order to have school capacity for continuous development, we need a school development process that is contextually-based and able to consider, reflect upon, and use data from evidence based programs and other sources as appropriate for particular problems and conduct their own experiments or assessments about how programs and processes work in particular contexts and with particular populations. For this, we need school development grounded in understandings of education and leadership as well as evidence.

For present purposes, we define school development as a continuous growth process for school teams supporting education amidst tensions between policy document expectations for use of evidence from experimentally designed programs and the needs of students in increasingly diverse school contexts. This volume features an ongoing project developed for culturally diverse Arizona schools and most recently applied to the South Carolina context as well as similar school development projects in Australia, Germany, and Sweden. School development projects are considered in relation to current national and cross-national policy trends toward evidence-based policies and changing demographics and in relation to particular contexts. We conclude with our thoughts about the need for further work in the area of school development.

Evidence-Based Policy Trends

Historically in the U.S., policy documents under both Republican and Democratic administrations have supported the need for evidence from externalized evaluations (standardized assessment data) to guide school decisions. Additionally, since 2002, there has been a drastic rise in the call for education research funded by the Office of Educational Research and Improvement (OERI) that addresses causal questions using random assignment designs [prior funding for randomized controlled trials represented 5% of federal funding for education research compared to 75% by 2002 (Morrison, 2012)]. Currently, funding applications for U.S. Department of Education grants must include research designs that are based upon prior studies with "strong evidence" (explicitly defined by large-scale quantitative studies with randomized controlled trials or quasi-experimental designs). In the international arena, multinational organizations (the Organization for Economic Co-operation and Development (OECD) and the World Bank) have also made evidence-based policymaking a priority, both in their own work as well as for their members (Wiseman, 2010).

In recent years, we can observe global changes in educational policies and governance systems with increased curriculum centralization, the advent of externalized evaluation policies and the increasing scrutiny of educational organizations at all levels, particularly public schools. More specifically, many nation states, including the U.S., have experienced both increased centralization (e.g., curriculum, evaluations) as well as increased decentralization (school-based decisions about improvements). New bureaucracies have emerged in relation to neoliberal policies, all of which demand strong leaders who can mediate among many different (and sometimes conflicting) policies, diverse student needs, and democratic education values. Further, school leaders now must work collaboratively within and between governance systems or levels, balancing evidence-based values and the humanistic values of education for increasingly diverse students. In Fig. 1.1 that follows, we illustrate some of the historical policy changes that have affected schools and leaders in the U.S. and internationally.

As the timeline demonstrates, evidence-based policies are not entirely new, however the political pressures have created more stringent external oversight. We can observe that "new" evidence-based policies can be categorized in terms of three interrelated intents, (1) to measure school quality on standardized tests, (2) to create equality among schools, and/or (3) to increase state control of schooling (Wiseman, 2010). For a full discussion of recent evidence-based policy intentions, see Wiseman (2010).

The most popular reason for using evidence as a basis for policymaking is that evidence provides an indicator of quality in terms of how much someone has learned or how much impact a certain educational technique has on students (Wiseman, 2010). Here the underlying assumption is that the more students learn, the more they know. The more students know, the better their test performance (a key source of evidence) will be. The better the students' test performance is, the better the teacher or school is. Most often summative assessments in the form of

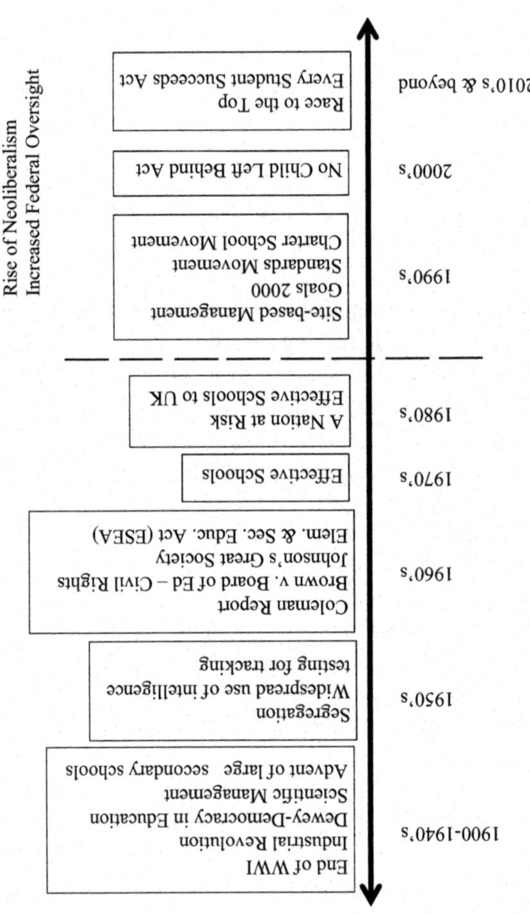

Fig. 1.1 Timeline of evolution of education trends and policies

norm-referenced standardized tests are used to summarize how well an individual or an organization is performing. This logic is flawed because these standardized assessments are normed on a bell curve designed to sort individuals; students with scores reflecting a single test question difference can be designated as deficient. Standardized tests are not designed to measure a student's mastery of content (e.g., Bond, 1995; Decker, 2008; Reynolds et al., 2010). Yet, summative assessments are a primary tool to measure educational quality and represent the final sum of knowledge that a student has been taught (or has learned) up to a particular point. It is important to note that with summative assessments, there is no opportunity for feedback, reflection, planning or further instruction to students. Moreover, norm-referenced standardized assessments have long been criticized for privileging children from White middle class households and communities (Reynolds et al., 2010). Yet the evidence resulting from their state, national or international test performance informs policymakers about the perceived quality of education.

In many nations, including the United States, there are a variety of external evaluations (state tests) given in different states and sometimes in different districts. For example, in Arizona, students currently take the AZMerit test of knowledge and skills. There is no longer a graduation exam[1] in Arizona, but some school districts additionally require all students to take the ACT exam. In South Carolina, beginning in grade 3, students take the South Carolina Palmetto Assessment of State Standards (SCPASS) in English/Language Arts, Mathematics, Science and Social Studies. The High School Assessment Program (HSAP) is first administered in grade 10, and South Carolina high school students must pass this test in order to receive a high school diploma. National tests, such as the National Assessment of Educational Progress (NAEP), provide nationally representative achievement information in core subjects. International assessments that are widely taken in many countries (e.g. PISA, TIMSS) have often driven national policy decisions toward an increased use of tests as evidence of school quality or success. Although there is a range in the extent to which the results of these assessments directly affect individual students, the average student scores for schools, districts, states and nations as a whole are widely accepted indicators of educational quality and have a major impact on educational policy-making (LeTendre et al., 2001).

The degree of equality attained in an educational system is another reason frequently cited for assessing the performance of students and schools. By seeing who performs highly and who does not, it is possible for teachers, administrators and policymakers to determine disparities among individual students, classrooms, and schools (Heilig and Darling-Hammond, 2008; Darling-Hammond, 2010). The logic behind using evidence to demonstrate equality suggests that policymakers can design policies and laws to close achievement gaps. For example, Arizona, like many other states, has a wide achievement gap between students from various social and economic groups. The state test (currently AZMerit) shows that this gap exists

---

[1] Arizona is in the process of changing vendors for a state test again. In the last 10 years, this will be the third test change.

and the extent to which it exists in particular content areas. Arizona politicians have used this evidence to reward high performing schools and to punish low performing schools. Analysis of standardized achievement scores clearly falls along socioeconomic lines across the nation (Perry et al., 2010; Baker and Johnston, 2010; Cunningham and Sanzo, 2002) and has contributed to the rise of charter schools, vouchers and public mechanisms to ensure greater equality among schools. Thus, politicians—with evidence from state tests— have passed legislation and policy targeting underperforming schools, requiring shifts in the curricular and classroom focus in order to close those achievement gaps. Under NCLB, if disaggregated data for each student subgroup (i.e., race, gender, language proficiency, etc.) do not demonstrate adequate yearly progress, then the U.S. Department of Education may withhold federal funding from the state or district within the state (McDermott and Jensen, 2005). In 2015, the reauthorization of NCLB resulted in the Every Student Succeeds Act (ESSA), which returned some control to states to determine their goals. Students are still required to be tested annually in grades 3 through high school, but the federal government removed many of the prescriptive pieces of the legislation (U.S. Department of Education, 2016). However, Arizona (as in many states) has not changed state legislation to reflect the greater flexibility of ESSA. It should also be noted that in Arizona, the state test was designed to have both criterion-references components and others that served as norm-referenced items by testing standards at, above, and below the grade level for which the test was designed.

Historically, federal and many state policy makers have attempted to address inequities through legislation. For example, the Coleman Report from the 1960s suggested that family and peer influences, not school resources, are the most important determinants of student performance (Baker and LeTendre, 2005). The Coleman Report was conducted in the wake of the court case *Brown vs. Board of Education of Topeka* that ruled that racial segregation of children in U.S. public schools was unconstitutional. "Evidence" from the landmark court decision and the latter Coleman Report changed the course of equity-driven policy-making in the United States and in many other countries. The Coleman Report was part of President Johnson's strategy in the Great Society program to level the playing field by identifying evidence of inequality in schooling. Coleman surveyed over 560,000 students across the U.S., a methodology partly due to the fact that the system was highly decentralized. And while recent externalized evaluation and curriculum policies have shifted toward centralization (e.g. Common Core curriculum), administration of education in the U.S. remains state-based. During the time of the Coleman Report, Johnson and other policymakers thought they could address inequality with additional resources for low-socioeconomic schools as a strategy for improvement. However, while they found unequal resources available according to class and race, Coleman's team found evidence that some equity indicators like resources did not predict achievement. Variations in family background and outside-of-school environment affected achievement at least as much as variations in school resources and quality. In other words, some policy impacts cannot be controlled by policymakers.

Closely related, Mexican American parents successfully sued school districts in California (Roberto Alvarez vs. the Board of Trustees of the Lemon Grove School District, 1931, and Mendez vs. Westminster, 1946), both of which attempted to segregate Spanish-speaking Mexican American students in inferior "Americanization" schools. The 1968 passage of the Bilingual Education Act (Title VII of the Elementary and Secondary Education Act) provided federal protections for culturally and linguistically diverse students. The Bilingual Education Act built from the *Brown v. Board of Education* case and the civil rights movement and promoted instruction that was both in a student's native language and culturally responsive. The act was far reaching, but it (and related state policies) remain at tension with the need to educate students in a common language and other common understandings and civic dispositions that create a nation state. For example, today's school leadership teams must balance tensions between recent shifts toward curriculum centralization in the Common Core (and state versions thereof) and related externalized evaluation policies designed to measure student performance.

Policy makers control school funding; at state and national levels, test results are increasingly tied to funding, with the most recent policy wave beginning with the No Child Left Behind Act and its requirement for schools to make adequate yearly progress. Because the U.S. Department of Education has the responsibility for evaluating schools' and states' performance, it can and does use test performance as evidence and a means to control the curriculum schools adopt, the content teachers teach and other components of schooling (Wiseman, 2010). Since the No Child Left Behind Act, schools identified as not making Adequate Yearly Progress (AYP) over a series of years have been in danger of losing federal funding, and as such this has become vital policymaking evidence for school systems in every state. Thus, some would argue that policymakers have opted toward evidence-based approaches over which they have control.

Globally, we can observe a policy convergence toward such compliance requirements, curriculum centralization and rankings for school quality and performance (Pilton, 2009; Steiner-Khamsi, 2006). As Pilton (2009) explained, there are several ways that policy convergence contributes to evidence-based policies, curriculum centralization, and comparisons or rankings of schools, states, and nations. One way is through imposition. Imposition is typically a result of political demand or pressure (e.g. Organization for Economic Cooperation and Development/OECD agenda, World Bank) and requires compliance with international policy or institutional arrangements. There is no legal obligation to participate in the Programme for International Student Assessment (PISA) with OECD; however, at OECD urging, member nations comply with evidence-based policies. Further, as Meyer (1977) and other institutional theorists would argue, when OECD identifies nation states with "high performing" schools, others emulate these practices (e.g. centralized curriculum) as they are legitimized. Such evidence-based policy convergence also contributed to research trends in funding applications, particularly research methods that are considered "scientific" and measure what works to improve schools.

Research Trends

In the U.S., federal grants legitimize "scientific" research designs and methods similar to the medical field that measure various interventions aimed at improved student outcomes on standardized tests, including randomized controlled trials and quasi-experimental designs Since the No Child Left Behind Act in 2002, education research funded by the Office of Educational Research and Improvement (OERI) that addresses causal questions using random assignment designs increased from 5% to 75% (Morrison, 2012). In current funding applications for the U.S. Department of Education grants, researchers must demonstrate that their research designs are based upon prior studies with "strong evidence" explicitly defined by large-scale quantitative studies with randomized controlled trials or quasi-experimental designs that primarily measure what works in terms of gains in student outcomes. That is, federally funded research channels future research in a particular and similar direction, and this research is considered legitimate with "strong evidence".

A number of influential scholars have argued persuasively for the use of such evidence to inform educational practice. Slavin is one of the most frequently cited proponents for the use of research and practice similar to the medical field. Using his Success for All project as an example, Slavin (2010) argues for the importance of studies that seek to make causal conclusions that include correlational and descriptive dimensions as he used in Success for All, one of the innovations featured in What Works Clearinghouse with strong evidence of effectiveness. The What Works Clearinghouse is sponsored by the Institute of Educational Science to provide educators with interventions designed and tested with scientific research that demonstrates effectiveness to improve student outcomes. The push for evidence-based policies is evident around the world. As noted earlier, this trend of convergence toward evidence-based policies has particular contextual challenges in nation states with federal systems of education and in schools serving increasingly diverse populations of students.

Australia, Germany, and the United States have a history of a state-based system with regards to education, but all three countries are experiencing an increasing centralization of curriculum, accountability systems, and evidence-based policy trends. Sweden has a much longer history of a centralized national curriculum; however, recent national policy has shifted to focus on equity within and between schools and municipalities. All of these policy trends have developed amidst changing demographics. Australia, for example, has experienced changing migration patterns from Europe to Asia and Africa. Since the 1970s, Sweden, too, has experienced significant demographic changes due to immigration. Demographic changes in the United States are due to both population migrations and refugees, as well as internal demographic changes. In certain ways, globalizing trends toward centralized curriculum and accountability policies are at tension with the needs of increasingly diverse students in schools.

Education and Humanistic Values

While diversity has increased and changed since Dewey wrote *Democracy and Education* with his philosophy of education, we see parallels with the contemporary situation for continuous growth in school development. Over the course of his career, Dewey (1897a, b, 1916, 1938) encouraged continuous growth and lifelong learning. Dewey (1916) argued, in particular, that an education which only emphasizes the achievement of "external aims" hinders students' capacity for continuous growth and leads students to view schooling as something to end as quickly as possible. In terms of school development, this might suggest that reliance on evidence from standardized test scores, grades, school letter grades, etc. inhibit school teams' ability to evolve and grow, resulting in seeing school development as a destination rather than a journey. In contrast, in a Deweyan notion of education and democratic growth, experience is key and growth is a continuous lifelong venture. Additionally, for Dewey, reality is constantly changing and no one has a monopoly on knowledge; this means that democracy requires everyone to continuously grow and adapt to changing conditions.

Dewey (1897/2000) sought to conceptualize education in an earlier time of social and political change. More specifically, Dewey (1900) discusses unifying the student with other students so that the school "gets a chance to be a miniature [democratic] community, an embryonic society. This is the fundamental fact, and from this arise continuous orderly sources of instruction" (p. 32). In our project, we incorporated these education theory perspectives and educative values for building leadership capacity in school development to include thinking, growth, reflection, and pedagogical interaction, as well as an emphasis on lifelong learning and growth. It is important to note that, like Dewey, we did not see the values as fixed but rather as guides to build leadership capacity.

It should also be noted that Dewey (1916) understood the significance, nature and utility of subject areas, or outcomes. In fact, in *Democracy and Education* (1916), Dewey addresses subjects such as geography, history, physical and social studies, as well as "play and work" and vocational aspects of education. He reinforces the aims of education for social direction, preparation, formation, and reconstruction. Thus, education is "based upon a consideration of what is already going on; upon the resources and difficulties of existing conditions" (p. 110), all of which require reflection and development or growth (democracy). More recently, Biesta (2010) renewed attention to democracy, critiquing contemporary "evidence-based" reforms and emphasizing how use of certain evidence-based programs threatens to replace professional judgment and the wider democratic deliberation about the purpose, outcomes and pedagogy of education. Biesta argues for a value-based education rather than an evidence-based education. "Calling the idea of value-based education an alternative is not meant to suggest that evidence plays no role at all in value-based education but is to highlight that its role is subordinate to the values that constitute practices as educational practices" (Biesta, 2010, p. 493). This project recognizes that education values, concepts and aims must interface with values and aims of educational organizations within increasingly diverse communities.

Changing Demographics

Currently, White people constitute the majority of the U.S. population (62%); however, the percentage is expected to fall below 50% by 2060 with Hispanic populations to experience the largest increase (Colby and Ortman, 2015). In Arizona, where we initially designed the school development project, Latino/Latina made up 31% of the population, but the traditionally marginalized non-White populations grew by 62.4% between 2000 and 2015 (Stepler and López, 2016). Poverty levels in Arizona averaged 16.4% with a range from 13.7% in Santa Cruz County to 36.2% in Apache County (Datausa, 2018).

In 2018, we extended the Arizona project to South Carolina, a southeastern U.S. state that has historically reflected a diverse population. At one time, South Carolina was recognized as a super-minority African-American state; current demographics continue to show increasing diversity with a rapidly growing Hispanic and refugee population (Colby and Ortman, 2015). In fact, South Carolina has seen the most rapid growth in Hispanic population of any state in the period between 2000 and 2010 (U.S. Census Bureau, 2011). During this 10-year period, the state saw a 147.9% increase in its Hispanic population (U.S. Census Bureau, 2011). Between 2000 and 2014 the Hispanic Population grew by 172% (Stepler and López, 2016). In addition to the shifting demographics, poverty levels remain high in South Carolina where 17.2% of children in the state live in poverty compared to 15.1% nationally (U.S. Census Bureau, 2018a, b). Minority and low-income students have historically been at-risk for school failure (Reardon et al., 2008). Student achievement data in South Carolina, including those high-needs schools along the I-95 corridor, corroborates the relationship between student demographics and student academic performance (South Carolina Department of Education, 2018).

Cultural diversity continues to bring multiple experiences, values, and views of knowledge to educational institutions and the academics within them. Since the 1960s there has been a significant increase in the number and diversity of immigrants coming to the U.S. The U.S. Census Bureau notes that the increasing number of international migrants will make the country "a "plurality" of racial and ethnic groups" (Colby and Ortman, 2015, p. 9). For example, the Hispanic population has grown from 6.5% of the U.S. population in 1980 to 17.6% in 2015 (Pew Research Center, 2015) while the Two or More Races population is projected to grow by 225% between 2014 and 2060 (Colby and Ortman, 2015). In the next section we consider the strengths and limitations of mainstream school development projects.

Strengths and Limitations of School Development: Research and Popular Models

Over the past five decades, school effectiveness and school improvement research has grown substantially around the globe. Many scholars, often in partnership with local school districts or municipalities, have designed and evaluated the effectiveness of various approaches to school development. Across the literature, we see an evolving approach to school development, beginning with an organizational health and development approach to studies of an application of findings from effective schools literature conducted in the wake of the Coleman Report, and a focus on change and comprehensive school reform to systems reform.

Early school improvement studies were most often aimed at *organizational* development, grounded in organizational theory (e.g. Lewin, 1947) as well as studies of effective schools (e.g. Edmonds, 1979). Lewin and others (e.g. McGregor, 1960; Miles, 1967) developed experiments to test the influence of the organization on group dynamics, culture and productivity. Miles (1967) applied concepts of organizational health to schools, looking at the relations between the organizational condition of schools and the quality of education they provide. His ten dimensions of organizational health included goals, the transmission of information, and the ways in which decisions are made, the effective use of resources, cohesiveness and morale, ability to deal with growth and change- notions of innovativeness, autonomy, adaptation to the environment and problem-solving. Early organizational development efforts were primarily focused on behavior changes aimed at efficiency with later studies to include an emphasis on how to "humanize" the organizational context. Here we see an emphasis on large-scale national reforms and school leader development (e.g. McLoughlin, 1990). Interestingly, scholars often provided evidence or feedback to school leaders and teachers in the form of survey results. Moreover, scholars who applied organizational development to education identified problems with top-down, externally developed projects that did not take into account the school context but contributed to understanding the leader's contribution to curriculum, instruction, and organizational change.

Although the U.S. Supreme Court's decision in *Brown vs. Board* did not achieve school desegregation on its own, the ruling (and steadfast resistance to it across the South and elsewhere) fueled the civil rights movement in the United States. As a prominent example, in 1955, a year after *Brown vs. Board of Education,* Rosa Parks refused to give up her seat on a Montgomery, Alabama bus. Her arrest sparked the Montgomery bus boycott that would lead to other boycotts, sit-ins and demonstrations, many of which were led by Martin Luther King, Jr.

We see evidence-based perspectives with less explicit attention to race and civil rights prominently displayed in later studies from the 1990s but these studies were influenced by the decentralization of schools and the increased prominence of site-based management in the U.S. and elsewhere. School development projects were frequently practitioner led during the 1990s in the UK and the US. During the 1980s, school-based review or self-evaluation became a major strategy for managing change and school development. The empirical support for school-based school reforms was mixed. For these reasons, school improvement during this time period was often seen as implementing an intervention or engaging in action research projects. In many countries, including the United States and Australia, it was also driven by federal funding to address passage of Title I legislation and Australia's mandate for school improvement councils. During this timeframe, in the United States, the publication of *A Nation at Risk* (1983) initiated what has become a widespread discourse about schools in need of improvements. For example, with this report, we see the earliest indication of the contemporary pressure toward externalized account-ability and change mandating school leaders to understand and apply concrete strat-egies for change for which they are held accountable.

Thus, in the early 1990s, in the U.S. and elsewhere, school development litera-ture focused on concrete strategies for the management and implementation of change at the school level. The emphasis on change emerged from previous research that indicated the need for more concrete approaches to school improvement as well as the increased need to prepare children for a world engaged in complex and rapid change. While earlier historical times also witnessed educational concerns about schools and education, this particular set of policies and resulting studies of school improvement focused attention on internal school practices in relation to the policy pressures. National policies (Goals, 2000) promoted the idea that school site-based management would free schools from the confines of external (district) control over substantive decisions and pedagogy. At the same time, national and state govern-ments assumed more control over school improvement efforts, a control that increased with the advent of comprehensive school reforms.

Some of these comprehensive school reforms included Levin's Accelerated Schools (1987, 1998) Comer's School Development Program (1996), and Slavin's Success for All (Slavin et al., 1996), mentioned earlier. These whole school design approaches combined elements from the school effectiveness and school improve-ment research and most often focused in varying degrees on school structures, inter-personal communications, professional development, explicit use of diverse measures of success, and curricula. Some whole school reform models, including Reading Recovery (Clay, 1993) and Success for All were approved for use in What Works Clearinghouse with versions of the models used in many different countries. This meant that schools could receive additional federal funding if they applied one of these particular reform models. Evidence to date indicates a mixed degree of effectiveness from these large scale, externally developed programs (Borman et al., 2003); however, others concluded that locally developed programs were even less likely to result in achieving initially desired outcomes (Nunnery, 1998). In particu-lar, success seemed to be much more elusive in large urban districts. Thus, and in response to the growing pressures for accountability from externalized evaluations and in response to international institutions and comparisons, school development approaches shifted toward system level change and building leadership capacity.

School development aimed at systems change and building leadership capacity for these changes focuses on collaboration and networking across schools and dis-tricts. These arguments were developed based upon research in the U.S., the United Kingdom (UK), and elsewhere. According to Harris and Chrispeels (2008) and oth-ers, district reform and network building, including professional learning communi-ties, need to occur simultaneously. The essential linkage is provided by an emphasis on building leadership capacity. Examples of such efforts include the National College of School Leadership in the UK (NCSL) and the Carnegie Foundation Project ILead in the U.S. In both of these approaches, the emphasis is on networking complemented by an increasing emphasis on leadership. Closely related, there is a growing body of research on school development and change, including Elmore's

(2004) study of successful school districts in California. In Elmore's (2004) study, participating schools showed a much greater clarity of purpose, a much greater willingness to exercise tighter controls over decisions about what would be taught and what would be monitored as evidence of performance, and a greater looseness and delegation to the school level of specific decisions about how to carry out an instructional program.

Stringfield and Yakimowski-Srebnick (2005) reported on district reforms in historically very low-performing, 90% minority Baltimore City Public Schools. Results from the Baltimore reform situation were mixed with early gains in student outcomes across most schools. However, as accountability systems and policies changed, the district and many of its schools situated in diverse, traditionally marginalized communities experienced many challenges. Early accountability systems did not produce measurable gains. Although some gains were made (graduation rates, outcomes), schools that had been reconstituted and turned over to for-profit management systems showed little to no gains, resulting in a need to be reconstituted again. Teachers and principals required additional professional development to gain skills in interpreting complex data. The study did not indicate any efforts to support teachers in terms of democratic values and practices or culturally responsive pedagogy in culturally diverse settings. Additionally, such reform efforts have not focused exclusively on the role of districts and local authorities in school development but also included other partners or entities, including state and/or national organizations and for-profit partners.

Hopkins (2011) summarized recent key variables in regional systems approaches to school improvement networks that contribute to student achievement. The variables were: (a) a clear and comprehensive model of reform; (b) strong leadership at the regional level; (c) substantive training related to the goals of the programme; (d) implementation support at the school level; and (e) an increasingly differentiated approach to school improvement. Across these studies and projects, the primary aim has been to link school improvement to student learning outcomes. We also see a strong focus on leadership with approaches focused on transformational leadership and change as well as instructional leadership (Leithwood et al., 2004) with more explicit attention to relations among multiple levels of leadership. Scholars are now working to understand the dynamics of improvement working simultaneously within and between levels (Barber, 2009).

Global Interest in School Improvement

Interest in school improvement knowledge is global, including understanding about how to mediate between international benchmarking and other evaluation policies and how to decide among strategies appropriate for both school and system reform (Hopkins, 2013). Here it is important to note that school development is a multi-level process, including the relations among individual schools and districts or municipal systems and state or nation-level systems (Datnow, 2006). Further, systems are culturally and historically situated; diverse nation states, nations and communities have, over time, developed very different systems for providing education to their children. Further, the systems and levers for systems improvement will vary greatly by national and local context. For example, in Hong Kong (Johnson, 1997), the state determines the core curriculum and the funding level per student. Under the state are a diverse series of school governing bodies, including churches, workers' unions, and so forth. The complexities of change in such a system are dramatically different from those of the United States. As noted in later chapters, schools and districts/municipalities vary considerably according to regional and state context as well as national context. At the same time, we can see growing similarities between school development efforts in Sweden, Germany, Australia and elsewhere. School development projects in these countries will be described later in this book.

Recent studies have examined highly effective educational systems across national contexts. According to Fullan (2009), Hargreaves (1982) and others, highly effective educational systems develop and disseminate clarity on goals and on standards of professional practice, ensuring that student achievement is the central focus of systems' schools; as a consequence, they (1) locate the enhancement of the quality of teaching and learning as central themes in systems improvement, (2) partially achieve their success through selection policies that ensure only highly qualified people become teachers and educational leaders, (3) put in place ongoing and sustained professional learning opportunities that develop a common practice, (4) emphasize school leadership and high expectations that focus on learning, (5) have procedures to enable this and provide timely data for feedback, (6) intervene early at the classroom level to ensure student performance, (7) address inequities in student performance through good early education and direct support for students, and (8) establish system-level structures that link together the various levels of the system and promote disciplined innovation as a consequence of thoughtful professional application of research. While these characteristics are helpful, they do not illustrate the complexity of systems change at multiple levels and in different contexts or the shift from implementation of standardized programs toward a new professionalism among leaders at different levels. Understandings of systemic school development continues to evolve and develop globally along with research understandings of how to scale reform.

Recent U.S. Leadership and School Improvement Programs

More current formal leadership development innovations or programs aimed at improvements in persistently underperforming schools promote such an evidence-based approach to effective leadership and school development, including most prominently the Virginia School Turnaround Specialist Program (STSP), the Mass Insight and Research Institute model based in New York, and the Chicago Reconstitution Effort. For example, the Virginia STSP is an intervention for principals with a focus on effective leadership practices with effective practices identified as mediators between leadership practice and gains in student outcomes, including data literacy, professional learning, motivation, and curriculum mapping as well as use of evidence-based strategies from the business field, including the development of a 90-day plan for rapid improvement, implementation support, long-term strategic planning and on-site visits. Since 2004, the Virginia STSP program has provided 95 principals with training in business strategies as well as individual coaching to school leaders in more than 82 school districts in numerous states, including Pennsylvania, Illinois, Florida, Missouri, Louisiana, Arizona, New Mexico, Nevada, Utah, Colorado, Texas, Ohio, and the Dakotas, as well as Virginia (Darden/Curry Partnership for Leaders in Education, ret. 2019). According to the Virginia STSP report (Harriman, ret. 2019), 46% of participants (44) made AYP compared to only 16% (15) prior to participation in the project.

The Mass Insight and Research Institute's project for rapid school improvement (Calkins et al., 2007) proposes a similar evidence-based focus on improvement but aligns schools and service providers into clusters of three to five low-performing schools. Districts and states commit to flexible operating conditions for zone schools with an emphasis on people (recruitment and retention), extended time, money or budget allocation, and program implementation of a rigorous standards-based curriculum and effective leadership practices (e.g. culture building, data literacy, professional learning communities). Results from the Partnership Zones indicated that two-thirds of participants reported gains and one-third reported declines in school performance. Researchers in the School Turnaround Group, a division of Mass Insight Education (2012), attributed the declines in performance to loose coupling between schools and districts.

Chicago's Academy for Urban School Leadership (AUS) drew on the Mass Insight project to improve student achievement in participating schools, including attention to positive school culture; parent engagement; setting goals; shared responsibility for achievement; standards-based, college-prep K–12 curriculum; aligned assessment systems; and engaging personalized instruction. Results indicated that some schools have attained high performance on district benchmarks; however, there were concerns about the sample of students included in the testing. Hood and Ahmed-Ullah reported that these schools have "pushed out the lowest performing children who could not attain the benchmark scores, thus artificially elevating their scores" (Hood and Ahmed-Ullah, 2012, p. 1). Surprisingly, despite the emphasis on instructional leadership in school effectiveness studies, education theory (Dewey, 1916, 1938; Slavin, 2008) with an emphasis on democratic growth and pedagogy has received little attention in educational leadership studies.

While not explicit, all of these innovations imply a primarily closed system for implementation of the innovation or program, meaning that if school leaders apply understandings from effective leadership and school development research within schools and decrease the use of other practices, schools will improve as measured on state tests. In these descriptors, we also see a void in the humanistic values of education and an ontology of education emanating from the later enlightenment and romantic heritage that impacted Dewey's early work (pp. 29–35). In other words, we see traditional education values and pedagogical methods that support being and becoming in a democratic way of living being replaced by numerical evidence-based values and data analysis methods that support the use of externally developed programs proven to improve student outcomes on standardized tests. Evidence-based programs value replication while Dewey values choice based on context and perspectives of the collective. Dewey values the process of growth (being and becoming) while evidence-based traditions value the outcomes. We return to this point in Chap. 6.

Moreover, despite recent demographic shifts, cultural relevance has not been explicitly addressed in the intervention models reviewed above. In other words, none of these popular evidence-based interventions explicitly considered the humanistic values of education for continuous growth and democracy. The project featured in this volume was designed to balance evidence-based values with the humanistic values of education for increasingly culturally diverse children in schools across the globe (Ylimaki et al., 2019).

In the remainder of this volume, we further highlight evidence-based policies in relation to democratic values in culturally diverse settings. Our discussion of evidence-based policy trends is culturally and historically situated. We then present lessons from school development projects, particularly including AZiLDR and lessons learned from that project as well as similar approaches across the globe. The volume concludes with implications for building capacity among scholars/researchers and practitioners in increasingly pluralistic and democratic communities with attention to leadership preparation, practice and policy.

References

Baker, M., & Johnston, P. (2010). The impact of socioeconomic status on high stakes testing reexamined. *Journal of Instructional Psychology, 37*(3), 193–199.

Baker, D., & LeTendre, G. K. (2005). *National differences, global similarities: World culture and the future of schooling*. Stanford University Press.

Barber, M. (2009). From system effectiveness to system improvement: Reform paradigms and relationships. In *Change wars* (pp. 71–94). Solution Tree.

Biesta, G. J. (2010). Why 'what works' still won't work: From evidence-based education to value-based education. *Studies in Philosophy and Education, 29*(5), 491–503.

Bond, L. A. (1995). *Norm-referenced testing and criterion-referenced testing: The differences in purpose, content, and interpretation of results*. ERIC.

Borman, G. D., Hewes, G., Overman, L. T., & Brown, S. (2003). Comprehensive school reform and achievement: A meta-analysis. *Review of Educational Research, 73*(2), 125–230.

Bryk, A. S., Gomez, L. M., Grunow, A., & LeMahieu, P. G. (2015). *Learning to improve: How America's schools can get better at getting better*. Harvard Education Press.

Calkins, A., Guenther, W., Belfore, G., & Lash, D. (2007). *The turnaround challenge*. Mass Insight Education and Research Institute.

Clay, M. M. (1993). *Reading recovery. A guidebook for teachers in training*. Heinemann.

Colby, S. L., & Ortman, J. M. (2015). *Projections of the size and composition of the US population: 2014 to 2060, current population reports* (pp. 25–1143). US Census Bureau.

Comer, J. P. (Ed.). (1996). *Rallying the whole village: The Comer process for reforming education.* Teachers College Press.

Cunningham, W. G., & Sanzo, T. D. (2002). Is high-stakes testing harming lower socioeconomic status schools? *NASSP Bulletin, 86*(631), 62–75.

Darden/Curry Partnership for Leaders in Education. https://curry.virginia.edu/faculty-research/centers-labs-projects/research-projects/dardencurry-partnership-leaders-education. Retrieved February 2019.

Darling-Hammond, L. (2010). Teacher education and the American future. *Journal of Teacher Education, 61*(1–2), 35–47.

Datausa. (2018). https://datausa.io/. Retrieved January 2019.

Datnow, A. (2006). Comments on Michael Fullan's, "The future of educational change: System thinkers in action". *Journal of Educational Change, 7*(3), 133.

Decker, S. L. (2008). Intervention psychometrics: Using norm-referenced methods for treatment planning and monitoring. *Assessment for Effective Intervention, 34*(1), 52–61.

Dewey, J. (1897a). My pedagogic creed. In *Curriculum Studies Reader* (2nd ed.). Routledge.

Dewey, J. (1897b). The psychological aspect of the school curriculum. In J. A. Boydston & F. Bowers (Eds.), *The early works of John Dewey 1882–1898: Vol. 5. 1895–1898.* Southern Illinois University Press. (Original work published in 1897).

Dewey, J. (1900). *The school and society.* University of Chicago Press.

Dewey, J. (1916). *Democracy in education.* The Free Press.

Dewey, J. (1938). *Experience and education.* Collier Books.

Dewey, J. (2000). My pedagogic creed (1897). *Philosophical Documents in Education, 2,* 92–100.

Edmonds, R. (1979). Effective schools for the urban poor. *Educational Leadership, 37*(3), 15–18.

Elmore, R. F. (2004). *School reform from the inside out: Policy, practice, and performance.* Harvard Education Press.

Fullan, M. (2009). Large-scale reform comes of age. *Journal of Educational Change, 10*(2–3), 101–113.

Hargreaves, A. (1982). The rhetoric of school-centred innovation. *Journal of Curriculum Studies, 14*(3), 251–266.

Harriman, D. *University of Virginia School turnaround report.* http://www.darden.virginia.edu/web/uploadedFiles/Darden/Darden_Curry_PLE/UVA_School_Turnaround/UVASTSPAnnualReport2008_Excepts.pdf. Retrieved February 7, 2019.

Harris, A., & Chrispeels, J. (Eds.). (2008). *International perspectives on school improvement.* Routledge.

Heilig, J. V., & Darling-Hammond, L. (2008). Accountability Texas-style: The progress and learning of urban minority students in a high-stakes testing context. *Educational Evaluation and Policy Analysis, 30*(2), 75–110.

Hood, J., & Ahmed-Ullah, N. (2012, February 6). School reform organization gets average grades. *Chicago Tribune Newspaper.*

Hopkins, D. (2011). *Powerful learning: Taking educational reform to scale.* Education Policy and Research Division, Office for Policy, Research and Innovation, Department of Education and Early Childhood Development.

Hopkins, D. (2013). Instructional leadership and school improvement. In *Effective leadership for school improvement* (pp. 65–81). Routledge.

Johnson, R. K. (1997). The Hong Kong education system. In *Immersion education: International perspectives* (p. 171). Cambridge University Press.

Leithwood, K., Louis, K. S., Anderson, S., & Wahlstrom, K. (2004). *How leadership influences student learning.* The Wallace Foundation.

LeTendre, G. K., Baker, D. P., Akiba, M., Goesling, B., & Wiseman, A. (2001). Teachers' work: Institutional isomorphism and cultural variation in the US, Germany, and Japan. *Educational Researcher, 30*(6), 3–15.

Levin, H. M. (1987). Accelerated schools for disadvantaged students. *Educational Leadership, 44*(6), 19–21.

Levin, H. M. (1998). Accelerated schools: A decade of evolution. In *International handbook of educational change* (pp. 807–830). Springer.

Lewin, K. (1947). Group decision and social change. *Readings in social psychology, 3*(1), 197–211.

Mass Insight Education. (2012). *The turnaround challenge.* http://www.massinsight.org/stg/research/. Retrieved April 16, 2019.

McDermott, K. A., & Jensen, L. S. (2005). Dubious sovereignty: Federal conditions of aid and the no child left behind act. *Peabody Journal of Education, 80*(2), 39–56.

McGregor, D. (1960). Theory X and theory Y. *Organization Theory, 358,* 374.

McLoughlin, J. (1990). *The demographic revolution.* Jane Hardback Book.

Meyer, J. W. (1977). The effects of education as an institution. *American Journal of Sociology, 83*(1), 55–77.

Miles, R. E., Jr. (1967). The case for a Federal Department of Education. *Public Administration Review, 27*(1), 1–9.

Morrison, K. (2012). *Causation in educational research.* Routledge.

Nunnery, J. A. (1998). Reform Ideologyand the locus of development problem in educational restructuring: Enduring lessons from studies of educational innovation. *Education and Urban Society, 30*(3), 277–295.

Perry, T., Moses, R. P., Cortes, E., Jr., Delpit, L., & Wynne, J. T. (2010). *Quality education as a constitutional right: Creating a grassroots movement to transform public schools.* Beacon Press.

Pew Research Center. (2015). *Population projections.* Retrieved at https://www.pewresearch.org/topics/population-projections/2015/

Pilton, J. (2009). *Policy convergence in education.* Unpublished manuscript, Lehigh University.

Reardon, S. F., Robinson, J. P., & Weathers, E. S. (2008). Patterns and trends in racial/ethnic and socioeconomic academic achievement gaps. In *Handbook of research in education finance and policy* (pp. 497–516). Routledge.

Reynolds, C. R., Livingston, R. B., Willson, V. L., & Willson, V. (2010). *Measurement and assessment in education.* Pearson Education International.

Slavin, R. E. (2008). Perspectives in evidence-based research in education – What works? Issues in synthesizing educational program evaluations. *Educational Researcher, 37,* 5–14.

Slavin, R. E. (2010). Experimental studies in education. In *Methodological advances in educational effectiveness research* (pp. 116–128). Routledge.

Slavin, R. E., Wasik, B. A., & Madden, N. A. (1996). *Every child, every school: Success for all.* Corwin Press.

South Carolina Department of Education. (2018). Retrieved at https://ed.sc.gov/

Steiner-Khamsi, G. (2006). The economics of policy borrowing and lending: A study of late adopters. *Oxford Review of Education, 32*(5), 665–678.

Stepler, R., & López, M. H. (2016). *US Latino population growth and dispersion has slowed since onset of the great recession.* Pew Research Center [Internet].

Stringfield, S. C., & Yakimowski-Srebnick, M. E. (2005). Promise, progress, problems, and paradoxes of three phases of accountability: A longitudinal case study of the Baltimore City public schools. *American Educational Research Journal, 42*(1), 43–75.

The National Commission on Excellence in Education. (1983). *A nation at risk: The imperative for educational reform.* The National Commission on Excellence in Education.

U.S. Census Bureau. (2011). Retrieved at https://www.census.gov/newsroom/releases/archives/population/cb12-tps83.html.

U.S. Census Bureau. (2018a). Retrieved at https://www.census.gov/programs-surveys/popest.html.

U.S. Census Bureau. (2018b). Retrieved at https://www.census.gov/topics/income-poverty/poverty.html.

U.S. Department of Education. (2016). *Every Student Succeeds Act (ESSA).* Retrieved from https://www.ed.gov/essa?src=rn, January 2020.

Wiseman, A. W. (2010). The uses of evidence for educational policymaking: Global contexts and international trends. *Review of Research in Education, 34,* 1–24.

Ylimaki, R. M., Brunderman, L., & Moyi, P. (2019). Balancing evidence-based and humanistic education in school development for underperforming Arizona and South Carolina schools. *Leadership and Policy in Schools.* https://doi.org/10.1080/15700763.2019.1695850

Chapter 2
A New Approach to School Development

Rose M. Ylimaki and Lynnette A. Brunderman

Abstract In this chapter, we further explore and contextualize school development amidst the tensions between contemporary policies and the educational needs of students. We conceptualize school development as a process that mediates among tensions that result in a Zone of Uncertainty. We then describe our application of school development in the Arizona Initiative for Leadership Development and Research (AZiLDR). Content was initially drawn from findings from the International Successful School Principalship Project (ISSPP) exploring leadership in high-needs, culturally diverse schools and related leadership studies. Our approach differs from other school development models in at least four ways. First, the approach is grounded in education theory as explicated by John Dewey and others. Closely related, our approach attempts to balance evidence-based values with humanistic values. Third, our approach is grounded in our empirical research and related studies of leadership in culturally diverse schools and communities. Fourth, our approach is process oriented and contextually sensitive for schools as they are situated in the larger community and serving culturally diverse populations. Finally, we develop leadership through a collaborative approach in that we work with school teams as a unit.

Keywords School development · Policy · Education theory · Research-based practice

In this chapter we further explore and contextualize school development amidst the tensions between contemporary policies and the educational needs of students. Figure 2.1 (below) illustrates our conceptualization of school development that mediates among tensions that result in a Zone of Uncertainty. As we described in

R. M. Ylimaki (✉)
Northern Arizona University, Flagstaff, AZ, USA
e-mail: rose.ylimaki@nau.edu

L. A. Brunderman
University of Arizona, Tucson, AZ, USA
e-mail: lbrunder@arizona.com

R. M. Ylimaki, L. A. Brunderman (eds.), *Evidence-Based School Development in Changing Demographic Contexts*, Studies in Educational Leadership 24,
https://doi.org/10.1007/978-3-030-76837-9_2

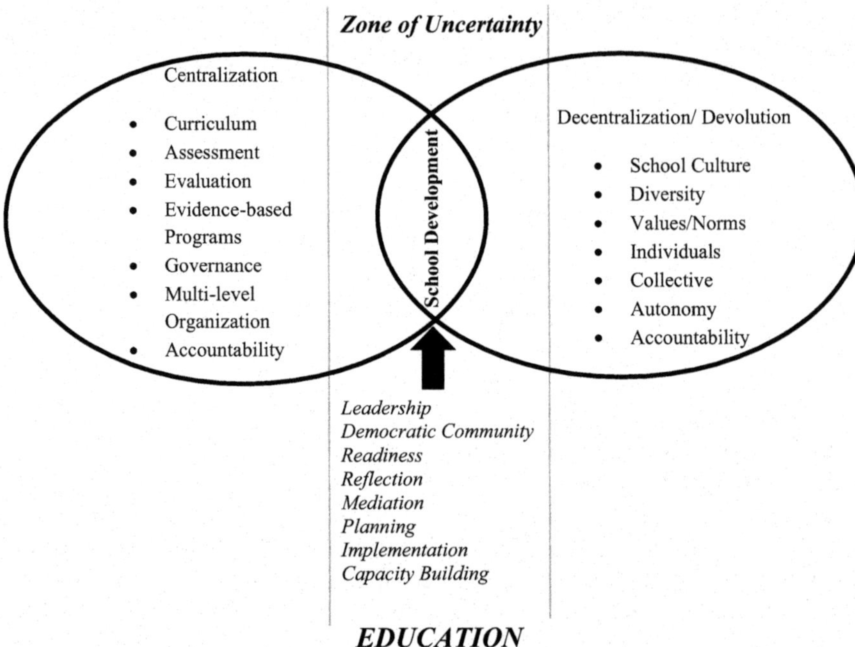

Fig. 2.1 Tension between Centralized and Decentralized Policies and Practices Research Base for School Development: ISSPP and Related Work

Chap. 1, school development is historically, culturally and politically situated. Contemporary policies have created new tensions between centralized expectations (e.g., curriculum, assessment, evaluation, evidence-based programs and governance) and decentralized trends that illuminate the importance of school culture, diversity, values/norms of individuals and groups. The policy trends toward curriculum and assessment centralization along with decentralization in school improvement efforts are common in many national contexts, including those highlighted in this volume. Mainstream school development approaches have been constructed to hold schools accountable and demonstrate evidence for quality and equality of outcomes as required by policy. The designers of these models recognize that schools must operate within what we refer to as the Zone of Uncertainty with its tensions.

Prior to our initial application of school development in the Arizona Initiative for Leadership Development and Research (AZiLDR), we had conducted research on principals in successful schools as part of the International Successful School Principalship Project (ISSPP) and related leadership studies. The ISSPP is a network of researchers from 27 different countries, including Sweden, Australia, and the United States. The methodology of the ISSPP includes (1) data collected from multiple perspectives (principals/headteachers, assistant principals, parents, students, support staff and teachers; (2) comparisons of effective leadership in diverse contexts ranging from small primary schools to large urban secondary schools, most of which were embedded in culturally diverse communities; and (3) the identification of principal/headteacher qualities and practices necessary but not sufficient for success in any school context. Case studies have been conducted in four strands, including a strand on leadership in high-needs, culturally diverse schools. Findings from those case studies from Arizona, other states, and other nation states were explicitly utilized for AZiLDR (e.g. Ylimaki et al., 2012; Bennett, 2012; Jacobson et al., 2005a, b; Gurr, 2015; Höög et al., 2005). Our approach differs in at least four ways. First, our approach is grounded in education theory as explicated by John Dewey and others. Second and closely related, our approach attempts to balance evidence-based values with humanistic values. Third, our approach is grounded in our empirical research and related studies of leadership in culturally diverse schools and communities. Fourth, our approach is process oriented and contextually sensitive for schools as they are situated in district, states, and nation-states and serving culturally diverse populations. Finally, we develop leadership through a collaborative approach in that we work with school teams as a unit.

Description of the Arizona School Development Project

The Arizona Initiative for Leadership Development and Research (AZiLDR) project also grew out of a desire to assist persistently underperforming, culturally diverse schools and to increase their capacity for continuous school development while mediating between policies and student needs. Our definition of school development again is a continuous growth process designed for school teams charged with education amidst tensions between the competing demands of tighter centralization and individual school needs. Leadership in our school development project is characterized by a leadership team approach. AZiLDR, thus, incorporated mechanisms to build leadership capacity among the team and others, and for diffusion of content and process throughout the organization. In addition, we purposely connected school leadership teams with district, regional and state leaders.

For our purposes, we assumed leadership capacity to be grounded in traditional humanistic values of education, as well as understandings about organizations and outcomes. In our design of the school development model (AZiLDR), we posited that school team members (teachers/administrator/coach/district representative) would function as a miniature democratic community, using evidence or data as a source of reflection and continuous growth for the organization. They would examine and make judgements about what worked in the past as well as trends across various sources of data in order to develop plans for future improvement, engage in change processes, and examine feedback on its effects. All of these leadership practices occur amidst the complexity and uncertainty of the contemporary policy and societal situation. Thus, leaders must not only mediate among policy, evidence-based values and humanistic education values to meet the needs of increasingly diverse students, but must also teach their school communities the meaning of the enacted policies, the needs of the students, how they are applying the policies, and how to think critically about policy implications for society. Unlike many dominant school development approaches, the AZiLDR approach focused explicitly on working with leadership teams, including formal leaders (principals, district leaders), state and regional leaders, as well as teacher leaders to build team leadership capacity with the ultimate goal of building whole school capacity.

Applying Dewey's arguments in *Schools and Society* (1907) and *The Child and the Curriculum* (1959) along with Biesta and Burbules (2003), we also highlight the tension between external and internal aims, further focusing on continuous growth for leadership teams as they engage in deliberations and pedagogical interactions for continuous school growth or development. At the same time, we recognized that school personnel bring their own individual habitus (Bourdieu, 1977) or funds of knowledge (González et al., 1995) to the democratic community deliberations (Eisner, 1979; Englund, 2006) and reflections around evidence and plans for growth (Ylimaki and Brunderman, 2019).

School members also bring conscious and unconscious biases to conversations, for example, around achievement gaps and racial inequities. In our model, therefore, we see education with (culturally responsive) pedagogical interactions and evidence-based interactions as interrelated. Thus, we incorporated understandings from culturally relevant leadership (Johnson, 2007; Khalifa et al., 2016) and funds of knowledge (González et al., 1995) along with our own evaluation results of the project (e.g. Ylimaki et al., 2014). For example, drawing on this body of research, we facilitated discussions and modeled ways that leaders could work with staff to identify inequities, disrupting the status quo, infuse students' cultural knowledge into the work of teaching and learning, and include parents and community leaders in the process of social change for the benefit of students.

In developing our model, we also used empirical research findings to inform the content provided to participants. Over time, many empirical leadership studies have focused on school and leadership practices that contribute to school development and ultimately student learning. Initially, we drew upon findings from the International Successful School Principalship Project (ISSPP) (Day et al., 2016; Gurr, 2015; Klar and Brewer, 2014; Drysdale et al., 2014; Ylimaki & Jacobson, 2013) that expanded the effective schools literature (e.g. Edmonds, 1979; Hallinger and Murphy, 1986; Purkey and Smith, 1982) to an international sample and to focus on the principal's leadership. Effective leadership studies (e.g. Edmonds, 1979; Hallinger and Murphy, 1986) provided important understandings about "best practices" common to schools that improved outcomes for all students regardless of socioeconomic status. These best practices included use of data for reflection, creating and maintaining a supportive school culture, building trust and relationships among all staff and with community, developing shared leadership team capacity, understanding motivation, and engaging professional learning communities focused on curriculum, instruction, and formative student assessments. Further, in light of increasing student plurality, the project considered studies regarding how to bridge students' funds of knowledge with academic knowledge (Moll et al., 2006), our previous studies of leadership in the sociocultural dimension (Ylimaki et al., 2012), leadership capacity at personal, interpersonal, and organizational levels (Bennett et al., 2013), and leadership as a multi-level pedagogical activity (Uljens and Ylimaki, 2017). Surprisingly, despite the emphasis on instructional leadership in the school effectiveness studies, education theory itself (Dewey, 1897, 1916, 1938) has received little attention. Additionally, despite global demographic shifts, cultural relevance has not been explicitly addressed in the intervention models reviewed in Chap. 1.

More specifically, the Arizona school development project was designed to provide district and school leaders with a sustained (18–36 months) process focused on curriculum/pedagogical work within and between school leadership teams, other teachers, and district and state leaders. The project conceptualized leadership as a shared, pedagogical, and often mediational activity within and between levels, grounded in trust, relationships, communication, and decision-making processes, all of which include using evidence (formative, external/summative) as sources of reflection. The project focused on three interrelated processes: (1) interpersonal, democratic (team member) interaction and reflection on content/pedagogy, (2) time for planning for diffusion of activities specific to the needs of each school site and (3) a research-based delivery system. It is important to note that we worked primarily with leadership teams that demonstrated a readiness to engage in this process; if the organizational culture was not developed to include open communication and trust, progress was slower. We worked with teams throughout the school development process to build collaborative processes and strategies to assist them at their school sites.

First, interpersonal interaction and reflection were integral components of the project, grounding the work accomplished by school teams. Teams received guidance in team development, reflection and mediation processes and conflict resolution skills. Time was provided throughout the project for team members to reflect at both the individual and team levels. Reflection was around the content they received as well as specific related issues at their own sites and ways to mediate those needs.

The second interrelated process centered on the planning stage. Teams were provided significant amounts of time to plan together to diffuse the content at their school sites. Additionally, using a structured planning and feedback cycle adapted from the Step-Back Consulting Model (Wagner et al., 2012), teams provided feedback to one another to enhance the refinement of their plans. During this structured feedback cycle, Team 1 presented their plan, then listened as Team 2 asked clarifying questions. Team 2 then considered the problem and plan as if it was their own, considering next steps, gaps in the plan, things to avoid, etc. During this time, Team 1 listened and took notes. Finally, Team 1 rejoined the conversation, reflecting on what they learned and how it felt observing another team take on their issue. Both teams together reflected on the implications that arose from the discussion, and prepared a written summary of the learning.

The third process was a research-based delivery system (Desimone, 2009). The delivery system featured direct instruction during institutes (10 days annually attended by all school teams), monthly regional network meetings for the purposes of both reflection and content follow-up, and in-school coaching and walk-through observations. Institute content was designed to address both the research-based best practices for school improvement and the information derived from the needs assessments completed by each school staff and the principals. Topics included, for example, professional learning communities, school culture, the state version of the Common Core (a national curriculum mediation), data as a source of reflection (i.e., survey results, summative/formative assessment data and other pertinent data), parent-community involvement, recognition of individuals, and culturally relevant practices. The ten institute days were distributed throughout the school year, thus providing sustained support. Institutes and regional meetings were experiential, modeling processes to intervene and mediate among common core standards, individual learner (student, teacher, leader) needs, and local school-community traditions. Importantly, institutes and other meetings also provided school team participants and district leaders with structured (discursive) spaces for dialogue and reflection within and between levels; time for school planning to diffuse the process and content was embedded within all meetings.

It is important to highlight the team composition throughout the project. Each school team was comprised of the principal, teacher leaders, the instructional coach (if applicable), and a district representative. Principals were encouraged to choose team members from the teaching ranks who had influence with their peers, representing a variety of experience levels and viewpoints. With the ultimate goal of diffusing the learning throughout the school as part of a microcosm of democratic education, this was imperative. The district representative was chosen in consultation with the superintendent; this individual was an integral part of the school team, offering insight and buffering them from competing district initiatives that could derail their progress. Additionally, regional coaches provided expertise to school teams, participating in all phases of the project. State representatives were also included in order to facilitate leadership team mediation with district and state policy.

The Arizona school development project was piloted and refined over several iterations. The racial/ethnic/gender demographics across phases are illustrated in Table 2.1.

During the initial project implementation (2011–12), schools were drawn from the statewide sample of Tier III[1] schools (252) with 45 schools selected for participation in the project. The selection was largely dependent on superintendent support and participant willingness to commit to all aspects of the project for the 18-month period. Schools were located throughout the state of Arizona. As indicated in Table 2.1, most principals had less than 3 years at their sites, with many in their first year.

Many lessons were learned from this phase of the project. Most participants were either single principal representatives from the schools or attending with one other teacher. At the initial Institute meeting, numerous attendees expressed that they did not know why they were at the training but had simply been told by their superintendents to attend. This lack of buy-in affected the retention rate of schools in the

---

[1]A Tier III school is defined as any state Title I school in improvement, correct action or restructuring as designated by the U.S. Department of Education (2009).

Table 2.1 Participants and demographics of schools served over three phases

	Phase 1	Phase 2	Phase 3
# Schools served	45	7	19
# Participants	80	35	101
% School-rural	56%	14%	53%
% Schools-urban	25%	72%	37%
% Schools-suburban	19%	14%	5%
% Community college	–	–	5%
Ethnicity—Latino/a/Hispanic			
Principals	27%	58%	57%
Staff	14%	32%	61%
Ethnicity—White			
Principals	60%	33%	43%
Staff	60%	68%	38%
Ethnicity—Native American			
Principals	11%	8%	–
Staff	3%	–	1%
Ethnicity—Other			
Principals	2%	–	–
Staff	23%	–	–
Gender—Female			
Principals	62%	25%	75%
Staff	74%	58%	88%
Gender—Male			
Principals	38%	75%	25%
Staff	26%	42%	12%
Principal tenure— <3 years	88%	17%	29%

project. Another aspect that impacted the retention rate was that many of the superintendents (who had agreed to the participation of their schools) mandated numerous competing initiatives that prevented those participants from fully attending and implementing what they were learning. Additionally, nationally recognized speakers were contracted to provide services at the Institutes throughout the project. Although they were well-received, participants were primarily passive recipients of information rather than active participants in processing and applying that information. Thus, moving forward, it was determined that school teams were critical to success, as was district representation on the team in order to mediate any competing demands of the district. Finally, Institutes were redesigned to provide work time for teams in order to process information and plan for dissemination and implementation at the schools.

The second pilot served seven school teams; each team was accompanied by at least one district representative. Teams ranged from four to six members, depending on the size of the school. As seen in Table 2.1, the majority of the principals in this study were experienced; in fact, 43% were near retirement with another 43% having between 5 and 10 years experience. This phase included state and regional representatives.

During this phase, in addition to offering Institutes, regional networking meetings were included and facilitated by project staff. This was designed so that teams would be supported at least monthly. The inclusion of the district representatives allowed teams to focus on the work without numerous competing demands. Additionally, the team structure ensured that the work of the team would be better diffused into the work of the entire school. It was determined through participant feedback and facilitator observation that more individualized coaching was needed to optimize the application of the learning at each site. It was also decided that group walk-through observations with immediate processing by multiple team members would facilitate understanding of instructional leadership.

The third phase of the project incorporated the team structure, district representation, team walk-through observations and processing, as well as individual site coaching visits. Prior to beginning the training, project staff met with each principal and district representative to assist them in determining the makeup of the school teams. Thus, each team was comprised of the principal, assistant principal if appropriate, instructional coach, and teacher leaders who had influence with the school staff. In this third phase, schools were located throughout the southern Arizona region, with 5% of the participants representing the local community college. Again, most of the administrators had a tenure of more than 3 years.

This group benefited from the team structure, regional networking groups with a facilitator, individual school coaching, facilitated walk-through opportunities, and district and regional representation. However, the large size of the group (over 100 participants) with 19 schools at different places in the development of school culture and trust, inhibited the individualized attention that they could receive. Thus, it was determined that a group size of 7–10 schools would be ideal.

Methods

Over the past 5 years, 71 Arizona schools participated in the project. Data collection and analysis has been ongoing. At the beginning of the project, participants took a survey (Bennett et al., 2013) modified by the authors as a pre-assessment prior to the beginning of the first training, and a post-assessment at the end of the project. Using this 181-item survey, the researchers examined principals' and teachers' leadership knowledge and practices essential for school turnaround, including principal-specific knowledge, skills and practices as well as capacity for progression through school development. Here, capacity was determined by the alignment between the principal responses and their staff perceptions of leadership skills and practice. All questions in sections 2–8 contain Likert-scale responses.[2]

---

[2] Both principal and staff surveys consisted of the same 137 Likert-scale items.

The principal survey was comprised of identical section content with the addition of one section that assessed the extent to which the principal perceived they demonstrated the practice of successful leadership characteristics in 16 different areas (e.g., reflection, relationship-building, planning, and professionalism).[3] Ten more open-ended questions were added to allow more elaboration in each section and at the end. All scales of the survey achieved acceptable levels of reliability in the pilot study (Alpha coefficients were .95 and .97 for teachers and principals, respectively). Survey results were shared with participants and used as a source for reflection and planning.

Finally, we used the Arizona Department of Education website to determine letter grades for schools with differing levels of participation (full participation, partial participation, and no participation). State assessments and data were used to analyze movement of lowest quartile students, within-school gaps, and graduation rate changes, all of which impacted the state letter grade designation. During the third phase of the project, Arizona changed the state assessment and suspended reporting letter grade determinations for 3 years; therefore, this information was not available for the third iteration of the project.

Results also informed semi-structured qualitative interviews (35–40 min) and observation settings in schools. Interviews were conducted by interviewers (outside of the internal researchers), paid by the grant and trained in qualitative interviewing techniques. Interview questions featured leadership practices in relation to the three stages of turnaround leadership (Leithwood et al., 2010), including levels of capacity building, collaboration, community involvement, assessment literacy, curriculum, and overall priorities. Interviews were designed to examine participants' (principals and teachers) understandings of turnaround stages, conceptions of leadership, and capacities. Specifically, semi-structured interviews were conducted during the last two institutes in order to determine the perceptions of changes in capacity building that occurred throughout the intervention period. Observational data was noted during walk-through observations, site visitations, and through observations of the team interactions.

Results

The Arizona model has served 71 focus and priority schools over a five-year period. Essentially, the model was designed to build team leadership capacity for sustainable school development in schools that were persistently underperforming but not yet designated for turnaround status. Results were analyzed using quantitative (a pre- and post-survey measuring leadership and school capacity; school letter grades based on student outcomes) and qualitative methods (interviews and observations). This section begins with an overview of pilot test results from the Arizona schools followed by results from refined iterations.

---

[3] Additional principal survey items contain Likert-scale responses.

Survey Results

According to Bennett et al. (2013), principal respondents in the first phase of the project gave themselves high-capacity scores on the majority (81%) of 16 additional Likert-scale items on the principal-only survey portion. Principals considered themselves as cultivating a supportive professional atmosphere. They scored themselves highly on their capacity-building efforts to help people feel honored and thrive (Mitchell and Sackney, 2009). They believed that they fostered respect, self-reflection, modeled professional attributes, and expected the same for others. Principals also noted confidence in their ability to foster staff commitment for change; principals believed they fostered a climate of ongoing renewal and improvement (Mitchell and Sackney, 2009). Additionally, the principals generally indicated few tensions related to their work in schools, feeling somewhat insulated from pressures that might require choosing between competing values or prioritizing compliance with district requirements over doing what was best for students, or avoiding participation outside the school (e.g., committees, professional development) altogether.

While these quantitative findings suggested principals possessed high self-capacity for developing people, commitments, setting direction, and effectively managing some aspects of the instructional program within their schools, these views were not equally shared by staff. Most capacities for building sustainable improvement at the beginning of the intervention period ranged from low to medium and revealed some discrepancies or weaknesses. Participants were keenly aware of accountability pressures and the need to comply with mandates requiring tools for curriculum change (e.g., curriculum maps, benchmarks), yet had difficulties in defining success. They valued a supportive, professional, collaborative, and democratic working environment in their schools, but lacked authentic connections with their communities and did not seem to value their contributions or support.

For Phase 2 of the project, generally the principals gave themselves very few high ratings, rather tending to focus on the growth that was necessary. Across all schools, the areas with the greatest need were Curriculum and Instruction, Assessment Literacy, and Culture and Capacity. These areas showed the largest gaps overall between teacher and principal perceptions. More specifically, respondents identified the lack of collaboration (among staff as well as with the community), articulation of the vision, the development and use of common formative assessments, and adequate resources as areas of need. Perceptions about students were often couched in deficit thinking.

Phase 3 survey results generally resulted in higher ratings of themselves by the principals than by the staff. Trends across all schools, however, indicated a lack of shared decision-making or soliciting input from stakeholders, and a lack of emphasis on instructional leadership, with both principals and teachers indicating little time spent in classrooms or assisting teachers to improve their practice. Additionally, little or no emphasis was placed on working with the community or engaging in culturally responsive practices.

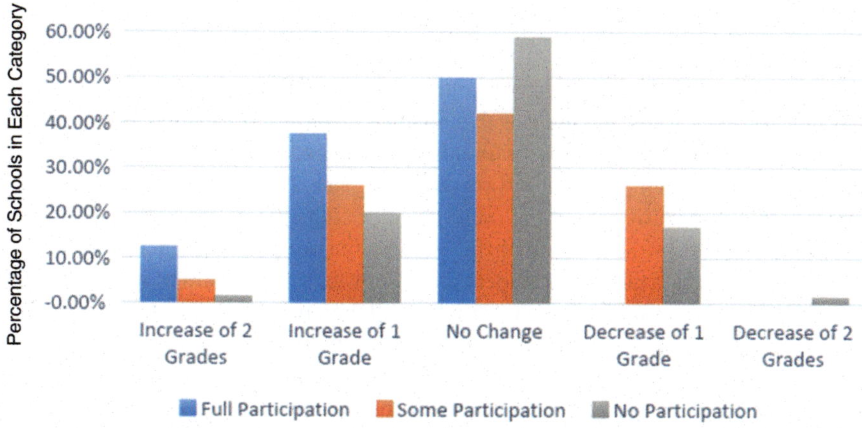

Fig. 2.2   Changes in school letter grades– Test group 1

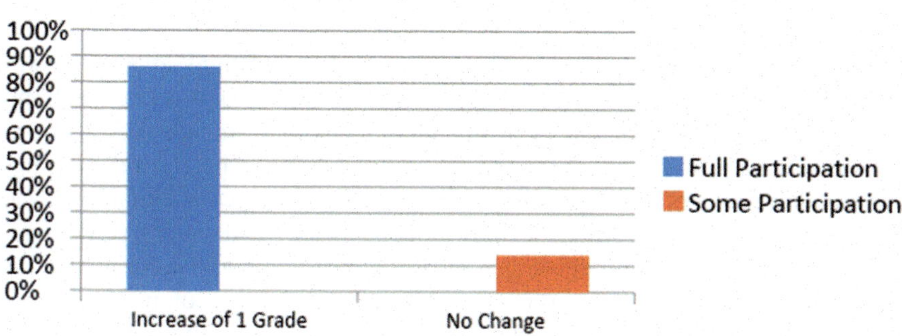

Fig. 2.3   Change in School Letter Grades – Test Group 2

Improved School Letter Grades

As stated earlier, Arizona changed the state assessment, and suspended the assignment of letter grades to all schools for 3 years, thus affecting the ability to present this data on Phase 3 of the project.

Figure 2.2 shows that, in the first test group, full participation in AZiLDR training increased the likelihood of an improved accountability rating by one to two grade levels. Specifically, over 50% of those schools that participated in all AZiLDR sessions and activities improved their letter grades by one or two letters. A few schools with lower levels of participation (i.e., some, none) were still able to make improvements. Those schools that had participated, either fully or partially, in the intervention showed greater improvement overall than those schools who had not participated in the training, with greater improvement defined by increased letter grades.

Figure 2.3 shows results for the test group 2. Over 80% of schools that fully participated improved their school letter grade by one grade.

Qualitative Interview Results

Results from interviews of principals and teacher leaders during Phase 1 indicated that their schools were making positive changes regarding formative assessments, data use, and growth in some community interactions, but noted that they were largely lacking in more authentic forms of engagement. Here we encouraged participants to retain clarity about the importance of authentic collaboration to education aimed at democracy. In much the same way, we encouraged teams to use student outcome data and other student data as a source of reflection; we worked to facilitate schools toward higher capacity for collaboration, using evidence from the survey as well as interview data. Participants also reported the need to move beyond their low capacity status and develop into high capacity learning communities but described little consciousness of the broader socio-cultural dimension and cultural-political shifts in developing the potential for sustainable improvement in the Arizona context (Ylimaki et al., 2012). The varied implementation of PLCs was evident in the multiple and sometimes conflicting district priorities, range of instructional leadership perspectives, and levels of resistance. As one principal stated, PLCs "forced us to look a little bit deeper at our data and think about who was involved genuinely and who might be excluded or ignored. That was kind of alarming…We maybe had that before and really didn't focus on it." In many cases, priorities shifted away from building authentic and culturally respectful relationships with families and communities, which served only to reinforce deficit thinking and lack of coherent direction within schools for collaboration and cultural responsiveness. This deficit thinking is illustrated by a principal in a high Native population school: "It's very important for us to try and help those students coming from those homes so that they have a better chance at the future. I live where the educated people live. And I said that if you get a good education, you can live down there too." In these instances, team members were asked to think about their agency to leverage changes in opportunities available for all students.

Prior to the beginning of Phase 2, interviews were conducted with a sample of teachers and principals within the project schools. Strong trust in the principals was evident; however, several issues were identified immediately by teachers. These included a lack of focused vision for the schools, limited capacity for collaborative leadership, and deficit thinking.

In all schools at the beginning of the project, the focus was on the state letter grade (outcomes) rather than on humanistic values of education and enhancing teaching and learning for all students. One teacher described,

> "You know, I really don't think we have a real, definite vision. I think right now we were a C-minus school… So I know that is definitely one of his visions, is to get us to improve our C-minus standing. But other than that, I don't think we all know…"

Deficit thinking was also revealed across the board. Yet teachers believed they were doing what was in the best interest of students.

"Well, right now, because the Hispanic culture tends to be very kind of laid-back, you kind of really have to push. They're very much, what's the word, "mañana," "tomorrow," that's the word., it's their culture. So they're not in any big rush, that's their culture. So I get that. So it's my job to not necessarily rush, but keep it steady. And I've learned that, because I came from the east where that wasn't the culture, it was okay to rush, it was okay to push, it was okay to rrrrr [car vroom noise] all the time. Here you can't do that."

This information was used to refine the curricular focus and processes for Phase 2.

By the end of Phase 2, participants were applying the leadership skills that they had learned over the course of the project. For example, interview data indicated that the principals and teacher leaders developed a shared mission for school improvement. As one principal put it,

"Since we started, I have seen changes in the school vision and mission, the directions that we are going in the capacity-building groups that we have, our curriculum action team, as well as the revamped and rejuvenated leadership council with better direction…We have better communication across the board and better professional development for our staff focused on student learning."

As another example, during the course of the project, participants increased their data literacy skills and use of data as a source of reflection in their daily practices. As another principal noted, "we are using data and the strategies we learned in the institutes in our PLCs…Primarily we've been modeling leadership processes and making data-based decision-making. Everyone has a voice at the table, but the voice needs to be informed by research and data. It is helping slowly."

Capacity building was key. One principal noted, "we executed a great turnaround so that when I left the school a couple years later, we had been recognized as an A+ school of excellence for the state of Arizona…" One assistant superintendent, who served as his district representative and attended all of the institutes, believed that the project made a difference to the capacity of the school to move forward. He stated,

"[The School Improvement Project] has provided the research, the systems, the applications to start small, look at the low-hanging fruit, start to build momentum, have clarity in purpose and direction, and get the buy-in to start moving forward…it's showing the principal how to build teams to have, for example, to help with issues on curriculum and culture. It is no longer just the principal trying to lead the way. It's all encompassing of staff trying to get on board."

Interestingly, during final interviews, no mention was made of culturally relevant pedagogy, yet at the same time, there was no evidence of deficit language.

Finally, Phase 3 began with school teams analyzing their own school data, including achievement data as well as the survey data. When talking about that analysis, one principal talked about the school survey results, stating, "I think looking at the trusting culture among the staff – that was a huge area, that they don't really trust; and collective efficacy was bad – they jump out at us…".

In contrast, at the end of Phase 3, a principal shared, "I think just reflecting through is that it's not me. It's this team of people communicating and determining these are the needs. This is what we need to do. This is where we get feedback from teachers what they need, and now let's put it together. That's what I think has been really wonderful this year." In other words, teams such as the one in this quote recognized the value of diverse perspectives engaged in collaborative deliberations and reflection using multiple sources of data.

Data suggested that participants had limited understanding about effective leadership practices, including the importance of trust and school culture, early in the project. School culture and a focused vision were areas of concern for many schools; however, progress was evident. One principal shared,

> "But, the biggest thing is we have been able to build our leadership team….and really look and see, what is our school culture? What defines [us]? So we have been able to refine our vision. We came up with our school beliefs. We have 4 core beliefs. And I have even come up with the Principal's Purpose. I also asked for the teachers to write about their purpose."

A teacher on her leadership team was enthusiastic about the changes occurring; she stated, "…definitely shared collaboration time, shared vision. I don't feel like Katie's telling us what to do. I feel like Katie's involving us in the process, and that has never happened before ever." Building the capacity of the site to continue was a focus of the project. One principal, who was retiring at the end of the school year, was excited about what could continue to develop:

> "It's on a positive note… I've enjoyed it. I'm still sitting here with my team going, "Okay, we need to do this next year, dah dah dah," and I have no idea if it's going to happen or not. They would like it to happen. I know they'll carry forward, or hopefully whoever takes over will be open to where we've been, and where we were thinking we would be going, and I'm sure they'll add their own expertise. We want it to be better, and it will be…"

Another principal focused on shared accountability. He stated,

> "We have increased accountability at [our school]. This does not mean people are scolded or face disciplinary action more often. This means we have made our goals and outcomes clearer. We have also further defined individual roles and what they look like so that people can truly be more included and feel their own importance to our shared goals. The further we move along with every individual having clearly defined roles/value/and importance to our team, the more people embrace that and make us more effective as a whole school."

Although there was still evidence of deficit thinking, the idea of asset-based instruction was at the beginning stages. One teacher reported, "I try to integrate things that are related, like topics that are related to the students…So, I chose a topic that they know in order to teach them a new strategy. So, that way, I'm now teaching a new topic and a new strategy. So, I try to integrate things that have to do with agriculture and things related that students can relate to…" And while the evidence-based reforms described earlier (e.g., Mass Insight, UVA, Chicago) all identify culture, these models do not go deeply into the cultural bias and deficit thinking that restricts or inhibits goals of equality and freedom.

Many participants spoke at length about the school development process itself. Both school leaders and team members were generally very positive. The interactions with other teams were highlighted, with one teacher sharing, "Just by talking to the other teams, some of them are also going through the same problems, seeing the same things. Some of the things that we're doing, a lot of times, sparks ideas for them. Some of the things they're doing sparks ideas for us." The walk-through process resonated with the participants, with one teacher highlighting this aspect of the process. "Walk-throughs…wow, that was an amazing … because I had an idea what my team does, but I don't have a chance to go into my 7th grade team, just as he doesn't have time to go into his 8th grade teams. What I expected them to see wasn't necessarily there. We actually collected data and then we shared it with our teams."

Finally, team members appreciated the structure of the institutes (taking teams away from their schools) although it was difficult. One principal shared, "…it gave us a time to think and really process, and maybe still not process as far as we need to, but I so appreciate that because it made the noise, all that outside noise, go away for a little while so we're going to do this, and now here we go with it, and then we'll come back to it again, and push forward with it. I think that was the helpful piece."

Across the three phases of school development implementation, we consistently observed the importance of providing teams with an immersion experience away from schools during the institutes. The other two delivery modes, however, were conducted within schools, including regional meetings and school observations.

In Part II of this volume, we provide additional detail on the key elements of the school development process: (1) values and culture, (2) leadership capacity, (3) use of data for reflection and feedback, (4) curriculum and pedagogical activity, and (5) strengths-based approaches for diversity. Within each chapter, we highlight, as appropriate, the processes of school development within the Zone of Uncertainty, including democratic community, readiness for change, reflection and mediation, planning and implementation for capacity building. All of these processes are grounded in education theory for democratic nation-states as well as understandings of culturally responsive practices. It is important to note that these elements and processes are not linear or isolated, but rather work together to support continuous school development.

References

Bennett, J. V. (2012). "Democratic" collaboration for school turnaround in southern Arizona. *International Journal of Educational Management, 26*(5), 442–451.

Bennett, J. V., Ylimaki, R. M., Dugan, T. M., & Brunderman, L. A. (2013). Developing the potential for sustainable improvement in underperforming schools: Capacity building in the socio-cultural dimension. *Journal for Educational Change.* https://doi.org/10.1007/s10833-013-9217-6

Biesta, G., & Burbules, N. C. (2003). Pragmatism and educational research.

Bourdieu, P. (1977). *Towards a theory of practice.* Cambridge University Press. Bourdieu Towards a Theory of Practice 1977.

Day, C., Gu, Q., & Sammons, P. (2016). The impact of leadership on student outcomes: How successful school leaders use transformational and instructional strategies to make a difference. *Educational Administration Quarterly, 52*(2), 221–258.

Desimone, L. M. (2009). Improving impact studies of teachers' professional development: Toward better conceptualizations and measures. *Educational Researcher, 38*(3), 181–199.

Dewey, J. (1897). My pedagogic creed (1897). *School Journal, 54*(3), 77–80.

Dewey, J. (1907). *The school and society: Being three lectures*. University of Chicago Press.

Dewey, J. (1916). *Education and democracy*. Macmillian.

Dewey, J. (1938/1997). *Experience and education*. Touchstone

Dewey, J. (1959). *The child and the curriculum (No. 5)*. University of Chicago Press.

Drysdale, L., Bennett, J., T. Murakami, E., Johansson, O., & Gurr, D. (2014). Heroic leadership in Australia, Sweden, and the United States. *International Journal of Educational Management, 28*(7), 785–797.

Edmonds, R. (1979). Effective schools for the urban poor. *Educational Leadership, 37*(1), 15–24.

Eisner, E. W. (1979). *The educational imagination: On the design and evaluation of school programs*. Macmillan.

Englund, T. (2006). Deliberative communication: A pragmatist proposal. *Journal of Curriculum Studies, 38*(5), 503–520.

Gonzalez, N., Moll, L. C., Tenery, M. F., Rivera, A., Rendon, P., Gonzales, R., & Amanti, C. (1995). Funds of knowledge for teaching in Latino households. *Urban Education, 29*(4), 443–470.

Gurr, D. (2015). A model of successful school leadership from the international successful school principalship project. *Societies, 5*(1), 136–150.

Hallinger, P., & Murphy, J. (1986). Instructional leadership in effective schools.

Höög, J., Johansson, O., & Olofsson, A. (2005). Successful principalship: The Swedish case. *Journal of Educational Administration, 43*(6), 595–606.

Jacobson, S. L., Johnson, L., Ylimaki, R., & Giles, C. (2005a). Successful leadership in challenging US schools: Enabling principles, enabling schools. *Journal of Educational Administration, 43*(6), 607–618.

Jacobson, S. L., Johnson, L., Ylimaki, R., & Giles, C. (2005b). Successful leadership in challenging US schools: Enabling principles, enabling schools. *Journal of Educational Administration, 43*(6), 607–618.

Johnson, L. (2007). Rethinking successful school leadership in challenging US schools: Culturally responsive practices in school-community relationships. *International Studies in Educational Administration (Commonwealth Council for Educational Administration & Management (CCEAM)), 35*(3), 49–57.

Khalifa, M. A., Gooden, M. A., & Davis, J. E. (2016). Culturally responsive school leadership: A synthesis of the literature. *Review of Educational Research, 86*(4), 1272–1311.

Klar, W. H., & Brewer, A. C. (2014). Successful leadership in a rural, high-poverty school: The case of county line middle school. *Journal of Educational Administration, 52*(4), 422–445.

Leithwood, K., Harris, A., & Strauss, T. (2010). *Leading school turnaround: How successful leaders transform low-performing schools*. Wiley.

Mitchell, C., & Sackney, L. (2009). *Sustainable improvement. Building learning communities that endure*. Sense Publishers.

Moll, L., Amanti, C., Neff, D., & Gonzalez, N. (2006). Funds of knowledge for teaching: Using a qualitative approach to connect homes and classrooms. In *Funds of knowledge* (pp. 83–100). Routledge.

Purkey, S. C., & Smith, M. S. (1982). Highlights from research on effective schools. *Educational Leadership, 40*(3), 67.

U.S. Department of Education. (2009). *Definition of SIG's transformation model*. Retrieved from https://www2.ed.gov›programs›sif.

Uljens, M., & Ylimaki, R. M. (2017). *Bridging educational leadership, Curriculum Theory and Didaktik*. Springer International Publishing.

Wagner, T., Kegan, R., Lahey, L. L., Lemons, R. W., Garnier, J., Helsing, D., … Rasmussen, H. T. (2012). *Change leadership: A practical guide to transforming our schools*. Wiley.

Ylimaki, R., & Brunderman, L. (2019). School development in culturally diverse US schools: Balancing evidence-based policies and education values. *Education Sciences, 9*(2), 84.

Ylimaki, R., & Jacobson, S. (2013). School leadership practice and preparation: Comparative perspectives on organizational learning (OL), instructional leadership (IL) and culturally responsive practices (CRP). *Journal of Educational Administration, 51*(1), 6–23.

Ylimaki, R. M., Bennett, J. V., Fan, J., & Villasenor, E. (2012). Notions of "success" in Southern Arizona schools: Principal leadership in changing demographic and border contexts. *Leadership and Policy in Schools, 11*(2), 168–193.

Ylimaki, R. M., Brunderman, L., Bennett, J. V., & Dugan, T. (2014). Developing Arizona turn-around leaders to build high-capacity schools in the midst of accountability pressures and changing demographics. *Leadership and Policy in Schools, 13*(1), 28–60.

Part II

Lessons from the Arizona School Development Model

In this part, chapters feature elements that emerged as important in the Arizona Initiative for School Development and Research (AZilDR). Specifically, Chaps. 3, 4, 5, 6 and 7 present these elements and how we worked to develop these among school teams over time—namely, values, culture and context; building and sustaining leadership capacity, using data as a source of reflection in a feedback loop, going deeper into curriculum and pedagogical activity, and strengths-based approaches to meeting the needs of culturally diverse students. Each chapter is organized to begin with a description of the element in the voices of participants in AZilDR, an explanation of the element using relevant literature as well as our experiences and evaluations from the project. Next, we provide a description of how we applied and learned from research in practice in the Arizona approach. Each chapter in this section concludes with lessons learned and case studies from school participants in AZiLDR.

Chapter 3
Values, Culture and Context

Rose M. Ylimaki and Lynnette A. Brunderman

Abstract This chapter presents our conception of culture for school development, including broader cultural aims and humanistic values of education for an increasingly multicultural society reflected in the micro-organizational culture of schools and the sub-culture of the leadership team. Specifically, drawing on the International Successful School Principalship Project (ISSPP) research, related studies, and education theory, we defined culture as the values, beliefs and norms of behavior embedded within the individual, the leadership team, the organization, and the larger community. The balance of the chapter presents application of theory and practice in the Arizona project (AZiLDR) as well as lessons learned. The chapter illustrates the critical importance of culture to readiness for school development. Often, during the project, teams were at different stages of readiness, resulting in the need to spend time building and solidifying the culture. In schools with less readiness, we found the diffusion process to progress much more slowly. We saw these schools existing in the Zone of Uncertainty much longer. We describe our process to develop school culture through leadership teams, using the AZiLDR delivery system of institutes, regional meetings and on-site coaching. Example case studies and activities are provided.

Keywords School culture · Human perspective · Organizational perspective

> *"Definitely at the start of this project, I would say we were pretty dysfunctional. We'd had 15 principals in the last 16 years...some teachers were ready to go but were still teaching. We had newbies who would last a year and then go. The kids, we have hard workers and we have kids who have zero GPAs...90% Hispanic, Latino. Part of the population comes from Mexico and into the United States for their education. Viably, it isn't like a hometown thing.*

R. M. Ylimaki (✉)
Northern Arizona University, Flagstaff, AZ, USA
e-mail: rose.ylimaki@nau.edu

L. A. Brunderman
University of Arizona, Tucson, AZ, USA
e-mail: lbrunder@arizona.com

© The Author(s) 2022
R. M. Ylimaki, L. A. Brunderman (eds.), *Evidence-Based School Development in Changing Demographic Contexts*, Studies in Educational Leadership 24,
https://doi.org/10.1007/978-3-030-76837-9_3

It's like a split...I would say probably 60% of our kids are bilingual. Then the others are bi-illiterate. where they speak Spanglish." -Principal

This chapter presents our conception of culture for school development, including broader cultural aims and humanistic values of education for an increasingly multicultural society reflected in the micro organizational culture of schools and the sub-culture of the leadership team. In this chapter, we discuss our understanding of culture that we developed from our work with AZiLDR, ongoing study of theoretical traditions and other empirical research. The balance of the chapter presents application of theory and practice in the Arizona project (AZILDR) as well as lessons learned.

Culture Defined in School Development

In order to better serve increasingly diverse students (with differing home and national cultures) in our schools, we see the need to define culture from a human (educational) as well as an organizational standpoint. Specifically, we considered sociology, education theory and leadership research as well as our experiences from facilitating school culture development. Thus, we define culture as the values, beliefs, and norms of behavior embedded within the individual, the leadership team, the organization, and the larger community.

In sociology, culture often refers to *the cumulative deposit* of knowledge, experience, beliefs, values, attitudes and religion by a group of people that (consciously and unconsciously) affects how people think and act (e.g. Bourdieu, 1990) or the ways in which the *organizational* culture influences how people think, feel and act. Leading leadership scholars agree and add that without a strong, positive culture, schools flounder and die. Based on their own research, Peterson and Deal (2002) and Fullan (2001) argue that culture is characterized by norms, values and beliefs that underlie thinking and is manifested through symbols and artifacts, stories that communicate meaning and herald values, a cultural network, heroes and heroines, and rituals, traditions and ceremonies. Further, Peterson and Deal (2002) note how these elements of culture can become toxic, featuring negative values and beliefs, a spiritually fragmented sense of purpose, negative and destructive relationships, heroes that are anti-heroic or negative, and few positive rituals, traditions or ceremonies to develop a sense of community and hopefulness.

Across the cases from ISSPP and related leadership literature, successful schools exhibited positive school cultures conducive to continuous school development work (Day & Sammons, 2013). There is evidence across 27 countries and almost 200 case studies that schools have a more positive culture when positively influenced by school leadership. Principals worked to build trust, shared values and a shared vision, thereby improving relationships and job satisfaction. Studies have also shown the opposite; inconsistent behavior, lack of trust and a work-and non-supportive approach from the principal produces a negative school culture and climate (Leithwood & Strauss, 2009). In sum, principals who build relationships and trust among teachers and interact with all staff members and students are key to positive school cultures in successful school. While terminology on school culture varies somewhat according to national context, results from cases studies in the U.K. (Day, 2005; Day, 2009), U.S. (Jacobson et al., 2005; Ylimaki et al., 2012; Klar et al., 2019), Australia (Gurr & Drysdale, 2012), and Sweden (Höög et al., 2005) and related studies (Hoy et al., 2002; Leithwood & Strauss, 2009) agree on areas of impact on school direction and goals: (1) support for learning; (2) stakeholder engagement; ((3) collaboration; and (4) principal leadership. More specifically, the principal's leadership was the umbrella area of impact on school culture through developing people through learning, stakeholder engagement in school activities, and collaboration embedded in the organizational design for decision-making and professional learning. These areas of impact were consistent in schools serving culturally diverse students where principals and others explicitly considered the socio-cultural affect (Ylimaki et al., 2012) and democratic values in education (Dewey, 1916).

From an education theory standpoint, according to Dewey (1916), culture is defined as a complex whole which includes knowledge, belief, art, morals, law, custom, tradition, folkways, religion, literature and any other capabilities acquired by individuals as members of society. Culture also comprises a vast array of inter-related knowledge, skills and values from rich experiences of humanity and society. From this perspective, the aim of education is to help individuals inherit rich cultural heritage of the past and to enrich it through activities that share culture with the next generation. Such shared culture of the older to younger generations is part of school organizational culture and education itself.

Dewey argues that the aim of education in the democratic countries of the world should be the cultivation of democratic values in the minds of the children and individuals - faith in a democratic way of living, respect for the dignity of other persons, freedom, equality of opportunity, justice, faith in tolerance, faith in change, and peaceful methods and faith in cooperative living and above all fellow-feelingness. Education takes place with the participation of the individual in social activities and relationships with his fellow human beings. Dewey holds that education is a necessity for healthy living in the society. It gives the child social consciousness. The school guides and controls propensities of the child in socially desirable channels. The teachers and principal must recognize the background of the child as well as the social demands. As such, the school is a social environment--simplified, balanced, and graded (Dewey, 1887).

With a view of schools as a microcosm of democracy, the fusion of learners' horizons--their capacities to shape common interests, project common ends, and converge upon common means despite their differences in perspective--is a primary educational goal. Within schools, leaders/learners (principals, teachers, children) develop an organizational culture around democratic educational values, including a shared system of democratic and intercultural norms, folkways, values and traditions, all of which infuse the school culture with passion, purpose, and a sense of spirit. Such cultural activity, in our view, is enhanced by leadership teams who embody and model democratic spirit and values. In the remainder of this chapter, we provide activities and examples that illustrate our definition of culture in school development.

video set, Collaborative Teams in Professional Learning Communities at Work (DuFour et al., 2010), teams worked through steps to move teachers to a culture of collaboration: define a collaborative team, analyze teams to determine whether they

---

Box 3.1: Assumption Card Stack and Shuffle (Lipton & Wellman, 2011)
Divide into groups of 3–5. Distribute one full set of cards to each group. The cards are then dealt to each member of the group. One individual will begin the round by reading a card aloud. The entire group then discusses the prompt using the following mediating questions as a guide:

- What is the thinking behind this assumption?
- What are some inferences that can be made from it?
- What might be some alternative interpretations?
- To what degree is this assumption generalizable or context specific?
- If _______________ were true, would this assumption still hold?

(Wellman & Lipton, 2004)
    Each individual in turn reads a card, and the team discusses the prompt until all cards are completed or time is exhausted. This activity could take up to an hour, depending on the group.
    The prompts which we used for the activity are as follows: (Hammond, 2014)

Assumption 1: As a leader, it is important for me to be able to communicate across cultures and to facilitate communication among diverse cultural groups.

Assumption 2: Cultural discomfort and disagreements are normal occurrences in a diverse society such as ours and are parts of everyday interactions.

Assumption 3: I believe we can learn about and implement diverse and improved instructional practices that will effectively serve all our students.

Assumption 4: I believe that all students benefit from educational practices that provide them with hope, direction, and preparation for their future lives.

Assumption 5: It is important to know how well our school serves the various cultural and ethnic communities represented in our school, and it is also important to understand how well served they feel by the educational practices in our school.

Assumption 6: I believe that all students benefit from educational practices that engage them in learning about their cultural heritage and understanding their cultural background.

Assumption 7: I am willing to ask questions about racism, cultural preferences, and insufficient learning conditions and resources that may be uncomfortable for others in my school.

Assumption 8: My personal goals and vision and our collective work at school focus on making our school more effective and equitable.

are operating collaboratively, identify team structures for assuring meaningful collaboration, list strategies for providing teams with time to collaborate, and the role of norms in functioning teams. Each team was provided with the video training set to use at their sites. This video set and facilitator's guide aligned with our process and aims, and we explicitly connected the activities with our approach, asking participants to reflect on what they saw and connect it to their own school values and assumptions.

With each Institute and Regional Meeting, some aspect of organizational culture was revisited and refined. For example, interculturality and communication styles were addressed through a North, South, East West (Lipton & Wellman, 2011) activity whereby participants identified their own styles: North (just get it done); East (look at the big picture); South (consider everyone's feelings) or West (pay attention to details). They were required to choose only one, then those individuals at each compass point generated a chart listing four strengths of the preference, four limitations, and what others needed to know in order to work together more effectively. Then individuals were asked to reflect on how they might individually stretch to work more collaboratively with individuals of varying styles.

Finally, we used the step-back consulting protocol, modified from the Change Leadership model (Wagner et al., 2012). Teams were asked to present an issue and their proposed solution to a partner team, answering clarifying questions. Then they became silent partners and observed the other team as they worked through the issue. The initiating team then rejoined the conversation, describing how it felt to observe and listen and what they learned. Finally, both teams considered the implications of the discussion, identifying any strategies or practices that might be useful moving forward. See the Activity Box 3.2 for our modified protocol.

Lessons Learned

Next we present some illustrative cases focusing on aspects of culture that were enhanced through the AZiLDR school development process. Psuedonyms are used for all schools and individuals presented within this book.

Case A: **Smithson High School**

Smithson High School is a public high school in southern Arizona, serving grades 9–12. It houses over 1500 students, although when built it was intended for 1100 students. The principal, Mr. Tierney, (at the time of the project) was a white male in his mid-thirties, who began teaching in 2005. After 5 years in the classroom, he was promoted to an assistant principal position, and 1 year later was thrust into the principal position with the abrupt removal of the previous principal.

Box 3.2: Step-Back Consulting Modified Protocol.
AZiLDR Institute.
Step Back Consulting: A Protocol for Building Communities of Practice.

Step Back Consulting is based on several learning principles:

- For powerful small group learning to occur, all members must have a role that matters to them and keeps them active.
- Groups are helped by a sense of urgency and momentum, a feeling that there is something important to do and hardly enough time in which to do it.
- The less the consultees talk, the greater the chance for the consultees to learn.

Steps	Explanation	Notes
Step 1	The consultees choose a spokesperson to present next steps and outcomes for competent PLC's and the organizational and belief changes associated with these. Once the spokesperson has concluded his/her presentation, others in the group may add information	Time guideline: 10 min
Step 2	The consultees answer clarifying questions from the consulting group.	Time guideline: 5 min
Step 3	The consultees "step back" and become silent observers. The consultees' job is to remain silent and listen actively, perhaps by keeping notes about ideas and internal reactions. The consulting group takes on the issue as if it were theirs, pondering questions such as:	
	What would we do if these were our next steps?	
	What would we avoid doing?	
	How do we find ourselves re-conceiving or re-defining the next steps and outcomes or the organizational/belief changes?	
	What may have been left out of consideration?	
Step 4	The consultees rejoin the conversation and describe how they experienced the process, what it was like to sit back and watch as others temporarily took on their issue, what they thought and what they learned.	Time guideline: 5 min
Step 5	Finally, the group collectively reflects on the implications of the discussion. Prepare a brief written statement summarizing the consultees learning	Time guideline: 5 min

Typically, consultees are often surprised to discover how challenging just sitting back turns out to be. Often this is a lesson in how difficult it is to reconstruct our experience or change our minds. We may be overinvested in our ideas and constructions and therefore have a hard time keeping an open mind, or simply not give new ideas a fair hearing. This process helps us with those realities.

Adapted from *Change Leadership: A Practical Guide to Transforming Our Schools*, Wagner et al., 2012.

Having moved up the ranks within the same school, Mr. Tierney had well-established, trusting relationships with most staff members. His focus during his first year was to establish a safe and orderly school environment, which was something his entire staff had asked to be addressed. When interviewed, one teacher stated, "And to be honest, I feel like [the principal] really wasn't ready to be a principal; ... He was still kind of in training. And yet, because he was a teacher and everybody knew him, there was a trust level. So we were all going to be supportive of him, knowing that he was going to be learning as he went, and that we were going to support him in that learning process. And he didn't just get this big head like, 'I'm in charge, do what I say.' So definitely from day one the transition was, 'We're in this together, we're a team. If there's a problem, let's see how we can figure it out together.'"

Another teacher at the school summarized the biggest concern from both staff and upper district administration. "We trust him; he is a good ethical principal, but he often hesitates. He does not make decisions that move the school forward." Additionally, other administrators on campus were not all on the same page. A teacher observed, "The leadership team seems a bit fractured. The assistant principal in fact is undermining some of his efforts."

At this point in his second year as principal, Mr. Tierney was unsure about how to move forward; he was operating solidly in the Zone of Uncertainty. He believed that he needed to do it all himself. At the direction of district leadership, he began working in the AZiLDR School Development training with a leadership team comprised of himself, three teacher leaders and an assistant superintendent. Mr. Tierney commented, "I started developing a leadership team….and we talked about what we saw as needs for the school and started making plans. It's been really helpful. These are people who are not formal administrators, mainly teacher leaders so they have the teacher perspective." At the same time, a veteran teacher noticed the efforts, offering, "There have been efforts by the leadership team to bring the school together around a theme, *Smithson Succeeds*. It's really made a difference in the culture."

Finally, when asked to reflect, Mr. Tierney offered, "I have been really thinking about what it means to be a leader. I knew when I was hired, I was moving into the principalship; it meant I had to be a transformational leader. I knew the four I's…but what did I know about taking that on? I didn't know anything. I had to engage myself as well as other people, and I have a long way to go, but I see us changing together. The trainings from AZiLDR have been incredibly powerful. It's a time to reflect and talk to teachers about where we are, what is the evidence, what do we know from research and then plan to move forward." He concluded, "Since we started, I have seen changes in the school vision and mission, the directions that we are going in, the capacity-building groups that we have, our curriculum action team, as well as the revamped and rejuvenated leadership council with better direction…We have better communication across the board, better professional development for our staff focused on student learning." The emphasis on democratic humanistic values and the needs of culturally diverse children resonated strongly with Mr. Tierney.

Observing Mr. Tierney and the leadership team as they worked through the school development processes during training, it was clear that the entire team felt empowered to make changes and build the culture of the school to move together in a positive direction. The trust by the team in each other was evident, and Mr. Tierney no longer felt the need to make decisions alone, thus impacting his ability to move forward with decisions. Through the school development process, the team was able to navigate the Zone of Uncertainty with deliberation. Interestingly, within 2 years after the training concluded, Smithson High School was recognized by the state of Arizona as an A+ School of Excellence.

Case B: **Ruth Bennett Middle School**

Ruth Bennett Middle School is in a rural community along the US-Arizona border, serving about 450–475 students in grades 6–8. They are housed in the oldest building in the district, 109 years old. The school is considered low socioeconomic, a Title I school. Many of the students are under guardianship with a grandparent or relative in the US, while parents reside in Mexico; there are a large number of students that transition back and forth across the border. The student population is primarily Hispanic/Latino/a/x (about 85–90%). There are approximately 22 teachers on staff, many who have grown up in the community and reflect those demographics. Only six of the 22 teachers are experienced.

The principal, Kim Wilson, is a white female in her 30's, who is also from the community, with family support in the area. She was in her first year as principal, having served 1 year as assistant principal prior to taking over. She is the 15th principal to serve this school in the last 16 years. In describing her own style, she states, "I'm trying to be more collaborative - more distributive in my style, trying to be a little bit more hands on, and trying to have more of an accountability which I think was lacking. My staff has had many principals in many years; the last few principals have been all 1-2 years...I'm sure they thought we can wait her out. I keep communicating to them unless the district moves me, I'm here for 5 years." Ms. Wilson was able to rather quickly mediate and teach the team about policy pressures and requirements in relation to student needs.

By the end of the AZiLDR school development training, one teacher discussed the changes that had occurred as a result of the project, commenting "definitely shared collaboration time, shared vision. I don't feel like Kim's telling us what to do. I feel like Kim's involving us in the process, and that has never happened before, ever. I trust Kim. I trust Kim to do what's best for the students." Another teacher offered, "I think we see Kim's vision. I don't think everybody realizes how many phases we're going to have to do to get there, but I think I see that we're more open to change."

Two teachers collaboratively described the new culture. "The way I'm seeing it, Kim's the train...conductor. We're on the train. We were the first ones to get on and we're like,"Okay." Then we started seeing it, so the train starts speeding up. Now we're pulling ...More passengers are getting on. They're starting to see it. It's like,"Okay." It's slowly ... it's going to take time. That's my biggest fear is if you truly look at it, it's going to be anywhere between five to seven years. Period."

Finally, when asked to describe the vision, a teacher stated unequivocally, "She wants to change the perception of Ruth Bennett. She doesn't want us to be the ghetto school. She wants our kids to succeed and she wants her teachers to succeed also. I really do see that we want to be the beacon of light."

Observing this team at work was enlightening. Initially, team members were quiet and hesitant to contribute. By the end of the project, they were fully engaged and eager to take the information back to the school site. The principal valued the ideas of her team, and allowed them to take the lead with staff, spreading the common vision and setting the direction together.

Final Thoughts

It was critically important that teams were ready to embrace the process of school development. Often, during the project, teams were at different stages of readiness, resulting in the need to spend time building and solidifying the culture. In schools with less readiness, we found the diffusion process to progress much more slowly. We saw these schools existing in the Zone of Uncertainty much longer. This was exacerbated by policy challenges at the district, state and national levels, as well as the churn of teachers and administrators. When schools were caught in the Zone of Uncertainty without a leader who could mediate the often conflicting demands on schools, the schools stagnated, or at best, moved very slowly.

References

Bourdieu, P. (1990). Structures, habitus, practices. *The logic of practice*, 52–65.

Day, C. (2005). Principals who sustain success: Making a difference in schools in challenging circumstances. *International Journal of Leadership in Education, 8*(4), 273–290.

Day, C. (2009). Building and sustaining successful principalship in England: The importance of trust. *Journal of Educational Administration, 47*(6), 719–730.

Day, C., & Sammons, P. (2013). *Successful leadership: A review of the international literature.* CIBT Education Trust. 60 Queens Road, Reading, RG1 4BS, England.

Dewey, J. (1887). My pedagogic creed. In M. S. Dworkin (Ed.), *Dewey on education.*

Dewey, J. (1916). *Education and democracy.*

DuFour, R., DuFour, R., Eaker, R., & Many, T. W. (2010). *Collaborative teams in professional learning communities at work: Learning by doing professional development video set.* Solution Tree.

Fullan, M. (2001). *The new meaning of educational change.* Routledge.

Gruenert, S., & Valentine, J. (1998). *School climate survey.* Middle.

Gurr, D., & Drysdale, L. (2012). Tensions and dilemmas in leading Australia's schools. *School Leadership & Management, 32*(5), 403–420.

Hammond, Z. (2014). *Culturally responsive teaching and the brain: Promoting authentic engagement and rigor among culturally and linguistically diverse students*. Corwin Press.

Höög, J., Johansson, O., & Olofsson, A. (2005). Successful principalship: The Swedish case. *Journal of Educational Administration, 43*(6), 595–606.

Hoy, W. K., Smith, P. A., & Sweetland, S. R. (2002). The development of the organizational climate index for high schools: Its measure and relationship to faculty trust. *The High School Journal, 86*(2), 38–49.

Jacobson, S. L., Johnson, L., Ylimaki, R., & Giles, C. (2005). Successful leadership in challenging US schools: Enabling principles, enabling schools. *Journal of Educational Administration, 43*(6), 607–618.

Klar, H. W., Moyi, P., Ylimaki, R. M., Hardie, S., Andreoli, P. M., Dou, J., … Buskey, F. C. (2019). Getting off the list: Leadership, learning, and context in two rural, high-needs schools. *Journal of School Leadership, 1052684619867474*.

Leithwood, K., & Strauss, T. I. I. U. (2009). Turnaround schools: Leadership lessons. *Education Canada, 49*(2), 26–29.

Lipton, L., & Wellman, B. M. (2011). *Groups at work: Strategies and structures for professional learning*. MiraVia.

Peterson, K. D., & Deal, T. E. (2002). *The shaping school culture fieldbook*.

Wagner, T., Kegan, R., Lahey, L. L., Lemons, R. W., Garnier, J., Helsing, D., … Rasmussen, H. T. (2012). *Change leadership: A practical guide to transforming our schools*. Wiley.

Wellman, B., & Lipton, L. (2004). Data-driven dialogue: A facilitator's guide to collaborative inquiry. *MiraVia LLC, 135*.

Ylimaki, R. M., Bennett, J. V., Fan, J., & Villasenor, E. (2012). Notions of "success" in southern Arizona schools: Principal leadership in changing demographic and border contexts. *Leadership and Policy in Schools, 11*(2), 168–193.

Chapter 4
Building and Sustaining School Leadership Capacity

Rose M. Ylimaki and Lynnette A. Brunderman

Abstract This chapter presents our approach to building and sustaining leadership capacity with attention to three areas: (1) personal capacity and commitment to growth; (2) interactions and interpersonal capacity grounded in a culture of trust, collective responsibility and appreciation of diversity, and (3) organizational capacity in high functioning teams that take responsibility for a child-centered vision and help diffuse that vision throughout the school. Leadership in high capacity schools incorporates both formal and informal leadership capacities (Mitchell and Sackney, 2009). Team leadership is essential for building and sustaining leadership capacity in a shared direction for continous school development and diffusion of educational improvements throughout the school. As formal leaders leave to take on new positions in the district or elsewhere, the shared direction and culture of continous improvement helps to sustain progress. In this chapter, we discuss our experiences with building and sustaining leadership capacity in *teams* that work to develop and diffuse a shared direction for continuous school development. We begin with a discussion of the research-based content from ISSPP and other studies that informed our project. The balance of the chapter presents application in our research-practice approach in the Arizona project (AZILDR) as well as lessons learned with case examples.

Keywords High-Functioning teams · Personal · Interpersonal · Organizational capacity

"As far as our PLCR leadership team, the ideas and what you've presented here have allowed us to pretty much congeal what we've been working on. All of a sudden it sparks something. It sparks something or if we're working on something and you have us go through an exercise and all of a sudden, oh this is a problem we were working on and all of

R. M. Ylimaki (✉)
Northern Arizona University, Flagstaff, AZ, USA
e-mail: rose.ylimaki@nau.edu

L. A. Brunderman
University of Arizona, Tucson, AZ, USA
e-mail: lbrunder@arizona.com

R. M. Ylimaki, L. A. Brunderman (eds.), *Evidence-Based School Development in Changing Demographic Contexts*, Studies in Educational Leadership 24, https://doi.org/10.1007/978-3-030-76837-9_4

a sudden oh, we've got a solution for it. We're saving up those papers ...It's kind of perfect. We're working on discipline, then the article today was talking about safety and discipline and instructional strategies we've been working on. It's kind of like we're progressing hand in hand, or what I see this training has enabled us to do is become a team. Before we were every two weeks for 30 minutes before school. Where we weren't given time to gel, to use your word, to become a unit. Then what we do, then we take it back to our teams. The last training here we had been was the close reading, I think, was one of the things that was offered. We went back and we have our thing ready to go. Our district took our Tuesday, so then we couldn't do it, but we're ready to roll. Basically it's ready to go. We're picking up on the strategies you're showing up here and we're applying them. And sharing them in our PLCs." -Teacher

This chapter presents our approach to building and sustaining leadership capacity with attention to three areas: (1) personal capacity and commitment to growth; (2) interactions and interpersonal capacity grounded in a culture of trust, collective responsibility and appreciation of diversity, and (3) organizational capacity in high functioning teams that take responsibility for a child-centered vision and helps diffuse that vision throughout the school. Leadership in high capacity schools incorporates both formal and informal leadership capacities (Mitchell and Sackney, 2009). In this chapter, we discuss our experiences with building and sustaining leadership capacity in *teams* that work to develop and diffuse a shared direction for continuous school development. We begin with a discussion of the research-based content from ISSPP and other studies that informed our project. The balance of the chapter presents application in our research-practice approach in the Arizona project (AZILDR) as well as lessons learned with case examples.

Leadership Capacity Defined for School Development

Our understanding of leadership capacity has been adapted from ISSPP cases, related leadership research, the work of Mitchell and Sackney (2009) on practices associated with sustainable improvement in high-capacity schools, as well as conceptual understandings about sustainable *education* improvements and our own experiences in Arizona. As noted in Chap. 1, ISSPP cases demonstrated the importance of building leadership capacity to school success with strands that examined sustainability of educational improvements over time. To review these major findings, principals of successful schools with sustainable improvements over 5 years or more, used the following common practices: setting direction, developing people, redesigning the organization, and managing the instructional program (Leithwood and Riehl, 2003). And while these findings are very important to guide new and seated principals toward school success over time, the findings are limited in terms of leadership capacity or *how* new leaders or leaders of struggling schools, particularly those in culturally diverse communities, make and sustain school changes over time. For this understanding of leadership capacity, we looked to Mitchell and Sackney (2009).

Mitchell and Sackney (2009) conducted interviews and observations in Canadian schools over a 10-year period and identified seven themes that must drive practices for sustainable improvement in an era of accountability; (1) shared vision, values and goals inclusive of all voices; (2) collaborative work culture; (3) collective learning and shared understanding; (4) a focus on reflective practice and experimentation, (5) presence of knowledge systems and data-based decision-making; (6) communities of leaders; and (7) a culture of high trust. Schools with evidence of all seven themes developed into high capacity learning communities and improved student learning and achievement. Mitchell and Sackney clustered these seven themes into three embedded but interactive layers of capacity building leadership necessary to develop the school organization into high capacity learning communities: building people, building commitments, and building schools. Building people or personal capacity was defined as a commitment to growth, expressed in a desire to help others to grow as they have grown. Building interpersonal capacity is based on the development of deep trust, collective responsibility, and appreciating diversity. Collaboration is developed through working together in teams and teachers understand the value of professional and authentic teamwork. Conflict is not ignored within collaboration but embraced as a learning opportunity to engage in honest, respectful deliberation and dialogue that encourages active listening, inquiry, and reflection. Organizational capacity is based in building networks, knowledge systems, leadership infrastructure, and organization.

Further, we extended leadership notions of capacity to include conceptual understandings from education traditions, including those applied in the U.S. by John Dewey. We will expand on this point in subsequent chapters, but it is important to note that we draw on education traditions as well as organizational theories and leadership approaches to work with people and the human relations and interrelations necessary for school development at any level, particularly culturally diverse schools.

Thus, in summary, we worked to develop groups as leadership teams for sustained school development in terms of personal, interpersonal, and organizational capacity for education within the Zone of Uncertainty. Team leadership is essential for building and sustaining leadership capacity in a shared direction for continuous school development and diffusion of educational improvements throughout the school. As formal leaders leave to take on new positions in the district or elsewhere, the shared direction and culture of continuous improvement helps to sustain progress. For AZiLDR, we worked with a leadership group (formal leaders, teacher leaders, coaches, district representatives) to take on the characteristics and dispositions of an educational leadership team. We drew on Leithwood and Riehl's (2003) synthesis of leadership practices in successful schools to include setting directions, developing people, redesigning the organization, and managing the instructional program, findings from ISSPP cases that supported Leithwood and Riehl's model, as well as Mitchell and Sackney's (2009) understanding of formal and informal leadership capacity in schools. As we describe in the next section, our application in school development (AZiLDR) extended this research with understandings about how leadership teams build and sustain capacity for school development over time.

Application

Throughout the Institutes and Regional Meetings, school teams engaged in a variety of activities designed to assist them to build capacity within their leadership teams, and ultimately at their school sites. First, teams explored the stages of group development, (1) dependency and inclusion, (2) counterdependency and fight, (3) trust and structure, and (4) work (Wheelan, 2013). They then examined the ten keys to productivity: goals; roles; interdependence; leadership; communication and feedback; discussion, decision-making and planning; implementation and evaluation; norm and individual differences; structure; and cooperation and conflict management (Wheelan, 2013). Each individual was asked to complete the Organizational Support Checklist (Wheelan, 2013), which elicited a grade of A, B or C for the overall organization as well as for each section. Individuals then divided into job-alike groups (principals, teachers, and District support) to discuss their similarities and differences as well as next steps that they might take. School teams then regrouped to look at the stage of development for their team, strategies for moving forward, and most importantly, how to think about and use the concepts of team development at their own sites. These activities, including the subsequent ones, provided teams with the tools to address their needs within the Zone of Uncertainty.

Teams were introduced to the structures and processes of professional learning communities, using the video set, Collaborative Teams in Professional Learning Communities: Learning by Doing (DuFour et al., 2010). Leadership teams learned how to structure professional learning communities at their own sites to focus on learning, embedding time for collaboration within the school day.

In conjunction with understanding how to create, structure and monitor professional learning communities, teams were instructed in how to deal with conflict and resistance. The video set, Leading Difficult Conversations: Professional Learning Communities at Work (DuFour and DuFour, 2011) prepared the team to address resistance, both around the work of PLCs as well as other changes that were being made. Schools received the video set for use in training their own staff. Understanding the change process involved in implementing professional learning communities effectively was imperative. Thus, we shared information on the Change Analysis Framework (Foord and Haar, 2008), asking participants to analyze their own situations and apply the 6 step process to their own needs. Innovation configuration maps (Hord and Roussin, 2013) were utilized to assist teams in planning for implementation of change efforts.

Time was also devoted to ensuring that both principals and other team members had the skills to coach their colleagues. We focused on how to give appropriate feedback, as well as understanding blended coaching and triple loop learning (Bloom et al., 2005). Participants were asked to use an example of Triple Loop Learning that needs to occur in their schools to develop the two to three next steps they could take prior to the following Regional Meeting. The were to present and discuss the results of those next steps at that Regional Meeting.

Finally, it should be noted that team planning for diffusion of content was provided at every Institute and Regional Meeting. The expectation was that they would apply and extend the learning to their entire staff. It should also be noted that teams were reminded and encouraged to consider evidence in terms of humanistic education as well as student outcomes.

Lessons Learned

In the following cases, we illustrate two examples of different ways that diffusion occurred and was supported (or not).

Case A: *Venture Inc.*

A small charter school in southern Arizona serving grades K-8, Venture, Inc. is located in a rural community. The student body is mostly White (77%) and low income (83%). Proficiency scores in both English/Language Arts and Math fall below the state average, at 29% and 25% respectively. The school is comprised of several modular buildings, connected with concrete walkways. Although not required by Arizona law, all of their teachers hold state certification, and 50% have 3 or more years of teaching experience. The school founder and executive director (principal), Mr. Vellan is a white male in his sixties. His main interest in participating in the school development project was to share the leadership in the hopes that he could someday retire.

This small team was comprised of the principal and two teachers. Since the school only had 6 teachers, the commitment to development was sincere. Observing the team at work was different than most, in that the principal made the conscious decision to not take the lead, but rather to allow the teachers to do so. When asked, Mr. Vellan would provide feedback or ideas, but tried to stay more in the background.

The teachers at this site rose to the challenge, taking the lead both during training and with staff when they returned to school. Even 3 years after the training ended, teachers continued to take the lead, with Mr. Vellan acting as cheerleader. He wrote: "Each Wednesday we work as a team to focus or refine the execution of a feature of our overarching mission: (1) Standards based instruction informed by relevant and timely data; (2) Our instructional framework Readers, Writers, Science and Math Workshop); (3) Building resiliency in students. Thank you, Margaret Hunter, Yvette Suni, Cathy Black for sharing expertise and coaching us as we apply the learning. And thank you, Susie, Tarrin, Lucy, DV, Kris, Lacey, Donald for sticking to it and for steadily improving "The Venture Way". Awesome is overused – so, how about a dose of "inspirational" with all that awe inspiring work and expertise."

Building capacity at this site was the purpose for their participation and was evident long after the project ended.

Case B: *Alexander High School*

Alexander High School is a comprehensive urban public high school serving approximately 1200 students. The student make-up is predominantly Hispanic (63%), followed by 18% White, 10% Black, 4% Asian, 3% Native American and 1% two or more races. Approximately 72% of the students come from low income homes. The school has a 71% four-year graduation rate, although this falls slightly below the state average. Academic performance, as measured on the state test, indicates that only 22% of students are proficient in English and 20% in Math; this falls significantly below the state average. And yet, the school as a whole has currently received a letter grade of B from the state of Arizona, based on its rate of growth.

> 'The principal, Jeffrey Long, has served in that capacity since 2011. He began his career at Alexander High School as a teacher, then served as assistant principal and principal for several years at different district schools. Jeffrey is of Native American heritage, and believes deeply that all students can grow and succeed. At the time of his entry into the AZiLDR school development project, Alexander High School was rated a D school, and Mr. Long was seeking ways to assist them to improve."

During the course of the project, both the district representative and several of Jeffrey's team expressed frustration with his unwillingness to share the load and trust in his team. Jeffrey believed he had to take charge of all areas of improvement, and did not seem to recognize the expertise of his team members. About halfway through the trainings, after diving deeply into the professional learning community model, Mr. Long changed his behaviors. He then embraced the concept of professional learning communities, turning the leadership of the process over to the leadership team. As one teacher stated, "It was a turning point in the work of the team; we were finally able to feel like a part of the process."

Final Thoughts

In order to truly build capacity at a school site, it is imperative that the leader be ready and willing to share the leadership. In one of the cases presented above, the leader was ready; in the other case, he was more hesitant, and it took time for him to understand that his role was to facilitate and encourage leadership in others. No single person is able to effect change without the support, help and willingness of others.

Additionally, in order to diffuse learning throughout the organization, it is essential to have teacher leaders with influence among their peers. Many times, school leaders want to choose only those individuals who agree with them, but in reality, it is necessary to include individuals who question and disagree, especially if they are influential at the site. Having them closely involved with the planning allows the team to anticipate issues, and address them early. Understanding the change process is critical to success, which includes understanding the stages of the change process itself as well as being able to assess the progress of individual staff members within that change process. Being able to support all staff to continue to grow and increase their own capacity is vital to success. Navigating the Zone of Uncertainty to embrace continual and sustainable school development is a team effort; leadership must be shared.

References

Bloom, G., Castagna, C., Moir, E., & Warren, B. (Eds.). (2005). *Blended coaching: Skills and strategies to support principal development*. Corwin Press.

DuFour, R., & DuFour, R. (2011). *Leading difficult conversations: Professional learning communities at work professional development video set*. Solution Tree.

DuFour, R., DuFour, R., Eaker, R., & Many, T. W. (2010). *Collaborative teams in professional learning communities at work: Learning by doing professional development video set*. Solution Tree.

Foord, K. A., & Haar, J. M. (2008). *Professional learning communities: An implementation guide and toolkit*. Eye On Education.

Hord, S. M., & Roussin, J. L. (2013). *Implementing change through learning: Concerns-based concepts, tools, and strategies for guiding change*. Corwin Press.

Leithwood, K., & Riehl, C. (2003). What do we already know about successful school leadership. *AERA division a task force on developing research in educational leadership* (pp. 1–60).

Mitchell, C., & Sackney, L. (2009). *Sustainable improvement. Building learning communities that endure*. Sense Publishers.

Wheelan, S. A. (2013). *Creating effective teams: A guide for members and leaders* (5th ed.). Sage Publications.

Chapter 5
Using Data as a Source of Reflection in a Feedback Loop

Rose M. Ylimaki and Lynnette A. Brunderman

Abstract This chapter considers recent policy trends toward evidence-based practices in Arizona, the U.S., and across the globe. The rise in the use of "scientific" evidence for educational policymaking rests on two common beliefs about knowledge: (1) the belief that school knowledge is universal, and (2) the belief that empirical evidence or data is the primary indicator of knowledge and learning. Recent U.S. policies have reflected the importance of data or numeric evidence from externalized evaluations to guide school decisions. Internationally, multinational organizations, such as the World Bank, have also made evidence-based policymaking a priority both in their own work as influential research and policy organizations as well as their members. Yet there are cautions against this particular use of evidence to replace professional judgement and the wider democratic deliberation about the aims, ends and content of education. Our school development project considers evidence-based values and humanistic, democratic values at tension. School development participants applied a balanced perspective on data with numerical evidence subordinated to educational values, using all as a source of reflection and growth. The chapter, thus, defines data as information that educators, school teams, and other agency members use to inform professional judgement and influence.

Keywords Evidence-based policies · Value-based education · Balance · Reflection · Pedagogical activity

> *"...the first one was understanding my responsibility is to always look at the data, from K through high school; even with juniors and seniors. There may not be state assessment, but there are a lot of things that we need to be looking at. Looking at all of that data driven instruction and that philosophy, my biggest push was for my teachers to understand and*

R. M. Ylimaki (✉)
Northern Arizona University, Flagstaff, AZ, USA
e-mail: rose.ylimaki@nau.edu

L. A. Brunderman
University of Arizona, Tucson, AZ, USA
e-mail: lbrunder@arizona.com

R. M. Ylimaki, L. A. Brunderman (eds.), *Evidence-Based School Development in Changing Demographic Contexts*, Studies in Educational Leadership 24,
https://doi.org/10.1007/978-3-030-76837-9_5

integrate that as being a valuable tool for themselves. Not because the principal said, I need to look at my data, but to fully understand the strengths and weaknesses of their curriculum map, of their instruction, of their materials, of surveys, of observation notes, and really use that data to improve what they're doing in the classroom. And they did it, and could see some direct results from it…" -Principal

As noted in chapter one, recently, education policies in the U.S. and elsewhere have reflected a trend toward "scientific" evidence-based practice and data-driven decisions. The rise in the use of scientific evidence for educational policymaking rests on two common beliefs about knowledge: One is the belief that school knowledge is universal, and the other is the belief that empirical evidence or data is the primary indicator of knowledge and learning (Ylimaki et al., 2019). Policy documents under both Republican and Democratic administrations dating back to the No Child Left Behind Act (2002) and the subsequent grant program, Race to the Top (McGuinn, 2012), have reflected the importance of data or numeric evidence from externalized evaluations to guide school decisions. Internationally, multinational organizations, such as the Organization for Economic Co-operation and Development (OECD) and the World Bank have also made evidence-based policymaking a priority both in their own work as influential research and policy organizations as well as for their members (Wiseman, 2010).

Yet as Biesta (2010) cautions us, this particular use of evidence threatens to replace professional judgment and the wider democratic deliberation about the aims, ends and content of education. Rather, Biesta calls for a value-based education as an alternative for evidence-based education. Here evidence plays a role, but that role is subordinate to the values that constitute practice as educational practices. Thus, as demonstrated in Fig. 5.1, our school development project, we recognized

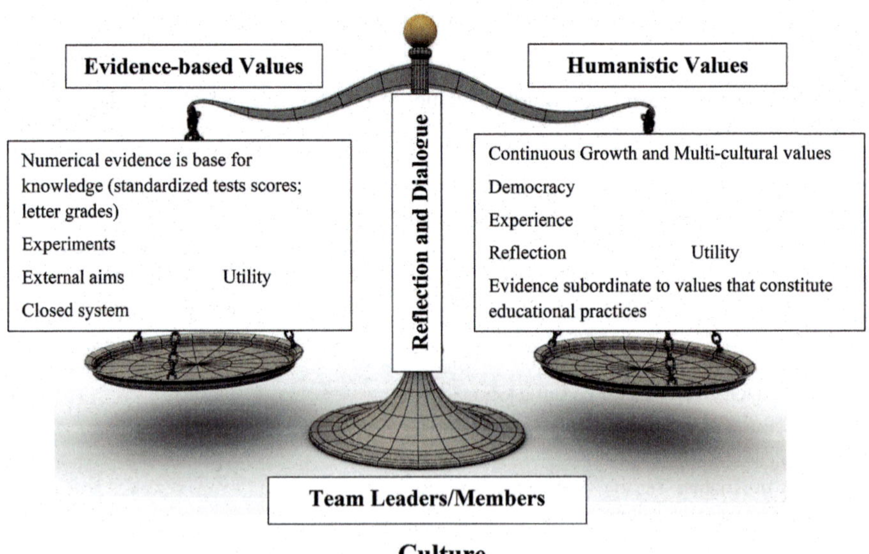

Fig. 5.1 Conceptual model for school development project. (Ylimaki et al., 2019)

that evidence-based values and humanistic values are at tension but held in balance through reflection and pedagogical activity in education.

In AZiLDR, institutes and other meetings provided school team participants and district leaders with structured (discursive) spaces for dialogue and reflection about a range of data as evidence within and between levels. In turn, participants applied a balanced perspective on data with numerical evidence subordinated to educational values, using all as a source of reflection and growth.

With an education theory grounding in mind, we define data as information that educators, school teams and other agencies use to inform professional judgment and influence. Data included student achievement tests, benchmark assessments in classrooms, and surveys of teaching-leading-studying practices in the school. Data literacy then means the capacity to understand, reflect upon, and make professional judgments about a range of data. As Ryan (2011) concluded in his explanation of Dewey & Bentley's concern about the future of humankind:

> Education is still fixed on rote memorization and standardized tests rather than the synoptic problem-solving that worked so well in Dewey's Chicago [lab] school. ...We can't work together until we begin to *see* together—not some preconceived *what*, some universal good, but a common *how* that is experimental, inclusive, and pluralistic (p. 76, *emphasis original*).

We considered the philosophy of transaction that Dewey and Bentley sketch in *Knowing and the Known* is an invitation, left for us to shape and refine in the social as well as the natural sciences. In the next sections, we present our application of theory and research as well as case examples.

Application

Our application featured a broad definition of data, to include student achievement data, attendance data, behavioral data, survey data, and observational data. As indicated in Chap. 4, teams began the process by taking the Bennett Survey for Leadership Capacity (Bennett et al., 2013) and reflecting on what it revealed about a variety of topics, including Leadership Characteristics and Practices, Curriculum and Instruction, Achievement (both current and previous levels), School Capacity, and Leadership Tensions and Dilemmas. This allowed teams to identify differences in perception between the principal and the rest of the team/staff. Teams then identified strengths and gaps in order to begin to set some goals for development.

Another survey that provided data for reflection was the Culture Survey, also discussed in Chap. 3. Again, teams were able to use that data as a source of reflection in order to plan activities for staff participation. Additionally, student achievement data was examined by the teams early in the process. However, we quickly discovered that not everyone understood the state achievement data, how to interpret it, or what use it was to them. Therefore, we spent time in building data literacy with team members. We began with looking at six assumptions about data (Love et al., 2008) and asking teams to have candid discussions about each statement. These statements can be found in Activity Box 5.1.

Activity Box 5.1: Assumption Card Stack and Shuffle (Lipton & Wellman, 2011)

Divide into groups of 3–5. Distribute one full set of cards to each group. The cards are then dealt to each member of the group. One individual will begin the round by reading a card aloud. The entire group then discusses the prompt using the following mediating questions as a guide:

- What is the thinking behind this assumption?
- What are some inferences that can be made from it?
- What might be some alternative interpretations?
- To what degree is this assumption generalizable or context specific?
- If ________________ were true, would this assumption still hold?

(Wellman & Lipton, 2004)

Each individual in turn reads a card, and the team discusses the prompt until all cards are completed or time is exhausted. This activity could take up to an hour, depending on the group.

The prompts which we used for the activity are as follows: (Love, N. Stiles, K.E., Mundry, S. & DiRanna, K., 2008. pp. 4–7.)

Assumption 1: making significant progress in improving student learning and closing achievement gaps is a moral responsibility and a real possibility in a relatively short amount of time – two to five years. It is not children's poverty or race or ethnic background that stands in the way of achievement; it is school practices and policies and the beliefs that underlie them that pose the biggest obstacles.

Assumption 2: Data have no meaning. Meaning is imposed through interpretation. Frames of reference, the way we see the world, influence the meaning we derive from data. Effective data users become aware of and critically examine their frames of reference and assumptions (Wellman & Lipton, 2004, pp. ix–xi). Conversely, data themselves can also be a catalyst to questioning assumptions and changing practices based on new ways of thinking.

Assumption 3: Collaborative inquiry – a process where teachers construct their understanding of student-learning problems and invent and test out solutions together through rigorous and frequent use of data and reflective dialogue – unleashes the resourcefulness and creativity to continuously improve instruction and student learning.

Assumption 4: A school culture characterized by collective responsibility for student learning, commitment to equity, and trust is the foundation for collaborative inquiry. In the absence of such a culture, schools may be unable to respond effectively to the data they have.

Assumption 5: Using data itself does not improve teaching. Improved teaching comes about when teachers implement sound teaching practices grounded in cultural proficiency – understanding and respect for their

(continued)

> **Activity Box 5.1** (continued)
>
> students' cultures – and a thorough understanding of the subject matter and how to teach it, including understanding student thinking and ways of making content accessible to all students.
>
> **Assumption 6:** Every member of a collaborative school community can act as a leader, dramatically impacting the quality of relationships, the school culture, and student learning.

Teams then explored the differences between summative and formative data, looking closely at the uses and value of common formative assessments. They were provided with resources to assist them in looking at a variety of formats. Teams were then expected to create a sample formative assessment for their sites, and were given feedback by other teams on what they saw and how it might be refined.

Another aspect of working with data as a source of reflection was inherent in the work we did with teams around Professional Learning Communities (DuFour and DuFour, 2011). The purpose of implementing professional learning communities (PLCs) is to examine and reflect on data in order to align instruction across content areas and grade levels, to provide for reteaching of concepts to students who did not grasp the material during initial instruction, and to support teachers in their own professional learning. Reflection on the data provided the impetus for action taken by the PLCs.

Finally, during the school development process, we provided information about the use of data gathered from classroom walk-through observations. We considered this concept from several angles. First, we talked about what kind of data to collect during walk-throughs, and how it could be best used. For example, if teachers were asked to implement new instructional strategies in mathematics, the walk-through data collected and analyzed should be specific to the goal. Secondly, we asked teams to create a walk-through protocol to meet their own individual school needs, defining the specific "look fors". An illustration of the goals, "look fors", and questions for group reflection (as created by one district) is included in Activity Box 5.2. The last piece of this process was to walk through classrooms at a variety of campuses together, working with team members to understand what they were seeing during the observation times, and then reflecting together about the observations and their implications. It was apparent that teams grew in their understanding of how to collect data as well as what it meant.

Lessons Learned

The following cases illustrate some aspects of the ways in which two different schools used data for reflection in order to move their schools forward in the continuous school development process.

Activity Box 5.2: Sample Walk-Through Protocol with Cues (Sunnyside USD, 2015)
Rubric Indicators with Mathematics Look fors Walkthrough form
   Goals for Mathematics Walkthroughs

- Calibrate through formative observations of mathematics instruction in classrooms across the district
- Build capacity for principals to provide feedback and lead mathematics improvement

Indicator: Mathematics Look Fors.
Instruction 1: EEI

- Alignment of instruction to common core standards
- Shifts in instruction - fluency, concept development, application

Instruction 2: Engagement

- Use of mathematical practices
- Use of math talk moves

Instruction 3: Differentiation

- Student Partners/Groupings,
- Menus
- Vocabulary support (anchor charts)
- Scaffolding prerequisite knowledge into grade level content instruction

Instruction 4: Checks for Understanding

- Journal prompts
- Use of white boards
- Questioning
- Chunking (10/2)
- Review of skills check data with students

Management 3: Learning Environment

- Organization of tools, computers, and materials
- Productive and cooperative environment (i.e. cooperative learning roles, student initiated and self-help processes - 3 before me, reference charts)

Guiding Questions for Classroom Debrief

- What did you see including examples and evidence from the indicators?
- How does this relate to our goals for mathematics instruction (content focus/pacing for grade level, shifts in instruction, mathematical practices)?
- What would be the priority for feedback and next steps (strength and stretch)?

(continued)

> **Activity Box 5.2** (continued)
> - How would you, as an instructional leader, coach the teacher to reinforce positive practices?
> - How would you, as an instructional leader, coach the teacher to grow in their use of math practices?
>
> ***Guiding Questions for Summary***
>
> - What trends did we see across the classrooms?
> - What would be the priority for next steps for the site (strength and stretch)?
> - How would you use the trends across the classrooms to inform professional learning in your building? How would you communicate that with staff?
> - Who will host the next visit (specific date and time frame)?

Case A: *Sylvester Middle School*

Sylvester Middle School is located south of the metropolitan area of Tucson, and is characterized as somewhat suburban, yet somewhat rural. Serving about 700 students in grades 6 through 8, the student population is approximately 50% Hispanic and 50% Anglo, with only about 10–20 students identified as English Language Learners. The principal, Susan Sussex, indicated that they are a growing school in a growing district, with many students moving into the area from out of state. For this reason, she suggested, the school is having an identity crisis, trying to decide who they are as a school; what does it mean to be a student at Sylvester Middle School.

The initial data that this leadership team looked at in order to see where they were was the data from the Bennett Survey of Leadership Capacity, (Bennett, et al., 2013) administered to all staff as well as the principal. The principal explained how they used that information.

> "And we decided that we would share all the data we have, all the staff, the principal survey as well as the other surveys and just give them time during the faculty meeting to just look it over, read it, look at trends, patterns, and it was very interesting to me that there were a lot of similarities and in how I rated myself and how my staff rated me. There may have been a few areas where I rated myself lower than they rated me or maybe I rated myself higher the they did me, but for the most part I felt like it was a good approximation. Our perceptions are similar."

She went on to discuss areas of concern that came out of this data examination and reflection.

> "I think looking at the trusting culture among the staff - that was a huge area - that they don't really trust; and collective efficacy was bad - they jump out at us…You know maybe a little bit of that, and then maybe just a sense of collaborative decision-making and shared leadership…it is certainly an area that we need to focus more on - using our teacher leaders, our curriculum team leaders, somewhat like department chairs in the middle school. How can we utilize them more?…Shared leaders on campus?…and then from their communica-

tion with their teams and their administration with communication, how do we solicit more important opinions and identifying ways for me to reach out for those opinions."

Teachers from the leadership team expanded on the principal's reflections, stating:

> "One of the things that came up was some of the teachers were reading the results and they were shocked at why some of the people said it this way in some of the written responses, and why would some of them be so negative. They were surprised. Sharing is a positive thing; if you just got negative results it sounds more horrible."

Trust in the administration emerged as an issue at this school, but by being open about the data, sharing the results of the surveys, both positive and negative, and reflecting on what the data were indicating, staff began the process of coming together to work toward a common goal.

Case B: *Mary Miller Elementary School*

Mary Miller Elementary School is located in a medium-sized urban school district in southern Arizona, hosting students in Kindergarten through sixth grade. The first elementary school in the district, it is known to serve students whose parents and grandparents had also attended the school.

The state testing results released in 2019 indicate that 31% of students at the school are proficient in English/Language Arts, and 26% are proficient in Mathematics. Understanding that these test results are just one data point from which to judge school success, the school website states:

> "The [State] Test measures how well our students are performing in English language arts and math. [State Test] scores are just one of several measures, including report card grades, classroom performance, and feedback from teachers, that can be used to measure your child's academic progress."

The principal, Cathy Ignacio, was asked about things that were meaningful from the School Development trainings. Upon reflection, she offered.

> "Another thing that we implemented, I think with Institute One, is we talked about how we look at the data, and that traditionally we've been all focused on the ground level, but we need to start taking more focus on where it was before it was that … I really enjoyed that session, because we took it back right away, and we did the activity with our staff, and talked about what we needed to really be looking at."

She continues,

> "We did data talks every week, like three grade levels at a time, on Wednesdays, and so that would either become goal setting, or we'd look at math or reading, and we'd look at strategies in the areas they were not doing as well, and what we could do for the reteaching, and what the focus was going to be. We changed our reading, as far as our comprehension questions, tailoring those to the story so that they focused more on the skills we were seeing. We were still on goals, and so that was helpful."

One use of data for reflection was highlighted in the School Assistance Team process. Cathy explained:

> Our school assistance team, some people call it TAT, we call it SAT…one of the things we've constantly struggled with is making sure what that referral process is, what teachers need to do on there, and how they document, how they do interventions…we had it nicely set up so when you come to meet with us, you need to bring this data, this data, this data. You need to talk about what's been going on, but we're going to come back with interventions. It's not like just because you come here we're going to do a child study. We had I think around over 30 referrals this year, but we really only went ahead with a handful of kids to really go through the child study process because we put the interventions in place, and it was just clearer. We did some inservices with teachers on things to know about it, what you're doing, what you need to do. It probably needs to be repeated each year so we remember, but what a difference. It was clarified, it was communicated, and it was successful with the strategies…and there's been this change in achievement, that all of a sudden it clicked."

Cathy and her team recognized that reflection on data was vital to the process of continuous school development, and worked to embed the practices on many different levels.

Final Thoughts

Schools are rich in data, but understanding how to use the data for reflection and continuous development is often lacking. In some cases, data is interpreted as solely test scores from summative state tests; in other instances, data as seen as a rich source of material upon which to reflect and to inform decision-making. The case studies presented above illustrated only small pieces of the process, but recognized that in order to use data appropriately, a culture of trust and collaboration needed to be in place. Teachers are often fearful about sharing student achievement or behavioral data because they are afraid of being judged. Thus, a trusting, collegial culture must be established in order to openly and honestly examine and reflect on data in a collaborative manner.

References

Act, N. C. L. B. (2002). No child left behind act of 2001. *Public Law*, 107–110.

Bennett, J. V., Ylimaki, R. M., Dugan, T. M., & Brunderman, L. A. (2013). Developing the potential for sustainable improvement in underperforming schools: Capacity building in the socio-cultural dimension. *Journal for Educational Change*. https://doi.org/10.1007/s10833-013-9217-6

Biesta, G. J. (2010). Why 'what works' still won't work: From evidence-based education to value-based education. *Studies in Philosophy and Education, 29*(5), 491–503.

DuFour, R., & DuFour, R. (2011). *Leading difficult conversations: Professional learning communities at work professional development video set*. Solution Tree.

Love, N., Stiles, K. E., Mundry, S., & DiRanna, K. (2008). *The data coach's guide to improving learning for all students*. Sage Publictions.

McGuinn, P. (2012). Stimulating reform: Race to the top, competitive grants and the Obama education agenda. *Educational Policy, 26*(1), 136–159.

Ryan, F. (2011). Seeing together: Mind, matter, and the experimental outlook of John Dewey and Arthur F. Bentley. *The Pluralist, 8*, 124–129.

Sunnyside Unified School District. (2015). *Mathematics leadership development: Mathematics walkthrough protocol*. Sunnyside Unified School District.

Wiseman, A. W. (2010). The uses of evidence for educational policymaking: Global contexts and international trends. *Review of Research in Education, 34*(1), 1–24.

Ylimaki, R., Brunderman, L., & Moyi, P. (2019). Balancing evidence-based and humanistic education in school development for underperforming Arizona and South Carolina schools. *Leadership and Policy in Schools*, 1–21. https://doi.org/10.1080/15700763.2019.1695850

Chapter 6
Going Deeper into Curriculum and Pedagogical Activity

Rose M. Ylimaki and Lynnette A. Brunderman

Abstract This chapter takes a deeper dive into curriculum and pedagogy as these are defined and applied within *education*. Here terminology like pedagogy, curriculum, leadership (including leadership teams) and education itself are defined in terms of a particular 'educational' interest. Such an approach also features a mediation among state and national standards and the needs and interests of children. This approach sees the task of educating children as necessarily occurring in the pedagogical relation between teacher and student in classrooms and between formal leader/principal and teacher in schools and between district leader/superintendent and principals. We recognize the value of understanding the foundations of education developed in earlier times of political and cultural uncertainty. We explicitly define key terms for education, curriculum, pedagogy and leadership in school development using foundational understandings amidst the contemporary situation. Application of the concepts is explored through case studies.

Keywords Education · Pedagogy · Curriculum · Leadership

> *"I love the ELA strategies. Anytime you guys do a … Like what you did this morning with the grouping, yesterday with the 3 cards. I find that … That's hands on. I can use that. I also really like the science where it was inquiry based. I had never done science that way. That hands on learning I really appreciate. Close reading was another one." Teacher A*
>
> *"We talked about the strategies and kind of the resources that you can look back into your toolbox. You can't possibly use everything and implement it. It just doesn't work that way. You use the things that you're problem solving now. Then, like you said, once you get the foundation for decision-making in place and you get this idea of what engagement looks like in place, and you've got these things that you've all agreed upon, then you can roll out your ELA strategies that you want to put in place. Consistency. Kids need structure and they need consistency." Teacher B*

R. M. Ylimaki (✉)
Northern Arizona University, Flagstaff, AZ, USA
e-mail: rose.ylimaki@nau.edu

L. A. Brunderman
University of Arizona, Tucson, AZ, USA
e-mail: lbrunder@arizona.com

R. M. Ylimaki, L. A. Brunderman (eds.), *Evidence-Based School Development in Changing Demographic Contexts*, Studies in Educational Leadership 24, https://doi.org/10.1007/978-3-030-76837-9_6

This chapter takes a deeper dive into curriculum and pedagogy as these are defined and applied within *education*. Here terminology like pedagogy, curriculum, leadership (including leadership teams) and education itself are defined in terms of a particular 'educational' interest. Such an approach also features a mediation among state and national standards and the needs and interests of children. This approach sees the task of educating children as necessarily occurring in the pedagogical relation between teacher and student in classrooms and between formal leader/principal and teacher in schools and between district leader/superintendent and principals. A relative degree of human freedom is assumed and guaranteed for the state, district, principal, teacher and ultimately for the child.

Educators in the U.S. and elsewhere must implement increasingly centralized state and national curriculum standards as measured by externalized evaluations. At the same time, schools across the U.S. and elsewhere are educating increasingly diverse students due to changing demographics as well as immigrants or refugees from globalization. As noted in the opening chapters, these challenges are not entirely new in the U.S. and elsewhere. In an earlier zone of uncertainty from the turn of the nineteenth century through two World Wars, John Dewey (1916) argued for a deliberative approach in his philosophy as the theory of education whereby schools functioned as a microcosm of a democratic society. Dewey's efforts to connect child, school, and society were motivated by more than just a desire for better higher standards or pedagogical methods. For Dewey, because character, rights and duties are informed by and contribute to the social realm, schools were critical sites to learn and experiment with the democratic prospect. Here democratic life consisted not only of civic and economic conduct but in habits of problem solving, compassionate imagination, creative expression, and civic self-governance. During World War II, Dewey (1944) wrote,

> "There will be almost a revolution in school education when study and learning are treated not as acquisition of what others know but as development of capital to be invested in eager alertness in observing and judging the conditions under which one lives. Yet until this happens, we shall be ill-prepared to deal with a world whose outstanding trait is change" (p. 463).

We are not arguing that we must strictly adhere to theories developed historically, but we recognize the value of understanding the foundations of education developed in earlier times of political and cultural uncertainty. In the next several paragraphs, we explicitly define key terms for education, curriculum, pedagogy and leadership in school development using foundational understandings amidst the contemporary situation.

Education is an explicitly interpersonal and ethical endeavor, one that regards the individual student or child as an end in himself—rather than in terms of predefined categories of social identity, psychological technique or academic achievement (Friesen, 2019). Such an approach does not ignore questions of politics but focuses on the task of educating children. Here we turn to Dewey as well as the traditions that informed his work since the Enlightenment to understand the task of educating children as necessarily occurring within and through the tensions between the individual and society, between freedom and constraint, between present realities and future possibilities (Friesen & Ylimaki, 2019; Price et al., 2019). That education finds its goal in the eventual autonomy of the student—in their ability to decide for themselves and to participate in social deliberation as well--means that its central purpose is a democratic one. Moreover, it seeks to achieve this goal not through psychological techniques or manipulations nor through sociological categorizations, but by taking informed risks, granting the student limited but ever increasing degrees of autonomy in a teacher-student relation in which they can also find trust and safety.

Pedagogy in this context is *not* the application of evidence-based teaching practices and models for teaching. Here we draw on historical perspectives as synthesized by Friesen (2019) to argue that pedagogy is an interpersonal, artful and relational calling and craft that possesses its own "dignity" outside of theory and "evidence." It appears as the formative cultivation of children and young people as ends in themselves, with a view to their becoming responsive members of society (e.g., Biesta, 2015). Pedagogy in this sense is also the theory of this engagement and cultivation, with the understanding that its relation to practice always relies on the artful and tactful mediation of the teacher (e.g., Herbart, 1896). Evidence is used as a source of reflection and planning for pedagogical decisions.

Curriculum is cultural aims and interests translated into content. Curriculum is not only a policy document that reflects cultural aims and interests like the state version of Common Core content, but is fully situated in an educator-student pedagogical relation or in the dynamic between the self-realization of the young person and the public, policy and curricular demands (e.g. see: Friesen, 2019; Klafki, 2000).

Leadership is, at heart, a pedagogical and mediational activity whereby principals are teachers of teachers, and superintendents are teachers of principals. This relationship is not unlike that of teachers and students in classrooms (Uljens and Ylimaki, 2017). Like teachers who must mediate between the curriculum standards and students, principals and superintendents must mediate between policies and other expectations and the needs of teachers and students in particular schools and communities. In order to support continuous improvement, leadership from multiple levels must work in teams to deliberate on problems of practice that support both policy interests or demands and the interests or needs of increasingly culturally diverse children.

Application

Throughout the school development project, participants were asked to explore state standards or cultural aims translated into content, and possibilities for pedagogy in particular situations. The first step was to explore the policy shifts from the old set of standards and assessment to the new state standards in terms of content in Arizona College and Career Readiness Standards (Arizona's version of the Common Core Standards) (2016) as well as pedagogical strategies or interventions in relation to the needs of young people. In the area of English/Language Arts (ELA) (2016), the new standards required students to build knowledge through content-rich non-fiction, to ground reading, writing and speaking in evidence from text (both literary and informational), and to have regular practice with complex text and its academic language. In Mathematics (2016), teachers were required to focus on coherence of standards across grade levels, with attention to rigor, conceptual understanding, procedural skill and fluency, and application. Participants then examined sample state assessment questions for format and what was demanded of the students in order to be successful. Moreover, teams were asked to bring examples of formative student assessments that reflected needs of particular children. They were asked to identify pedagogical strategies that would support the child's development academically and otherwise. Finally, the school teams reflected on the needs of teachers and how to support them to be immediately successful with particular children and cohorts of children.

Teams were also asked to plan how to address parents and community in a 1–2 min timeframe, like an "elevator speech". The whole concept of common core standards was receiving backlash nationally for a variety of reasons. Mainly, the belief that these common core standards were being forced on states by the federal government, and a lack of understanding about what they were and what they asked students to know and be able to do, caused tensions in many communities.

Additionally, experts in ELA and mathematics were asked to share strategies for teachers to use in classrooms to mediate among the greater rigor of the new standards and needs of children. Groups were divided into elementary and secondary so that the information could be geared to the levels of interest.

Using the strategies outlined in *The Core Six: Essential Strategies for Achieving Excellence with the Common Core* (Silver et al., 2012), participants experienced using each strategy as they learned about them. The six strategies outlined and practiced included: Reading for Meaning, Compare and Contrast, Inductive Learning, Circle of Knowledge, Write to Learn, and Vocabulary's CODE (Silver et al., 2012). Then as school teams, participants discussed the comfort level and facility of their own staff to implement the new reading strategies in order to support and mediate among the complexity of the new state standards and children in their schools. Finally, school teams worked together to create a plan to share and diffuse the information they had gained about standards and strategies to teachers, other staff and parents/community members. In other words, our application of contemporary school development grounded in education, curriculum and pedagogy was culturally sensitive to the Arizona context and individuals within it. We will expand on this point in the next chapter.

Interestingly, when working with school teams, we were stunned by the lack of knowledge and understanding about curriculum and pedagogy. Generally they understood standards, knew they needed objectives, but were mandated to use prepackaged programs which did not allow for deep thought about how children learn to read or do mathematics. In some of the more urban districts, teachers had the benefit of internal experts who understood content specific curriculum and pedagogy and were providing professional development for teachers on an ongoing basis. In the more rural settings, however, this ongoing development was lacking.

Lessons Learned

The following two cases highlight some aspects of the implementation of evolving curricular and pedagogical activity at the school level.

Case A: *Sun City Elementary School*

Comprised of approximately 730 students in grades K-6, Sun City Elementary School serves 77% Hispanic students, 20% Native American students, and the remaining 3% identify as White or 2 or more races. The free and reduced lunch rate is about 91%. They see themselves as primarily a neighborhood school, although most of the native American students reside on the local reservation lands. Principal Isaac Elias has led the school for over 10 years, and was able to reflect on several aspects that resulted from their time with the School Development Project.

First, Isaac focused on the implementation of lesson study and peer observation.

> "So, one of the things that did come up that we did this year that we had never done in the past…was having lesson studies done at each grade level…each grade level presented lessons and the rest of their teamates observed…them and afterwards gave them feedback, then the next teacher and the next teacher. So we did that with every grade level this year. So we are really looking to build upon that for next year to make it even more effective."

He elaborated further on the collaborative aspect of curriculum development and planning.

> "I think the biggest impact has been in the area of collaboration and trying to continually improve that process and make it more productive. We're seeing a greater focus on the actual planning, especially with the new standards and having a better process for breaking those down…you know the process for that, the fact that the whole focus on collaboration and working together and having those PLCs in place and teachers having that system of planning and continually meeting and having our coaches being a part of that as far as supporting them and helping to drive that process of breaking down the standards."

Additionally, Mr. Elias recognized the need for school leaders to work with teachers, coaching them as they implement new standards and different pedagogies.

> "There was a lot of dialogue around the topic of coaching and looking at those different scenarios and strategies and ideas that she presented. It was just a good discussion with myself and our coaches and our teachers to be able to get into specifics or some different ideas of approaches to working with teachers and coaching."

Sun City Elementary School was fortunate to be located in an urban school district that did provide ongoing development opportunities in pedagogy, allowing this staff to take what they gained from the AZiLDR Institutes and expand on it with internal support.

Case B: *Smithson High School Revisited*

As a reminder, Smithson High School is a public high school in southern Arizona, serving grades 9–12 and over 1500 students. The principal, Mr. Tierney, (at the time of the project) was a white male in his mid-thirties, who began teaching in 2005. After 5 years in the classroom, he was promoted to an assistant principal position, and 1 year later was thrust into the principal position with the abrupt removal of the previous principal.

Smithson High School and Principal Tierney entered the project at the direction of the superintendent due to declining test scores and community pressure to improve. The associate superintendent, Bob Burlington, attended each training with the Smithson principal and team so that he could support them in their endeavors.

However, during this time, the district purchased a curriculum package that included pacing guides, materials, lesson plans, etc. Every school within the district was mandated to use the curriculum with integrity, adhering to all parts. As the school team and teachers learned more about curriculum and pedagogy, and Principal Tierney enrolled in a PHD program with particular emphasis on leadership of curriculum and pedagogy, they requested permission to adjust the pacing guide and to supplement the curriculum to meet the needs of their students, They were denied.

In his own words, Principal Tierney explains:

> "We began to discover that the mandates of No Child Left Behind and Race to the Top and the Arizona Career and College Readiness standards (that are common core) were difficult to bring about the changes necessary in the curriculum in order for us to be able to adhere to and to excel in the new paradigm. That created some problems. One is it exposed the communication issues that we have. Schools weren't talking to each other. People within departments were rarely talking to each other and it was just kind of the relic of the past and how it had been, and so we got together as a leadership team (principals) and we basically said we need something to help us get there; and we were excited about the Beyond textbooks…because it was billed to us as 'here is a template for you to do things. You still get to choose how to teach it but this gives you a template', which was exciting. We were, okay, this is from a district that has consistently been at the top or the second best in the entire state for many years. This is going to be a helpful thing. Like most things, it is complicated.

Final Thoughts

Deep understanding of curriculum and pedagogy have taken a backseat to prepackaged programs which were often designed to be "teacher-proof." It has been our observation (as well as that of many of our content experts) that we have an entire generation of teachers, and increasingly a generation of leaders, who grew up under No Child Left Behind and the increased accountability that drives decisions. They have only known packaged programs, many of which are scripted, and have never been asked to make decisions about the needs of their students and how to best approach their learning. It is our hope that calling attention to this issue will help as we go forward in school development work around the world.

References

Arizona Department of Education. (2016). *Arizona's English/language arts standards final draft*. Retrieved at https://k12standards.az.gov/sites/default/files/media/ELA%202nd%20DRAFT%20STANDARDS-%20Clean%20Copy_1.pdf

Biesta, G. J. (2015). *Beyond learning: Democratic education for a human future*. Routledge.

Dewey, J. (1916). *Democracy and education: An introduction to the philosophy of education*. Macmillan.

Dewey, J. (1944). Challenge to liberal thought. *Fortune, 30*(2), 155–157.

Friesen, N. (2019). Educational research in America today: Relentless instrumentalism and scholarly backlash. *Erziehungswissenschaft, 30*(59), 77–83. https://doi.org/10.3224/ezw.v30i2.09

Friesen, N., & Ylimaki, R. (2019, April). *Renewing education theorizing for curriculum, teacher education and leadership*. A paper presented at the annual meeting of the American Educational Research Association, Toronto, ON.

Herbart, J. F. (1896). *The science of education*. DC Heath & Company.

Klafki, W. (2000). *Didaktik analysis as the core of preparation of instruction* (p. 114). Rethinking Schooling.

Price, T., Castner, D., & Watson, L. (2019). *After Currere: The meaning of education in North American curriculum studies*. Paper presented at the European Conference on Educational Research, Septmber 6, 2019.

Silver, H. F., Dewing, R. T., & Perini, M. J. (2012). *The core six: Essential strategies for achieving excellence with the common core*. ASCD.

Uljens, M., & Ylimaki, R. M. (2017). Chapter 1: Non-affirmative theory of education and foundation of curriculum studies, Didaktik, and educational leadership. In M. Uljens & R. M. Ylimaki (Eds.), *Bridging educational leadership, curriculum theory, and Didaktik: Non-affirmative theory of education* (pp. 3–145). Springer.

Chapter 7
Strength-Based Approaches to Meeting Culturally Diverse Student Needs

Rose M. Ylimaki and Lynnette A. Brunderman

Abstract A strengths-based approach to education is essential for successful school development in culturally diverse schools. Chapter 7 reflects that education lies in the pedagogical relations and provocations into the self-realizations and growth of young people. In this arena, provocation refers to intentions to provoke thoughts, ideas, and actions that help students to learn and grow. A provocation should be grounded in the child's cultural background strengths. We explicitly worked with school teams to *recognize* the equal value of different cultures in their students' ethnic and linguistic backgrounds and to lead in culturally responsive ways with regards to pedagogy, curriculum, data-analysis, education and community engagement. We drew on research to include positive perspectives of parents and families, communication of high expectations, learning within the context of culture, student-centered and culturally mediated instruction, reshaping the curriculum, and teacher as facilitator. Thus, culturally relevant teaching requires teachers to embrace diversity, build on strengths, and recognize that students learn in a variety of ways. It is the job of the leader to help teachers gain an understanding of those cultures, and how to incorporate that into their classrooms. Sample activities and case studies expand the concepts.

Keywords Culturally responsive pedagogy · Culturally responsive leadership · Funds of knowledge

"…we have somebody in Navajo enrichment class in kindergarten, first, and second and third grade. And we have a teacher who taught in kindergarten and has an aide in the classroom and they were both Navajo, Native Americans, and they would teach the language and culture infused into the core, into the curriculum. And, the same with kinder. And in 2nd grade, we have a Navajo teacher who is not as competent, or feels as capable of teaching

R. M. Ylimaki (✉)
Northern Arizona University, Flagstaff, AZ, USA
e-mail: rose.ylimaki@nau.edu

L. A. Brunderman
University of Arizona, Tucson, AZ, USA
e-mail: lbrunder@arizona.com

R. M. Ylimaki, L. A. Brunderman (eds.), *Evidence-Based School Development in Changing Demographic Contexts*, Studies in Educational Leadership 24, https://doi.org/10.1007/978-3-030-76837-9_7

the language or the culture. We have a foster grandparent who is there every day for seven hours that helps with her and so, even though that foster grandparent doesn't have the certification, she...knows the language and the culture... She can reinforce skills using the culture and the language of the standards...And so, it's not just the principal of the school. It's the facilitators, the parapros, it's the anybody who touches the child in their educational career has that capacity of having that. And, you have to help build that within them."
-Principal

A strengths-based approach to education is essential for successful school development in culturally diverse schools. As noted in Chap. 6 and elsewhere, education lies in the pedagogical relations and provocations into the self-realizations and growth of young people. Here, provocation in educational literature refers to intentions to provoke thoughts, ideas, and actions that can help to expand on a thought, project, idea or interest. A provocation can come in many different forms, but it is always intended to provoke thoughts, ideas, or actions that extend current thinking, interests, and ideas. Pedagogical relations and interventions or provocations are grounded in recognition (Taylor, 2004) of the child's cultural background strengths or funds of knowledge (Moll et al., 2006). Recognition in this sense means that the teacher recognizes or sees all features of each student and the strengths of these features for teaching and learning.

Moll et al. (1992) and González et al. (2005) reflect the notion of recognition through a research project that helped classroom teachers understand and acquire knowledge about families within their communities. Specifically, Moll et al. (1992) conducted a collaborative ethnographic study of the classroom and household practices of working-class Mexican-American families in Arizona. The authors defined the key term, *funds of knowledge*, as the skills and knowledge that have been historically and culturally developed to enable an individual or household to function within a given culture, and argue that integrating *funds of knowledge* into classroom activities creates a richer and more highly-scaffolded learning experience for students. Research findings from this study (Moll et al., 1992, p. 132–141) include:

1. Families have abundant knowledge that programs can learn and use in their family engagement efforts.
2. Students bring with them *funds of knowledge* from their homes and communities that can be used for concept and skill development.
3. Classroom practices sometimes underestimate or constrain what children are able to display intellectually.
4. Teachers should focus on helping students find meaning in activities rather than learn rules and facts.
5. Group discussions around race and class should promote trust and encourage dialogue.

Gloria Ladson-Billings also argues that culture is central to teaching and learning (i.e. pedagogical relations and provocations); it plays a role not only in communicating and receiving information, but also in shaping the thinking process of groups and individuals. As she put it, pedagogy that recognizes and celebrates diverse cultures offers equity and access to education for all students (Ladson-Billings, 1994).

Culturally Responsive Teaching is a pedagogy that recognizes the importance of including students' cultural references in all aspects of learning (Ladson-Billings, 1994).

A number of scholars have recently applied principles of culturally responsive teaching to leadership (e.g. Horsford et al., 2011; Johnson, 2006; Johnson, 2014; Scanlan and López, 2014). Johnson (2006) was one of the first to extend the asset-based approach of culturally responsive pedagogy to leadership. Johnson (2006) defined culturally responsive leadership as leadership that involves philosophies, practices, and policies that create inclusive schooling environments for students and families from ethnically and culturally diverse backgrounds. Common practices include (1) emphasizing high expectations for student achievement; (2) incorporating the history, values, and cultural knowledge of students' home communities in the school curriculum; (3) working to develop a critical consciousness among both students and faculty to challenge inequities in the larger society; and (4) creating organizational structures at the school and district level that empower students and parents from diverse racial and ethnic communities (Johnson, 2007). Other researchers (e.g. Scheurich, 1998; Johnson, 2006, 2007; Riehl, 2000) identified similar characteristics and practices of culturally responsive leadership.

Horsford, Grosland and Gunn (2011) incorporated antiracist pedagogy and leadership in diverse contexts to create a framework for culturally relevant leadership, including four dimensions: (1) knowledge of the political context; (2) inclusion of a culturally relevant and antiracist pedagogical approach; (3) a personal knowledge of cultural proficiency and challenges to it; and (4) the professional duty to work for educational equity. As Johnson (2014) and others have noted, culturally responsive leadership often overlaps with leadership for social justice approaches, a term that has been prevalent in the U.S. educational leadership literature and focuses on improving the educational experiences and outcomes for all students, particularly those who have been traditionally marginalized in schools. Most recently, Johnson (2014) applied culturally responsive leadership to practices that bridge school and community concerns, advocate for cultural recognition and revitalization, and position educational leaders as advocates for racial equity and community development in diverse neighborhoods (p. 7).

Scanlan and López (2014) agree and add explicit attention to cultural and linguistic diversity. Scanlan and López draw on culturally responsive leadership practices that reduce marginalization and successfully educate what they term the new mainstream of students. Based upon their analysis of the literature, Scanlan and López identified three essential dimensions to effectively educate culturally and linguistically diverse students, including promoting sociocultural integration, cultivating language proficiency, and ensuring academic achievement. They proposed a theory of action that school leadership most effectively creates the learning architecture for successfully educating culturally and linguistically diverse students through an integrated service delivery.

In our project, we explicitly worked with school teams to *recognize* the equal value of different cultures in their students' ethnic and linguistic backgrounds and to lead in culturally responsive ways with regards to pedagogy, curriculum, data-analysis, education, and community engagement. We drew on the above research to include:

1. Positive perspectives on parents and families - Whether it's an informal chat as the parent brings the child to school or in phone conversations or home visits or through newsletters sent home, teachers and principals can begin a dialogue with family members that can result in learning about each of the families through genuine communication (Nieto, 1996; Moll et al., 1992).

2. Communication of high expectations- All students should receive the consistent message that they are expected to attain high standards in their school work, and this message must be delivered by all that are involved in students' academic lives including teachers, guidance counselors, administrators (Horsford et al., 2011). Teachers and others should understand the students' behavior in light of the norms of the communities in which they have grown.

3. Learning within the context of culture – The increasing diversity in our schools, the ongoing demographic changes across the nation and the movement towards globalization dictate that we develop a more in-depth understanding of culture if we want to bring about true understanding among diverse populations (Wilson-Portuondo, 2002). People from different cultures learn in different ways. Their expectations for learning may be different. For example, students from some cultural groups prefer to learn in cooperation with others, while the learning style of others is to work independently.

4. Student-centered instruction - In our multicultural society, culturally responsive teaching reflects democracy at its highest level (Dewey, 1916). It means doing whatever it takes to ensure that every child is achieving and ever moving toward realizing her or his potential. Here learning is a socially mediated process whereby children develop self-realization and autonomy by interacting with both adults and more knowledgeable peers. These interactions allow students to hypothesize, experiment with new ideas, and receive feedback. Here it is also important to create classroom projects that involve the community and its resources.

5. Culturally mediated instruction - Ongoing multicultural activities within the classroom engender a natural awareness of cultural history, values and contributions (Severian-Wilmeth, 2002; Moll et al., 1992; Scanlan and López, 2014; Johnson, 2006). Instruction is culturally mediated when it incorporates and integrates diverse ways of knowing, understanding, and representing information. Instruction and learning take place in an environment that encourages multicultural viewpoints and allows for inclusion of knowledge that is relevant to the students. Learning happens in culturally appropropriate social situations; that is pedagogical relations and human relationships among teachers and students are congruent with students' cultures (Hollins, 1996).

6. Reshaping the curriculum - Schools must take a serious look at their curriculum, pedagogy, retention, and tracking policies, testing, hiring practices, and all other policies and practices that create a school climate that is either empowering or disempowering for those who work there (Nieto, 1996). The curriculum should

Application

In this section, we describe our process to develop school culture through leadership teams. When we first met with school teams for the first Institute, we understood that they needed to develop as a strong team before they could work productively or be expected to diffuse the learning throughout their school sites. Thus, they were initially asked to creatively introduce their school team. The result ranged from artistic visual displays to raps, songs, and poetry. The activity allowed teams to identify what was special and unifying about their own team. Group norms are vital to a well-functioning team, so teams were then asked to imagine that the were viewing their team functioning well, recording what they were seeing and hearing. This became the basis for their team norms. At this point, we felt that teams were ready to address some of the hard work. We structured an activity, Assumption Card Stack and Shuffle (Lipton & Wellman, 2011), in which teams had deep conversations about the values and aims of education. See the Activity Box 3.1 for additional detail. Teams were able to coalesce around some basic values and aims of education that they would use as their guide going forward.

At this time, we provided information to the teams, both through short lecture and sharing of scholarly articles, including particularly articles from our research on the ISSPP project and related research studies. Articles focused on, the socio-cultural affect and the southern Arizona context, emphasizing the value of building relationships in an ethic of community. They also examined their own conscious-ness and awareness of the border context and political environment, all of which contribute to the organizational culture.

The next step in the process was to ask each team member to individually com-plete the School Culture Survey (Gruenert & Valentine, 1998). The dimensions explored in the School Culture Survey included Collaborative Leadership, Teacher Collaboration, Professional Development, Collegial Support, Unity of Purpose, and Learning Partnership. Team members were directed to compare their responses, discuss areas of strength and areas needing additional development, and finally to infer how closely they believed their responses would reflect those of their staff as a whole. We then defined a culture of collaboration, asking each team to describe their existing school culture, explicating the unwritten rules by which everyone operated. They rated their faculty on their readiness as a whole to work collaboratively (on a scale of 1–5) and identified what, if anything, they wanted to change. Participants were provided with additional information about what constitutes positive school culture, then asked to apply their learning. Specifically, they were asked to identify something from a recent staff meeting for which they would have liked to see more staff engagement, and then to find/create a strategy to help and determine why that strategy would be appropriate. Finally, they were asked to plan the next faculty meeting to address their concerns, considering specifically goals to improve culture and team building strategies.

Subsequent institutes sought to refine and enhance the development of inclusive, democratic cultures in schools as a microcosm of society. Using the Solution Tree be meaningful and student-centered as well as aligned to cultural aims and interests (state versions of Common Core). Here Nieto and others recommend using resources other than textbooks for study, developing learning activities that are more reflective of students' backgrounds, and developing integrated units around universal themes.

7. Teacher as facilitator – Teachers should develop a learning environment that is relevant to and reflective of their students' social, cultural, and linguistic experiences. They act as guides, mediators, consultants, instructors, and advocates for the students, helping to effectively connect their culturally- and community-based knowledge to the classroom learning experiences (Scanlan and López, 2014). Ladson-Billings (1995) adds that a key criterion for culturally relevant teaching is nurturing and supporting competence in both home and school cultures. Teachers should use the students' home cultural experiences as a foundation upon which to develop knowledge and skills. Content learned in this way is more significant to students and facilitates the transfer of what is learned in school to real-life situations (Padrón et al., 2002; Moll et al., 2006; González et al., 2005).

Culturally relevant teaching, in the simplest terms, requires teachers to embrace diversity, build on strengths, and recognize that students learn in a variety of ways. Building on the knowledge and skills that students bring from their home and community cultures provides the hook for students to be able to grow in understanding as they relate what they know to what they are learning. The difficulty comes when teachers are not familiar with the home cultures from which students come. It is the job of leaders to help teachers gain an understanding of those cultures, and how to incorporate that into their classrooms.

Application

In order to legitimately address culturally responsive pedagogy, individuals must first be willing to talk about race and culture, and confront their own inherent biases. This is uncomfortable for most people. Jack Mezirow (1997) discusses transformative learning in adults, and how that occurs. As humans, we all have core beliefs and basic assumptions that grow out of our experience, culture and the way we were raised. These are most often unconscious, and as long as things that happen around us or learning in which we engage fit into this framework, we do not question it. It is only when something does not fit well into our personal framework that we seek to understand in different ways. Mezirow (1997) suggests that we transform our learning when we question our own centrality of experience, our frame of reference, through critical self-reflection on our own assumptions (and the assumptions of others) and rational discourse with others in order to arrive at collective understandings. When challenged about your beliefs, values and assumptions, at a below-conscious level it can often be interpreted as challenging your identity, and can result in the fight-flight response. Another key piece to this process is affirmation; affirmation can help to separate identity from evidence and facts. At the core of this type of learning is centrality of relationship.

Thus, when approaching culture, race, ethnicity, gender, sexual orientation, etc. with adults, it was important to help them self-reflect and feel comfortable discussing these issues and how they impact schooling. First, each individual was asked to reflect on their own biases and assumptions by completing a worksheet, identifying key factors from their personal backgrounds that shaped the way they see the world. These included gender, generational, culture, personal style, sexual orientation, family background/values, professional experience and race/ethnicity. Then in their teams (with whom they had built a trusting relationship) they discussed their own biases/assumptions as well as any they may have heard from others about the culture at their own school sites. They were also prompted to identify affirming statements about culture that they may have heard at their schools.

With a partner, participants then explored facets of their own culture, and how, if at all, their own teachers incorporated their culture (or funds of knowledge) into lessons. They were asked to reflect about what it felt like when their culture was not included at school. Finally, participants read about *funds of knowledge* (Moll et al., 1992), discussing what resonated with each individually, what strategies from the article they could incorporate into their own school setting, and how they might bridge the students' *funds of knowledge* with the expectations of the common core standards.

We also used the gender caucus as an activity to explore the way we see the world. Participants self-divided into 2 groups, male and female, and together created a chart answering the question, "What unique needs and challenges do you as a female or male leader have? After sharing with the other group, they then discussed in pairs their perceptions of what biases might come into play if they were coaching each other, as well as how those biases might influence their coaching of others.

Participants were engaged in activities using a variety of cases and scenarios. One example was "A Case Study of a New High School Principal" (Cortez et al., 2012) with its different scenarios for discussion. In small groups, members discussed the issues in the scenario they were given, addressing the question of how schools in the southwest attempt to meet the cultural needs of non-white students. They then discussed how they would have responded as the leader, as well as how the scenarios related to the funds of knowledge concepts, and how the assets of groups or individuals might apply in the scenarios. See Activity Box 7.1 for an example scenario.

Please note that the above activities were not all accomplished in a single meeting, but were spread throughout the project. We came to understand that culturally responsive pedagogy and leadership required an ongoing effort in order to effect lasting change.

Activity Box 7.1: Sample Scenario for Small Group Discussion (Cortez et al. 2012)
Scenario V: *Curricular and Instructional Issues and the Hispanic Culture*

1. A 16-year old "recent immigrant" student enrolls in a predominantly white school system in the southern United States. The student has a fair command of the English language but to help support his family, the student has decided to work in a recently opened Mexican food restaurant across the thoroughfare from the high school he attends. As a result of his work schedule, he is missing numerous classes. To what extent do schools in the United States attempt to understand the culture and experiences of Hispanic students and their families most notably when it comes to teaching, learning, and scheduling of classes? To what extent do the schools in the southwest attempt to meet the cultural needs of Hispanic students through specialized courses, programs, and scheduling adaptations to include the Hispanic culture in the curriculum?

2. Salvador Vargas is a recent Hispanic immigrant who, along with his family, fled Mexico for the safety and security of the United States and for greater educational and career opportunities. Salvador wants to be a civil engineer. In Mexico, Salvador was an honor student in his high school. Today, Salvador attends Sun Valley High School in a major metropolitan city in the Midwest. A growing pocket of immigrant Hispanics have moved to the northwest side of town, where they have found work, homes, and security. At Sun Valley High School, Salvador is immediately placed into remedial coursework even though he was an outstanding student in his homeland community of Puerto Escondido, Mexico. Salvador is highly intelligent in all academic areas but especially in mathematics and the sciences. He is eager to succeed, ambitious in his goals, and ready to enroll in Advanced Placement coursework at the high school. However, his command of the English language is limited.

   Salvador's counselor, Mildred Dunn, has problems communicating with him as do other counselors or teachers because they are not fluent in Spanish. Ms. Dunn has referred him for testing to determine his level of cognitive ability. After parental consent has been given, a bilingual school diagnostician administered a cognitive evaluation to establish his general intellectual ability and an achievement test to determine his present level of performance. Both tests were administered in his native language because IDEA mandates that a student must be tested in his native language or nonverbally. Salvador's scores reveal that achievement and cognitive scores were in the average range. Based on the results of the assessment, Ms. Dunn places Salvador in the regular general education curriculum core courses with ESL and remedial services (tutoring) support.

(continued)

Activity Box 7.1 (continued)

Interestingly, while Salvador cannot complete the class work at school, he has a brother-in-law at home that speaks English and who is willing to help him with translating the class work and other assignments. When Salvador brings the work back to class, his teachers generally deduct points from the work exclaiming to one another: "You know it's not his work. Someone else is doing the work for him. Just look at his grades. They are exceptional. Most of these Mexican students are low achieving and lazy. There is no way he can do this work on his own!"

How relevant to the culture and experiences of Hispanic students is the curriculum adopted in schools across the nation, especially in quick growing Hispanic population pockets? Consider Hispanic immigrant students, such as Salvador, who may experience language barriers, or have instructional issues such as grade retention, ability grouping, and the over-identification of learning disabilities resulting in Special Education placement. How do these practices affect Hispanic immigrant students in U.S. schools? What must principals, teachers, and counselors in predominantly White communities do to meet the instructional, curricular, and academic needs of students such as Salvador? What about the attitudes exhibited in the teacher conversations in the scenario? Are these conversations realistic assessments of the students being described? Do people really think and talk as is quoted in the scenario?

Lessons Learned

We found that schools needed much more work on cultural responsiveness, thus we will share only one case that illustrated both progress and a consciousness about the importance of cultural responsiveness for ongoing school development.

Case A: *Santo Domingo Mission School*

Santo Domingo Mission School is located in southern Arizona on reservation lands. With a student population K-8 of approximately 90% Native students, 6% Hispanic students and 4% Other students, Santo Domingo Mission School has been serving the commnity for more than 150 years. The free and reduced lunch rate hovers between 83% and 87%. Many students live in a single parent home or reside with a relative; approximately 10% of the school population are in foster care, resulting in a high rate of transiency. Many students travel an hour to school, resulting in a high tardy and absence rate. To combat this, the school provides a bus for about 40% of their students, but on days when the bus breaks down, about half of those students are unable to get to school at all. A private parochial school, they rely on the community for donations in order to operate. In 2000 they were able to launch a capital campaign that allowed them to expand from 4 classrooms to their current 11 classrooms.

The principal, Shelly Kerr, had been at the school for 10 years. Understanding that she was an outsider to this community without deep cultural understanding, she sought to build trusting relationships quickly and learn about the assets of the community as well as the needs. A white female, Princial Kerr describes her challenge when starting at the site:

> "…one of the things that you have to know when you're out there is one year is not enough for them to feel comfortable with you. Two years is not enough. I got my first hug at six years…so they're not going to trust someone that was kind of pushed on them, which is how I came into being…It's a pretty interesting dynamic that goes on, but the more and the longer that I'm there, the more confidence they have so they pretty much feel like they can say anything."

Mrs. Kerr talks about communication with the school community.

> "Trying to get into that community is very, very difficult, so you have to work constantly on your relationships. How you deal with one person in a negative manner is going to get out to the entire village (and so the community is called a village) and so you had to be careful about that; you had to be careful about little things…word of mouth, …everybody knows what's going on at the school."

Mrs. Kerr also understands that students have more to offer than what might appear initially to someone who does not understand the community dynamics.

> "Any stranger coming in, maybe even a speaker to talk, especially to my big kids, they are silent, so silent, and I always have to assure them, these guys are not silent, they talk non-stop, or giggle non-stop, you just don't see it. If they don't know you, there's nothing. You won't get anything out of them."

Recognizing that diabetes affects about 50% of the native population, Shelly describes some efforts at school to help combat that.

> "We do employ a full time RN at the school, which does seem necessary for the…people; they have the highest rate of diabetes in the world. The likelihood of a student who is Native American getting diabetes is 50% at this time, so we take that very seriously in what we provide for them in food and in physical activity. So they do have…PE and they do have…a no sit recess. They have a lap that they have to go every time they go out (it's a quarter mile); they walk the lap…or run, depending on their age and what they want to do, but they can't sit down, they can't come out, and [say] 'oh, I'm so tired', 'well, get up and walk around; 'I know that, I've been sitting all day too.'"

Santo Domingo Mission School provides a safe place for students to do homework after school, requiring their athletes to attend prior to practice. Principal Kerr also talks about the school as a safe place for students who bring issues from home or the community. Although bullying is considered an issue around the reservation, it is not typical at this school. She describes her approach:

> "There are times when I have to do counseling with students and their behavior when I know that it's something that happened off campus and they're bringing it on campus, and we just talk about how our campus is a safe place; we don't do those things at the school and this is your school, and this is how I would be saying it to them, 'this is your school; is that some-

thing that you want in your school? Do you want someone disrespecting you like that?', and boom, they step up to the plate and it doesn't happen again. We really are very lucky, [bullying]…doesn't happen in our school on a regular basis because we jump on it and we call it what it is. So, if I am talking to a student I ask them, 'would you like to be called a bully? Your actions could be seen as that, and if I talk to your parent about that, what do you think they would think?' And boom, it just stops. It's the reality that you can't hide anything; you need to take care of each of these different things in this particular community. I think it would have to help in any community, but it's been really successful. I mean, I don't have graffiti in the bathroom, I don't have graffiti anywhere. When they graffitied the mission really badly a few months ago, they didn't touch the school. Why didn't they touch the school? We're right next door. You know, they touched the plaza, that was 100 feet further than we are, but they didn't touch the school, they touched the graveyard which was all the way down the road, why didn't they touch the school? It's because we are building this culture of respect at the school.

Santo Domingo Mission School recognizes the importance of building relationships with students and their families as the basis for being culturally responsive. They seek to build on the assets that the students bring while emphasizing academic achievement. The principal and staff recognize that they could do more, and continue to work with their community.

Final Thoughts

A focus on culturally responsive pedagogy within a school is predicated on the willingness of all staff members to confront their own biases (and each other), to build relationships with students, families and communities, and to work from an asset-based mindset rather than a deficit-based outlook to build upon the *funds of knowledge* in the students and community. To do this, it is vital to learn about the community and its assets; this is the basis for education. Knowing the strengths, however, is meaningless from an education standpoint unless those assets are utilized in educational relationships - curriculum, pedagogy, critical thinking, reflection for a democratic way of living. In most schools across the U.S., there is much work to be done in this area. We have only touched the surface.

References

Cortez, M. T., Sorenson, R. D., & Coronado, D. (2012). A case study of a new high school principal: Instructional challenges and administrative interventions relating to immigrant students and teacher apathy on the US/Mexico border. *Journal of Cases in Educational Leadership, 15*(1), 7–24.

Dewey, J. (1916). *Education and democracy*. Macmillan.

González, N., Moll, L. C., & Amanti, C. (Eds.). (2005). *Funds of knowledge: Theorizing practices in households, communities, and classrooms*. Routledge.

Hollins, E. R. (1996). *Culture in school learning*. Mah-wah.

Horsford, S. D., Grosland, T., & Gunn, K. M. (2011). Pedagogy of the personal and professional: Toward a framework for culturally relevant leadership. *Journal of School Leadership, 21*(4), 582–606.

Johnson, L. (2006). "Making her community a better place to live": Culturally responsive urban school leadership in historical context. *Leadership and Policy in Schools, 5*(1), 19–36.

Johnson, L. (2007). Rethinking successful school leadership in challenging US schools: Culturally responsive practices in school-community relationships. *International Studies in Educational Administration (Commonwealth Council for Educational Administration & Management (CCEAM)), 35*(3).

Johnson, L. (2014). Culturally responsive leadership for community empowerment. *Multicultural Education Review, 6*(2), 145–170.

Ladson-Billings, G. (1994). *The dreamkeepers: Successful teachers of African American children.* Jossey-Bass.

Ladson-Billings, G. (1995). But that's just good teaching! The case for culturally relevant pedagogy. *Theory Into Practice, 34*(3), 159–165.

Mezirow, J. (1997). Transformative learning: Theory to practice. *New Directions for Adult and Continuing Education, 1997*(74), 5–12.

Moll, L. C., Amanti, C., Neff, D., & González, N. (1992). Funds of knowledge for teaching: Using a qualitative approach to connect homes and classrooms. *Theory Into Practice, 31*(2), 132–141.

Moll, L., Amanti, C., Neff, D., & González, N. (2006). Funds of knowledge for teaching: Using a qualitative approach to connect homes and classrooms. In *Funds of knowledge* (pp. 83–100). Routledge.

Nieto, S. (1996). "I like making my mind work": Language minority. In *Education reform and social change: Multicultural voices, struggles, and visions* (pp. 147–164). L. Erlbaum.

Padrón, Y. N., Waxman, H. C., & Rivera, H. H. (2002). *Educating Hispanic students: Effective instructional practices* (Practitioner brief# 5). Center for Research on Education, Diversity & Excellence.

Riehl, C. J. (2000). The principal's role in creating inclusive schools for diverse students: A review of normative, empirical, and critical literature on the practice of educational administration. *Review of Educational Research, 70*(1), 55–81.

Scanlan, M., & López, F. A. (2014). *Leadership for culturally and linguistically responsive schools.* Routledge.

Scheurich, J. J. (1998). Highly successful and loving, public elementary schools populated mainly by low-SES children of color: Core beliefs and cultural characteristics. *Urban Education, 33*(4), 451–491.

Severian-Wilmeth, K. (2002). *Culturally mediated instruction.* Brown University: The Education Alliance.

Taylor, F. W. (2004). *Scientific management.* Routledge.

Wilson-Portuondo, M. (2002) *Teacher as facilitator.* Brown University: The Education Alliance.

Part III
Extending the Process to Other Contexts

This part widens the lens to consider school development processes in other contexts, beginning with a description of work in another U.S. state, South Carolina, with a similar and distinct history, policy demands, and culture. The South Carolina school development processes (Moyi, Hardie, & Cunningham, this volume) drew on lessons from the Arizona approach (e.g. leadership team capacity, clear direction, cultural relevance, use of data as a source of reflection, strong curriculum and pedagogical practices) and added elements necessary for another state context, including a focus on place-based education for rural schools and understandings about improvement science from the Carnegie project ILead of which the University of South Carolina is a member. Across the U.S., despite the policy demands for strong evidence and the use of methods legitimized in the What Works Clearinghouse, there are a number of distinct, school development approaches proposed by for-profit agencies, universities, and others, some of which are funded at least in part by states. The South Carolina state curriculum and Arizona state processes were developed for increasingly diverse students in a decentralized system for curriculum and evaluation policies as well as distinct cultural and historical traditions. At the same time, in recent years, the U.S. has moved toward more centralization of curriculum and evaluation amidst demographic shifts toward increasing diversity.

The next chapter features a national policy approach in Sweden (Johansson & Ärlestig, this volume), a country with a longer history of centralized curriculum and evaluation policies as well as inspections from the nation state and OECD. Here lessons from analysis of policy and inspection documents provide important understandings about school development and a language for communication within and between multiple levels. More specifically, the Swedish government project for school development illustrates the importance of institutional capacity for sustained school improvement and coherent language and processes within and between levels (schools, districts/municipalities, nation). Although the focus of school development in this chapter is at the national level, we see similar insights (trust and capacity, goal attainment, coherence, common language for leaders within and between levels).

Next, the chapter from Australia (Gurr, Acquaro & Drysdale, this volume) features school development approaches that operate distinctly at national, state and local levels. Understandings from school development in Australia further contextualize and explain school development with positive results at the different levels. Findings from the Australian cases indicate the importance of leadership and institutional capacity, professional autonomy, a commitment to education and a fundamental desire to improve student outcomes, all of which align with the Arizona school development process.

The chapter from Germany features an approach within a city and a state, one that adapted school turnaround processes from the U.S. and U.K. but reveals nuances and opportunities amidst the contemporary situation; it is interesting to note that the adaptation of turnaround occurs in Germany with a strong historical education tradition quite different from organizational and educational traditions in the U.S. and U.K. (e.g., Bildung upbringing, Didatik and Lehrplan). In particular, Huber and Skedsmo (this volume) indicate the importance of autonomy and school development coaching that explicitly accounts for the needs of children in surrounding communities as well as within specific schools. The focus on context, autonomy and goal attainment are consistent with the findings from the Arizona project.

Interestingly, the similarities that emerged among all national contexts include (1) leadership capacity, (2) importance of school culture, (3) focus on individual needs of diverse students, (4) the importance of leadership, (5) strong school-community relationships, (6) clear goal setting and attainment, (7) recognition that school development occurs within and between levels and is more successful if there is coherence between goal setting processes, (8) use of data and evidence (broadly defined); the importance of teaching and learning to school development, and (9) the ongoing nature of the process and the need for time. Commonalities of practice are not entirely surprising given the global policy trends and policy borrowing trends toward evidence-based practices and improvement processes, including school turnaround as well as global population migrations that lead to increasing student diversity in all contexts.

In school development processes within the U.S. (Arizona, South Carolina), and in Sweden, Australia, and Germany, there are some differences that emerged, primarily around cultural and historical traditions of education (e.g. religious base in Australia, Bildung tradition in Germany) as well as governance and policy structures (e.g. centralized, decentralized) in the different national contexts. Moreover, regardless of policy requirements and governance structures, the local community contexts and needs of increasingly diverse children greatly affected the ways in which school development (and evidence of success) was thought about and implemented. In other words, the chapters illuminate contextually relevant elements of globalized policy trends for school development.

Chapter 8
School Development in South Carolina - Building Leadership Capacity for Evidence-Based School Development in South Carolina Schools

Peter Moyi, Suzy Hardie, and Kathleen M. W. Cunningham

Abstract This study presents two U.S. school development projects aimed at building leadership capacity for continuous school development that attempts to use "evidence-based" ideas from the standpoint of education values and understandings with a renewed sensitivity to culturally diverse students in South Carolina schools. The Lowcountry Educator Initiative (LEI) uses a professional development program designed for educators from various schools. School Improvement through Improvement Science (SITIS), stems from a larger university-school partnership initiative that includes other institutions around the United States. The two projects serve as compelling examples that push on the limited scope that federal and local policy requirements place on educational institutions to provide evidence of improvements that lead to educational success. This work offers qualitative evidence that honors, recognizes, and leverages the strengths of the participants' contexts to facilitate improvement in practice. The projects implemented offer evidence for (1) providing leadership support for school improvement efforts, (2) the use of local context in improving practice, and (3) the valuing of various data to engage in locally-relevant and appropriate work. We recommend centering the local context and improvement science approaches in research design, research funding, and educator preparation.

Keywords Place-based education · Improvement science · Leadership development · Educational equity

P. Moyi (✉) · S. Hardie · K. M. W. Cunningham
University of South Carolina, Columbia, SC, USA
e-mail: moyi@mailbox.sc.edu; sehardie@mailbox.sc.edu; katiemwc@mailbox.sc.edu

Introduction to the Chapter's Purpose

This study presents two U.S. school development projects aimed at building leadership capacity for continuous school development that attempts to use "evidence-based" ideas from the standpoint of education values and understandings with a renewed sensitivity to culturally diverse students in South Carolina schools. The aim is to help schools mitigate the gaps in educational opportunities experienced by culturally diverse students who have been historically marginalized. The two projects are different and distinct. One project, the Lowcountry Educator Initiative (LEI), uses a professional development program designed for groups of educators from various schools in South Carolina. This project focuses on place-based learning as a vehicle to improve educational opportunity and achievement through instruction that leverages the assets of schools' local communities. The other project, School Improvement through Improvement Science (SITIS), stems from a larger university-school partnership initiative that includes other institutions around the United States. This initiative uses an improvement science (Bryk et al., 2015) framework to address problems of practice in the partner school. Outside these differences, however, the projects are connected in their overarching values and aims and the policy contexts in which they operate. We present findings from semi-structured interviews, observations, and fieldnotes that highlight key processes and outcomes related to teacher and leader development including effective organizational structures, professional development processes, and changes in practice. Due to the stages of both projects, we dedicate more attention in this chapter to the LEI.

Through partnerships, both projects help schools (1) build internal professional capacity to address problems of practice, (2) strengthen human connections both within the school as well as with the community, and (3) improve instruction through improving their students' experiences. The two projects serve as compelling examples that push on the limited scope that federal and local policy requirements place on educational institutions to provide evidence of improvements that lead to academic success. Further, many U.S. research funding sources now require the use of prior school improvement models that produced "strong evidence" of improved student outcomes and school development, all of which is currently subject of debate in the literature (e.g. Biesta, 2010; Slavin, 2008). This work offers qualitative evidence, that honors, recognizes, and leverages the strengths of the participants' contexts to facilitate improvement in practice.

In this chapter, we first offer a brief description of the U.S.'s national educational context through a synopsis of federal laws and policies. Next, we focus on one state, South Carolina. This section describes the history of education in the state and how national policy has impacted and continues to impact the education system locally. Following, we offer some challenges stemming from the policy contexts related to school improvement. We then shift focus and describe both the LEI and SITIS, their overlapping purposes, and the lessons learned that shape our recommendations for educational practice and policy moving forward.

South Carolina Policy Context

South Carolina was impacted by the federal context policy evolution; and the goal of federal and state policies have been the closure of the achievement gap as described in Chap. 1. The U.S. education system has struggled to address issues of educational inequality. Despite outlawing segregated schools, Black and Latinx students and low-income students attend the most under resourced schools (Orfield et al., 2016). South Carolina has a long history of unequal education with poor rural, mostly minority, students facing the biggest challenge (Tran et al., 2020). The racial divide between White and Black students was evident with the early settlers in South Carolina with a mindset that education was only for affluent white people who could afford a private education through a personal tutor. As a result, poor White and Black students did not receive an education. Education of children of color was formally limited through 1740s by laws criminalizing teaching Black students to read and write. By 1927 in South Carolina, there were 279 high schools for Whites, but only 10 high schools for Black students (Switzer & Green, 2016).

South Carolina was slow to institute the 1954 *Brown v. Board of Education,* the landmark case that made segregation of schooling unlawful. Schools in South Carolina were not desegregated until the 1970–1971 school year (Switzer & Green, 2016). Even after desegregation major disparities between the education of White and Black students persisted. Funding of schools was not equal between schools with majority White students compared to schools with a majority of Black students. According to the South Carolina Constitution's education clause, the General Assembly must provide a "minimally adequate education" (Tran et al., 2020); unfortunately there are major disparities among school districts.

In 1993, the state of South Carolina was sued by 36 school districts for failing to provide adequate funds for education – *Abbeville County School District* et al. *v. the State* (Hart, 2015). These school districts are found in a region of the state along Interstate-95 between North Carolina and Georgia. This area became known as the "Corridor of Shame" after the 2006 documentary, *Corridor of Shame: The Neglect of South Carolina's Rural Schools* by Bud Ferillo. Well-known South Carolina author, Pat Conroy, who had taught Black elementary students on Daufuskie Island in Beaufort County, South Carolina, chronicled his experiences in the memoir, *The Water is Wide* (1972). Conroy described the neglect of rural students in South Carolina, especially Blacks. In the introduction to the *Corridor of Shame* documentary, Conroy, argued that the "water is even wider" three decades later, illustrating the justification the rural school districts had in suing the state of South Carolina for not providing adequate funding to offer quality education for its own students.

In 2014, the South Carolina Supreme Court, in the *Abbeville County School District* et al. *v. the State* case, ruled that a wide opportunity gap existed in South Carolina due to insufficient state funding. The Court, in essence, told the State to do more to ensure equal opportunity for South Carolinian children. However, in 2017, the Supreme Court vacated the landmark decision that held the state accountable for poor, failing schools citing judicial overreach (Black, 2017). Nevertheless, schools are continually and negatively impacted by state funding policies and this case exemplifies the challenge of improving schools in parts of South Carolina.

As South Carolina has not provided equitable opportunities for its students, it is no surprise students' performance ranks among the lowest in the nation. The U.S. News & World Report ranks South Carolina number 43 out of the 50 states (U.S. News, 2020). Further, since 1998, South Carolina has consistently performed below the national average in NAEP 4th grade reading (NCES, 2020). When the NAEP scores are disaggregated by race and income, the gaps are even more pronounced. For example, in 2019, Black 4th graders had an average reading score that was 31 points lower than their white classmates. At the same time, poor 4th grade students, as measured by those eligible for the National School Lunch Program, scored an average of 32 points lower (NCES, 2020).

Federal policies such as NCLB, Race to the Top, and ESSA, reflect a paradigm of school leadership defined by performance outcomes and standardization. Under ESSA, states have more flexibility regarding holding the school leader responsible for achievement, yet some states like the South Carolina Department of Education embeds student achievement in all 10 of the principal evaluation standards titled *Program of Assisting, Developing, and Evaluating Principal Performance* (PADEPP). For example, Standard 3, describes school leaders' responsibility for ensuring that each student has equitable access to highly effective teachers, learning opportunities, academic and social support, and other resources necessary for success. In Standard 9 (SCDE, 2017), the focus on performance outcomes is evident as

> The principal develops and implements an appropriate annual professional development plan on the basis of three required areas: identified strengths and weaknesses, the district strategic or school renewal plan, and area(s) for student growth. For each of the three goals, principals must develop an action plan and monitor their progress towards meeting those goals (p. 8).

Limitations in Research Priorities: Accountability and the Role of Research and Evidence

Symptoms stemming from a long history of inequitable practices, perceptions, and policies include the evident gaps in opportunities and academic achievement. The policy context in South Carolina illuminates challenges for educational professionals in K-12 and higher education. These include accountability requirements and delimitations with research priorities.

To mitigate the inequities, researchers and policymakers in the U.S. and in other countries promote scientific evidence-based interventions. The effectiveness of these interventions is typically measured by standardized tests and empirical research that use randomized controlled trials (RCT), quasi-experimental designs (QED), regression discontinuity designs, and single-case designs. Consider the federal law, the Every Child Succeeds Act (ESSA) of 2015. It encourages school districts to use federal funds to support evidence-based interventions. While we argue there is value in the use of evidence from quasi-experimental or randomized control designs, we also argue that a hyper-focus on these studies limits the learning that could happen from other types of research focus and goals. Unfortunately, the way policy and research funding is currently focused, limited explicit attention in these types of measurement is focused on values that can drive promising practices, including humanistic values (Dewey, 1916), or culturally responsive (e.g. Scanlan & López, 2012), or those that value mutualistic research-practice-partnerships (RPPs) (Coburn & Penuel, 2013), or those that center context to make educational decisions that are place-based (Dewey, 1916), or those that ask for whom does something work, when, and under what conditions (Cohen-Vogel et al., 2015). Instead, neoliberal pressures for competition and achievement exacerbate the pressures for researchers and school leaders, especially those in low performing educational contexts. Funding for educational research endeavors reflect this trend. Educational reform tends to focus on the improvement of students' performance outcomes, which can be seen in how and where the Office of Educational Research and Improvement (OERI) have awarded their funding. Since 2002, 75% of the education research funded by OERI addresses causal questions using random assignment design compared to prior randomized controlled trials which constituted only 5% of the federal funding (Morrison, 2012).

Recent U.S. education policies have moved toward "scientific" evidence-based practice. Policy documents under both Republican and Democratic administrations from the No Child Left Behind Act (2002) to more recent Race to the Top (2008) have reflected the importance of evidence from externalized evaluations to guide school decisions. The U.S. Department of Education now requires researchers applying for grant funding to demonstrate that their research designs are based upon prior studies with "strong evidence" explicitly defined by large-scale quantitative studies with randomized controlled trials or quasi-experimental designs. Internationally, multinational organizations, such as the Organization for Economic Co-operation and Development (OECD) and the World Bank, have also made evidence-based policymaking a priority both in their own work as influential research and policy organizations as well as for their members (Wiseman, 2010).

Researchers have also argued for the use of natural scientific evidence to inform educational practice (Eisenhart, 2005; Hattie, 2008; Schneider et al., 2007; Slavin, 2008). While scientific evidence-based interventions which link research to practice are useful, we see limitations in the lack of traditional humanistic values of education for growth and democracy (e.g. Dewey), cultural diversity, and contexts. In *Democracy and Education,* Dewey (1916) argued that an education which only emphasized the achievement of "external aims," (e.g., standardized tests) hinder students' and teachers' capacities for continuous growth and leads them toward viewing learning as an overly burdensome activity which they should seek to end as quickly as possible. Drawing on Dewey, Biesta (2010) argues, "Calling the idea of value-based education an alternative is not meant to suggest that evidence plays no role at all in value-based education but is to highlight that its role is subordinate to the values that constitute practices as educational practices" (p. 493). Biesta's critique of evidence-based reforms is supported by research on culturally responsive leadership.

Culturally responsive leaders are not only aware of the increasingly diverse student demographics, but they respond to the changes through culturally responsive practices. These leaders strive to develop teachers who legitimize students' funds of knowledge and acknowledge the histories of students through their teaching (Gay, 2002). Thus, culturally responsive leaders encourage their teachers to utilize the knowledge of their students' culture and their knowledge of the dominant culture to construct intercultural bridges that acknowledge differences "without shining the deficit light on students' cultural knowledge" (Ladson-Billings, 2009, p. 18). Moreover, culturally responsive leaders recognize the impact of deficit thinking on student learning and work to remove those and other barriers.

Aim of the Two Initiatives: LEI and SITIS

The two initiatives featured, LEI and SITIS, offer a counter narrative to making school improvements through a greater focus on development and improvement by prioritization of humanistic values and continuous improvement. Further, this work is done through two types of partnerships, where both help educational professionals (1) build internal professional capacity to address problems of practice, (2) strengthen human connections both within the school as well as with the community, and (3) improve instruction through improving their students' experiences.

Conceptual Model for the School Development Projects in South Carolina

We draw on a conceptual model developed by Ylimaki et al. (2019). Ylimaki et al. (2019) argue, "as U.S. schools are becoming increasingly diverse, we see a need to renew a focus on humanistic education values, including a focus on culturally responsive practices that support increasingly diverse students in schools" (p. 17). Therefore, the authors argue for the need to balance scientific evidence-based values and humanistic education values. Scientific evidenced-based and humanistic values are at tension; however, with reflection and pedagogical activity there can be a balance. Culturally responsive practices consider the diversity of the students and incorporate the values and cultural funds of knowledge in pedagogical activity in the classroom (Ylimaki et al., 2019; Ylimaki & Jacobson, 2013).

This is in line with the continuous improvement framework of improvement science, which is anchored by six principles of improvement for education: (a) "Make the work problem-specific and user-centered"; (b) "Variation in performance is the core problem to address"; (c) "See the system that produces the current outcomes";

(d) "We cannot improve at scale what we cannot measure"; (e) "Anchor practice improvement in disciplined inquiry"; and (f) "Accelerate improvement through networked communities" (Carnegie Foundation for the Advancement of Teaching, 2020). Terms like user-centered, system, and networked improvement communities invite a humanistic approach to interventions, improvement and research while also valuing measurement and data as a way to guide improvement efforts.

Leadership and School Development Project 1: Lowcountry Educators Initiative (LEI)

The LEI was modeled after the previously implemented, research-based, and studied Arizona Initiative for Leadership Development and Research (AZiLDR) project. AZiLDR focused on four-prongs of improvement: leadership, education, and school development as well as its delivery system (Cohen et al., 2002; Garet et al., 2001; Wenglinsky, 2000; Ylimaki et al., 2019). The AZiLDR project was developed to assist persistently underperforming, culturally diverse schools and increase the capacity for continuous school improvement. In the design of AZiLDR, school team members (teachers, administrators, and coaches) got the chance to use evidence or data as a source of reflection and continuous growth, drawing on what has worked in the past and trends across various sources of data to develop plans for future improvement. Professional development such as coaching meetings, institutes, and/or improvement team meetings offered opportunities for participants to reflect on the assets of their communities thoughtful and in culturally responsive ways, leveraging these strengths to improve practice.

Place-Based Education   The LEI introduced the teachers to placed-based education, a form of experiential education, where learning is grounded in the resources and values of the local context. John Dewey (1916) promoted the importance of experiential education in relation to the local context. Place-based education typically includes outdoor education methodologies as advocated by John Dewey to help students connect with their particular locality. As noted by Dewey (1916), an education which only emphasizes the achievement of "external goals" (e.g. standardized test scores, grades, school letter grades, etc.) hinders students' and schools' capacities for continuous growth and leads them toward learning as an overly burdensome activity which they seek to end as quickly as possible.

LEI Participants

The LEI involved participants who were employed at multiple layers of the educational organization. Participants were from multiple school districts and worked at the school level and the district level. Within South Carolina there are extreme variations in the economic resources depending on the school district where the students attend school. Of the five school districts that had attendees at the LEI, three school districts had a poverty index of 90% or higher (NCES, 2019c). Hampton 2 and Barnwell 19 had a poverty index of 91% and Allendale had a poverty index of 94% (NCES, 2019c). One school district had a poverty index of 76.04% and the other school district had 58.32% (NCES, 2019c). The five school districts that attended the LEI were not only some of the most economically challenged in the state, but the one school district had a graduation rate of 76.54% (NCES, 2019a). The other four school districts with attendees at the LEI had graduation rates of 83.94%, 87.13%, 88.33% and 89.35% (NCES, 2019b).

The LEI targeted thirty rural teachers who worked in the region of the state known as the lowcountry. Participants were invited from six counties: Beaufort, Allendale, Jasper, Hampton, Colleton and Barnwell. Most of these districts are located in economically challenged and underdeveloped rural communities, known as the aforementioned "corridor of shame". The majority of the schools within these districts are severely resource constrained as a result of declining state funding and diminishing tax bases as businesses leave the area. While many of these issues require national and state level responses, one key focus of the LEI was to help educators within these districts identify and leverage their local resources.

The LEI Participant Demographics The LEI participants were drawn from Beaufort, Colleton, Hampton and Jasper counties. The 30 participants had spent an average of 7.79 years teaching at their current school, 9.74 years teaching in the rural schools in the lowcountry and 4.6 years teaching in rural schools outside of the lowcountry. In contrast, they spent an average of 2.85 years at a non-rural school, although 66% of participants indicated that they had no teaching experiences in such locales and about 17% had less than 5 years' experience teaching in non-rural settings. The majority (63.63%) of participating educators were from elementary schools, although there was also representation from middle (12.12%) and high schools (15.15%), and the district office (6.1%).

To provide further context about their daily work lives, participants noted that they traveled an average of 18.23 miles in their commute from home to work. While most indicated only having to travel 1–10 miles to work, a significant portion of participants traveled more than 60 miles to work daily.

Implementation of the LEI

First, meetings took place with school superintendents in the lowcountry to learn the needs of the area. After the initial meeting we developed the Lowcountry Educator Institute (LEI). Specifically, LEI used the lessons learned from Arizona to help educators better understand what is available in the rural community and how to better leverage these resources to build on the capacity of the local education system. While some aspects of rural living and rural communities have been described in deficit terms in the media and elsewhere (e.g. lack of economic diversity; slow internet speed; long distance to urban/suburban commerce, lack of social life, and recreational opportunities), the LEI aimed to change the narrative as it values what the communities *do* have: a strong sense of community, K-12 schools serving as a cultural hub, little traffic/congestion, low cost of living, and a sense of pride in supporting locally owned and managed business in rural communities.

In the summer and the fall of 2018, the team implemented the LEI centering around two major themes: (1) building the capacity and sustainability of local rural educators and (2) familiarizing educators with local resources. Thus, LEI sought to highlight the advantages and resources of the lowcountry communities. It provided the tools to encourage students and teachers to appreciate the area and tap into its agricultural, tourism and historical resources. The LEI helped the teachers better connect to their students as well as other teachers. A similar theme of *connection* will be described later in the SITIS portion of the chapter.

The LEI provided the tools to encourage teachers to appreciate their local community and tap into its resources in to two sessions. The first session of the LEI was held in early August 2018. At the start of the session participants used words like "country," "agriculture," "small towns," and "farms" to describe rurality. While these descriptions are primarily neutral, several connoted rurality with negative descriptors such as "less resources," "an area away from major development and amenities" "lots of unused land, limited development, poverty and low income earners", and "less things to do, less attractions." Only 39% of responding participants indicated that they had heard of (although may not understand) the term place-based education, and an even lower percentage (25%) of the participants were not familiar with the term place-based education.

The LEI provided training and curriculum for rural teachers so that they could better introduce their students to the possibilities of science and agriculture-related careers. During the September 2018 follow-up session, teacher participants presented how they planned and implemented place-based education in their schools. Some teachers from the same school presented in teams, while others developed individual lesson plans.

We conducted a mixed methods evaluation, including a survey and semi-structured interviews with a random selection of participants. Further, we collected and analyzed artifacts from the participants' projects. The LEI activities were grounded in effective professional development research (Cohen et al., 2002; Garet et al., 2001; Wenglinsky, 2000). Garet et al. (2001) study, endorsed by the What Works Clearinghouse, was the first large-scale empirical comparison of effects of different characteristics of professional development on teachers' learning.

Results of the evaluation indicate that there are more positive outcomes from professional development activities when all the structural features (form, duration, collective participation) and the core features (content focus, active learning opportunities, coherence) are included. These findings align with prior professional development research. Desimone et al. (2002) conducted a national mixed methods research study of curriculum directors to examine implementation strategies to diffuse professional development content throughout schools. Building on the earlier work of Garet et al. (2001) the study by Desimone and her colleagues (Desimone et al., 2002) suggests three additional characteristics of high quality professional development include: (1) alignment to standards and assessments, (2) continuous improvement efforts, and (3) involving teachers in the planning. Wenglinsky (2000) conducted a multi-level structural equation modeling of NAEP data and the relationship between teachers' professional development and eighth-grade achievement scores. Specifically, Wenglinsky (2000) found that extended periods in professional enhancement activities are closely linked to effective classroom practice. Furthermore, results indicated that significant gaps among teachers in their professional development contribute to differences in teacher quality, which substantially impact on student achievement, especially with the most disadvantaged students.

Findings: Participant Projects and Application of Place-Based Education

There was a range of understanding of implementation of place-based education. Some of the teachers truly embraced place-based education and developed and implemented effective place-based lessons for their classes.

Examples of Place-Based Design One of the teachers from Allendale-Fairfax involved the superintendent and school principal who were supportive of place-based education. The high school principal works in a rural area surrounded by cotton fields but had yet to see cotton up close. The teacher taught the school principal about cotton. Many teachers drove by cotton fields to get to school, but they had never touched a cotton pod. He stated, "place-based education is a necessary element in our schools today more than ever." Like the principal, the students had not seen cotton up close. They thought cotton was still handpicked and that farmers would water with a garden hose.

The teacher also involved eight community farm leaders who were willing to work with the school. To advertise the farmers coming to school, the teacher involved the technology teacher to create posters and electronic media to advertise the farmers and other community members such as EMT and firefighters coming to school. The farmers came to school and educated the students on how technology is used for farming. The farmers also helped the students create a school garden. This teacher really understood the goals of place-based education and he not only impacted his classroom, he impacted the whole school.

A group of teachers from an elementary school organized a field trip to a local pumpkin patch where the students learned the entire life-cycle of a pumpkin. The lesson plans and the field trip also included the students learning about farm animals such as pigs, cows, horses, and goats. While on the field trip, the students also learned about the life cycle of animals and what each of the animals produces. The students would also learn about the production of hay from growing, to bailing and to use of hay. Due to the training one of the teachers said that she has a greater appreciation and greater awareness of local farms and farmers. She really valued getting to meet one of the local farmers at the training.

One of the teachers started a school garden to teach students about growing vegetables, but this year she added a composting component so students learn to preserve their community by taking care of the land and water. In addition, she asked a developer to aid the students in creating a walking tour for their town of Bluffton. The students got to explore their town to create the walking tour. One of the teachers stated that she would use Beta Club to clean historical sites in their community.

Example of Principal Support for Place-Based One principal attended LEI with eight of her teachers. This principal embraced the learning, as she led by example in her school. She conducted the back to school staff development off campus at Lake Edgar Brown and Barnwell State Park, which is approximately ten miles from the school. By conducting the staff development at a local site, she taught the teachers what they can do to use the resources in their part of the state to enhance the students' learning. Since the school is Title One and 79% live in poverty according to the South Carolina 2016–2017 school report card poverty index, the principal knows that the parents do not have a lot of money for field trips, so learning about the community is beneficial. The principal even worked with transportation to reduce the cost of the school buses to take the students to the local sites.

From the initial training, the entire fifth grade level developed a unit based off a field trip to Lake Edgar Brown and Barnwell State Park. Prior to the place-based education institute, the big field trip for fifth grade was going to Barrier Island, but due to resources the class could only take 60 of the 200 fifth grades. The teachers realized that they could take all of the fifth graders to two sites by selecting to stay local. By taking the students off campus, the students were able to apply their learning to their own local communities.

While on the local field trip, the students also were exposed to science and math involved in road construction. One of the teachers said that the most valuable takeaway from the training was "integrating the classroom experiences into the wider community." One fifth grade teacher shared that place-based education "gets kids involved in real problem solving that is relevant to their community." The students can make connections between abstract science concepts to the local lake or apply math problems in solving community issues like measuring how much fencing needed to be purchased to mark the parking lot at Barnwell State Park. The evidence showed that the teachers approach lesson development and instructional design differently after attending the conference as they are thinking how they can relate the content standards to the students' community.

In fourth grade, the teachers organized a field trip to the local news station and local museum. The students learned about weather phenomena from meteorologists from a local news station. After learning about weather phenomena, the students then saw the path of destruction from a tornado that occurred at the Barnwell State Park. While in the park the teachers designed lessons to incorporate weather, the water cycle, and shadow movements. The fourth-grade teachers understood the concept of place-based education and designed lessons that would effectively implement place-based education.

A benefit from several teachers from the same school attending LEI is that regular education and special education teachers had the opportunity to plan together. The sixth-grade teachers and the special education teacher created place-based education lessons to incorporate all learners. Part of place-based education was to get to know the culture of the students who are attending the school. In the special education classes, the students were to share about their culture by sharing about an heirloom or something that was passed down from generation to generation. One student brought in a photo of his house. He shared how his great grandfather built the house and now his family is living there. The students learned about their families as well as the communities in which they live. The principal wants to continue to approve and support place-based experiences for the students at her school. The culture at the school has changed as teachers are looking for ways to connect all learning to place-based learning.

Increased Understanding of Place-Based Education Results of the evaluation indicate that participants gained a better understanding of place-based education and assets of the rural community. We also verified the importance of school teams for implementation and sustainability as well as positive outcomes from professional development activities when all of the structural features (form, duration, collective participation) and the core features (content focus, active learning opportunities, coherence) are included. Some schools were represented by only one teacher while others had large teams of teachers. As mentioned earlier, one principal attended alongside her teachers. The results as presented by the participants clearly illustrated the need for working as a team. Specifically, we recommend training for school leadership teams to include the principal, teacher leaders, and a district representative. This team composition will allow teams to plan for diffusion of the concepts/practices throughout the schools.

Further, while valuing inclusion of teacher assistants in the training, their ability to deeply apply the learning was predicated by the support from teachers and school leaders. For future institutes, participants commonly suggested more specificity and lesson modeling/ideas on how to link place-based education into lesson plans for more subject matters and methods to overcome barriers for implementation, such as "how to deal with less than enthusiastic administrators as making a reasonable chance..." for teaching place-based education in their classrooms.

Leadership and School Development Project 2: School Improvement Through Improvement Science (SITIS)

The SITIS involves the development of a university-district partnership centered on addressing a problem of practice: the achievement gap between the students of color and the white students. This focus area for improvement was originally identified by the school district and confirmed as a problem by school leaders, and is evidenced by assessment data.

The partnership began from an opportunity to participate in an initiative, initially designed to bring university-district partnerships together to use and infuse improvement science practices in educational leadership preparation programs in order to be more effective in developing the school leaders of today and tomorrow. Improvement science is a type of continuous improvement that prioritizes root cause analyses, planning and testing, then scaling changes in a systematic way (see e.g., Bryk et al., 2015). An improvement science framework also values the local context as a source of expertise and as a locus for change.

SITIS Participants

The partnership consists of stakeholders affiliated with the university (e.g., faculty) from the College of Education. The university is a large, public research intensive university. The school district has four high schools, three middle schools, and sixteen elementary schools and is in a city, but is isolated and surrounded by a very rural area. The district is located about an hour and a half drive from the university. At the inception of the partnership it was anticipated that multiple schools within the district were to participate in improvement work. However the reality of the contextual factors (e.g., leadership churn) led to the participation of faculty from one university department and one committed school leader – a first year principal named Dana. Partnering with one school is aligned with the spirit of improvement science, where tests and trials start small. The partnership between the school and the university department shares an explicit priority of educational equity for all students.

Dana has worked at Woodlawn High School for multiple years, but the beginning of the university-district partnership was the same year she began her leadership position. Woodlawn serves about 1700 students in grades nine through twelve. Fifty-six percent of the students are Black and 44% are White students. The certified teaching staff is approximately 33% teachers of color and 67% White and the non-certified staff is 75% of color and 25% White.

The partnership work prompted the creation of a school-based improvement team who would spearhead the school-based work learning and using improvement science. This group was organized purposefully by Dana and consists of five full-time classroom teachers, each representing different content areas. One administrator (i.e., the principal) is also a member of the team. The team is made up of all women. Four are Black and two are White. From the university-side of the partnership, multiple faculty members are involved and between two and four faculty members typically attend each meeting at the partner school. The university faculty involved include three white women faculty members and four men of color. More about the work of the improvement team will be described in the next section.

Implementation of the SITIS

Although the partnership technically began before the organization of the formalized improvement team at the school, for the purposes of this chapter, the information about the progress and learning of the work begins after the improvement team was formed. The school-based improvement team involves five teachers and a building administrator. The teachers were purposefully selected by the administrator and she invited teachers who were well-respected. The partnership typically meets monthly and each meeting at this stage is dedicated to understanding an identified problem of practice. Determination of the focus problem has been a journey. Focused on a value of equity, the team, at the overarching level, is focused on closing opportunity and achievement gaps between students of color and white students. However, the complexity of addressing this problem calls for an examination of the causes of the problem and how the problem manifests in schools. The team used focused brainstorming and questioning activities to examine the problem and what might be contributing to it. Often, when attempting to address educational challenges, such as test scores and other indicators of achievement, educational professionals put together an intervention to help increase test scores (e.g., a reading comprehension program), implement it "with fidelity", and then observe what happens. However, this approach is vulnerable to the threat that the proposed intervention is addressing a symptom of the problem and not an underlying issue leading to the symptom connected to the problem.

In efforts to push against this threat, the improvement team used tools such as brainstorming then using their input to organize thematically the brainstormed ideas into a fishbone diagram. Recall that the LEI helped the teachers better connect to their students, as well as other teachers, strengthening the capacity of the community in the process. The SITIS team, with an overarching aim to address the achievement gap, is similarly focusing their efforts on relationships and connections in their building. Their current theory of improvement is that if there is a genuine connection between teachers and students, then the educational professionals will be able to cultivate and contribute to a positive building culture, will be able to improve their practice (e.g., training and development on mitigating racial biases and/or culturally-responsive teaching), and then students will be better positioned to find a higher level of educational opportunity and success. In line with a tenet of improvement science that reminds improvers that our understanding and identification of a cause of a problem is "possibly wrong and definitely incomplete" (Russell et al., 2015, p. 35) and to gather additional understanding, the team also conducted empathy interviews so that they may understand the problem from other stakeholder groups' perspectives while also gathering data on if the team is focusing their improvement efforts on the right area. For example, they interviewed students to learn how connected they felt to the school and the teachers. In summary, the team is currently using qualitative and quantitative data to help make sense of the phenomena of focus and is willing to identify the specific places to target efforts for improvement.

It is important to note that this work is within an intentional partnership. It is driven by the expertise at the school with the school improvement team and is supported by the university faculty who serve in reflective and guiding roles since the school team is simultaneously learning about how to use an improvement science approach while engaged authentically in this work. Future directions will blend the expertise of those at the local site with other sources, such as existing previously published research. What will not happen is a rapid, wholesale adoption of an intervention that has evidence of success somewhere else. However, learning from other successful models or approaches (e.g., culturally-responsive teaching and leadership) will be utilized, shaping the action steps of the team in ways appropriate for their context.

There is a critical ingredient to the partnership and that is the leadership at the school. Dana's role cannot be overstated. In this initiative, Dana was the critical leadership lever who shepherded the work. Without her insights, commitment, and willingness to try a new approach to address problems of practice within her context, the work would not have progressed and likely would not have even truly begun. She demonstrated, and continues to demonstrate, different leadership qualities that have been particularly helpful. She was explicitly enthusiastic about the work and communicated this commitment to her team. Her intentional selection of the team members demonstrated her recognition of the types of talent needed for this work, her belief in, and her observation of the selected teachers' reputations within their school community that would position them well for this continuous improvement work focused on equity. This is an important note since "as an organizational trait, positive efficacy beliefs in the capacity of the collective provide a boost to teachers' morale, tenacity, and resilience as they pursue increasingly ambitious student outcomes, rendering themselves likely to achieve their goals" (Forman et al., 2018, p. 185).

The improvement science approach is an alternate framework that will yield findings, that may not include experimental designs. Other researchers such as Lewis (2015) and Cobb and Virella (2019) propose that some data and research cannot appropriately address problems that schools, each with unique context, aim to improve. The SITIS work is approaching school improvement that utilizes prior research while leveraging the context in order to understand and determine appropriate change ideas to help meet their aim of closing the opportunity gap between their students of color and white students so that the achievement gap will also close.

Recommendations for Practice

The programs implemented offer evidence for (1) providing leadership support for school improvement efforts (2) the use of local context in improving practice and (3) the valuing of various data to engage in locally-relevant and appropriate work.

Leadership Support

Our observations of the role that leadership support plays aligns with prior research. Just as Halverson and Kelley (2017) point out, the "principal's leadership works by engaging and building leadership capacity throughout the school" (p. 12) and that "the principal's role shifts to creating supporting structures…" (p. 14). Leadership support, in the challenging work of educational improvement, will be critical. Support from school and district leadership comes in the form of valuing approaches to learning such as place-based instruction or approaches to addressing problems of practice, such as improvement science. Actions that convey support include, but are not limited to (a) attending professional development with teachers, (b) participation on the improvement team, and (c) allowing teachers to make decisions, try new approaches, and provide resources (e.g., time, space) to meaningfully engage in the work.

In the LEI, the most successful place-based designs were those that had support from the school and district leaders. With SITIS, the principal is an integral part of the improvement team providing necessary support and leadership. Leadership can come from different sources. On some occasions, leadership may come from the district level, while in others, school-level leadership may be a primary driver of the work.

Using the Local Context in Improving Practice

Prior research highlights challenges teachers face when working to improve practice. In the LEI, the valuing of the local context not only changed instructional practice, but also was changing the narrative of living, working, and learning in a rural context to an assets-based approach, valuing and leveraging the resources and benefits of rural communities. It focused on local connections and relationships to be cultivated to provide a high-quality education for students. The SITIS improvement team, due to the insights and experiences of the educational professionals who were included on the team, also focused on the relationships and connections to impact the educational experience of students. Looking to the resources and knowledge already available in a local site and building off of those strengths provide opportunities for educational improvements due to the appreciation of the context.

Valuing of Data

The fourth principle of the Carnegie Foundation for the Advancement of Teaching's Six Core Principles of Improvement (2020) argues, "We cannot improve at scale what we cannot measure" and goes on to state, "Embed measures of key outcomes and processes to track if change is an improvement. We intervene in complex organizations. Anticipate unintended consequences and measure these too" (para. 4). Data are critical in improvement work. Gathering and organizing data offers guidance to what is or is not working, for whom, and under what conditions (Cohen-Vogel et al., 2015). We argue, as others have (e.g., Lewis, 2015), that research in educational improvement broaden the acceptance of which types of data typically hailed (such as RCTs) and also value data that provides information to catalyze the ability to scale improvement efforts, such as context-specific, value-focused, and humanistic data.

Recommendations for Policy

The U.S. and South Carolina have had an extremely long and shameful history of educational inequities based on race and class. For years, many interventions with goals of addressing and mitigating challenges such as the student achievement gap have not found wide success. We, through the success of AZiLDR and its successor, LEI, used humanistic, values-based approaches to improvement—demonstrated positive changes in teacher mindsets and practice. SITIS, although too soon to report changes in instruction, is similarly using local expertise to harness changes. Through the centering of the local context in place-based education and improvement science approaches to educational improvement, we recommend that this type of prioritization be valued in research design, research funding, and educator preparation.

The work described in this chapter was and continues to be done through partnerships between schools and universities. This type of professional relationship requires the distribution of decision making and collective learning (Goldring & Sims, 2005). Through different types of partnering, both the LEI and SITIS helped educational professionals (1) build internal professional capacity to address problems of practice, (2) strengthen human connections both within the school as well as with the community, and (3) improve instruction through improving their students' experiences. López Turley and Stevens (2015) argue that public schools and universities can both benefit from partnerships especially as these institutions face increased accountability despite budget cuts.

Findings noted the importance of leadership, of the local context and data. Therefore, policy to support leadership could include components such as partnerships, developing robust connections to the community in which they live, the value of continuous improvement when addressing problems of practice, and offering the latitude for school leaders to be able to engage in ways outside of what has traditionally been done to push on the status quo to forward a more equitable school environment. Further, the role of context and data is embedded in continuous improvement and root cause analysis work where improvers interrogate why and for whom something is working or not working and under what contextual conditions (Bryk et al., 2015).

As organizations that want to value improvement and place-based learning embark on this work, they will likely come across some institutionalized factors that do not fully align. For instance, the mechanisms in place for leadership assessment and feedback across different states may want to consider how elements such as these are infused into their evaluative practices. For example, Standard 5 in the principal evaluation system in South Carolina called the Program for Assisting, Developing, and Evaluating Principal Performance (PADEPP) is focused on School/Community Relations. The LEI study findings provide evidence that would invite policymakers to evaluate the wording to explicitly encourage the school to not only invite the community in, but also encourage school and district leaders to cross the traditional school and district boundaries to engage *with* the community *in* the community.

Standard 9 is focused on Principal Professional Development. From our work in the LEI and SITIS, engagement with the various stakeholders is critically important. Thus, principals who look to various stakeholders (i.e., the "users" of education and those who experience education) to help determine where professional learning resources should be targeted are arguably aiming to be improvers and effective school leaders. Building principals should be supported and allowed to make professional learning choices and goals that fit their unique context, since they are positioned to know their context more intimately than those who work outside of the school building – in central office, for example.

The relationship that the district has with the university can also help shape institutions of higher education. Educational leadership preparation programs can help forward some of the key findings and practices presented in this chapter. Curriculum, coursework, and activities could offer powerful learning experiences including authentic opportunities for leadership candidates to practice meaningful engagement and relationship building with internal and external educational stakeholders (Cunningham et al., 2018). Preparation programs are also well-positioned to help future school leaders in their approach to addressing problems of practice though ongoing support, guidance, and the continuous bridging of theory to practice (Sanzo et al., 2011).

Leadership preparation programs or other leadership professional development programs should also help leaders be successful in meeting the professional standards referenced above. Professional development should be centered on how to identify problems, deeply understand problems, and how to systematically address problems of practice in a way that is appropriate for their own context in a continuous improvement framework.

Policy could serve as a legitimizing level in articulating support, funding, and research designs that values approaches to educational improvement that are not traditionally prioritized, such as continuous improvement with its recognition of the important role of context, as the place-based education also recognizes. The prioritization of positivist, large-scale quantitative research has not yet provided the panacea that the public is in search of. We argue that an intervention tested and then implemented in other contexts with fidelity is not necessarily the way to "achieve" educational equity and improvement. Addressing problems of practice in ways beyond What Works Clearinghouse, for example, will support the field of education in its pursuit of improving education so every student is offered a high-quality and impactful experience. The work in the LEI and SITIS is exploring a new way of thinking about approaches to teaching and approaches to addressing problems of practice. It is much more focused on shifting the way we conceptualize and interpret the work rather than implementing a "thing". These initiatives challenge educators to reflect deeply about the work, the context, and why something exists in order to appropriately move forward.

References

Biesta, G. J. J. (2010). Why 'What Works' still won't work: From evidence-based education to value-based education. *Studies in Philosophy and Education, 29,* 491–503.

Black, D. W. (2017). Kids will suffer because court refused to do its duty. *The State Newspaper.* Retrieved from https://www.thestate.com/opinion/op-ed/article186489863.html

Bryk, A. S., Gomez, L. M., Grunow, A., & LeMahieu, P. G. (2015). *Learning to improve: How America's schools can get better at getting better.* Harvard Education Press.

Carnegie Foundation for the Advancement of Teaching. (2020). *The six core principles of improvement.* Retrieved from https://www.carnegiefoundation.org/our-ideas/six-core-principles-improvement/

Cobb, C. D., & Virella, P. (2019). *The legitimization of improvement science in Academe.* Retrieved from https://pdfs.semanticscholar.org/2cf4/685d3b2e0459a63bea79f99a710e645903ee.pdf

Coburn, C. E., & Penuel, W. R. (2013, January). *Research-practice partnerships at the district level: A new strategy for leveraging research for educational improvement.* Wiilliam T. Grant Foundation.

Cohen, D. K., Hill, H. C., & Kennedy, M. (2002). The benefit to professional development. *American Educator, 26*(2), 22–25.

Cohen-Vogel, L., Tichnor-Wagner, A., Allen, D., Harrison, C., Kainz, K., Socol, A. R., & Wang, Q. (2015). Implementing educational innovations at scale: Transforming researchers into continuous improvement scientists. *Educational Policy, 29*(1), 257–277.

Conroy, P. (1972). *The water is wide.* Dial Press Trade.

Cunningham, K. M. W., Van Gronigen, B. A., Tucker, P. D., & Young, M. D. (2018). Using powerful learning experiences to prepare school leaders. *Journal of Research on Leadership Education, 14*(1), 74–97. https://doi.org/10.1177/1942775118819672

Desimone, L., Porter, A., Birman, B., Garet, M., & Yoon, K. (2002). How do district management and implementation strategies relate to the quality of the professional development that districts provide to teachers? *Teachers College Record, 104*(7), 1265–1312.

Dewey, J. (1916). *Democracy and education.* The Free Press.

Eisenhart, M. (2005). Hammers and saws for the improvement of educational research. *Educational Theory, 55*(3), 245–261.

Forman, M. L., Stosich, E. L., & Bocala, C. (2018). *The internal coherence framework.* Harvard Education Press.

Garet, A., Porter, A., Desimone, L., Birman, B., & Yoon, K. (2001). What makes professional development effective? Results from a national sample of teachers. *American Educational Research Journal, 38*(4), 915–945.

Gay, G. (2002). Preparing for culturally responsive teaching. *Journal of Teacher Education, 53*(2), 106–116.

Goldring, E., & Sims, P. (2005). Modeling creative and courageous school leadership through district-community-university partnerships. *Educational Policy, 19*(1), 223–249. https://doi.org/10.1177/0895904804270777

Halverson, R., & Kelley, C. (2017). *Mapping leadership: The tasks that matter for improving teaching and learning in schools.* New York, NY: John Wiley & Sons.

Hart, L. C. (2015). *Abbeville County School District v. State of South Carolina: How did we get here and what happens now?* Retrieved from http://scasbo.net/wp-content/uploads/2015/11/1-Abbeville-vs-State-of-SC-Laura-Hart.pdf

Hattie, J. (2008). *Visible learning: A synthesis of over 800 meta-analyses relating to achievement.* Routledge.

Ladson-Billings, G. (2009). *The dreamkeepers: Successful teachers of African American Children* (2nd Ed.). San Francisco: Wiley Publishers.

Lewis, C. (2015). What is improvement science? Do we need it in education? *Educational Researcher, 44*(1), 54–61. https://doi.org/10.3102/0013189X15570388

López Turley, R. N., & Stevens, C. (2015). Lessons from a School District–University research partnership: The Houston education research consortium. *Educational Evaluation and Policy Analysis, 37*(1_suppl), 6S–15S. https://doi.org/10.3102/0162373715576074

Morrison, K. (2012). *Causation in education research.* Routledge.

National Center for Education Statistics. (2019a). *Graduation rates.* Retrieved from https://nces.ed.gov/ccd/tables/ACGR_RE_and_characteristics_2015-16.asp

National Center for Education Statistics. (2019b). *High school graduation rates.* Retrieved from https://nces.ed.gov/fastfacts/display.asp?id=805

National Center for Education Statistics. (2019c). *The Condition of Education 2019 (NCES 2019-144).* Retrieved from https://nces.ed.gov/fastfacts/display.asp?id=16

National Center for Education Statistics (NCES). (2020). *Reading state snapshot report.* Retrieved from https://nces.ed.gov/nationsreportcard/subject/publications/stt2019/pdf/2020014SC4.pdf

Orfield, G., Ee, J., Frankenberg, E., & Siegel-Hawley, J. (2016). *Brown at 62: School segregation by race, poverty and state.* Retrieved from https://civilrightsproject.ucla.edu/research/k-12-education/integration-and-diversity/brown-at-62-school-segregation-by-race-poverty-and-state/Brown-at-62-final-corrected-2.pdf

Russell, J. L., Bryk, A. S., Dolle, J., Gomez, L. M., LeMahieu, P., & Grunow, A. (2015). A framework for the initiation of networked improvement communities Jennifer. *Teachers College Record, 113*(12), 2897–2921. Retrieved from https://www.learntechlib.org/p/90771/

Sanzo, K. L., Myran, S., & Clayton, J. K. (2011). Building bridges between knowledge and practice. *Journal of Educational Administration, 49*(3), 292–312. https://doi.org/10.1108/09578231111129073

Scanlan, M., López, F. V. (2012). How school leaders promote equity and excellence for bilingual students. *Educational Administration Quarterly, 48*, 583–625.

Schneider, B., Carnoy, M., Kilpatrick, J., Schmidt, W. H., & Shavelson, R. J. (2007). *Estimating causal effects using experimental and observational design.* American Educational & Research Association.

Slavin, R. E. (2008). Perspectives on evidence-based research in education—What works? Issues in synthesizing educational program evaluations. *Educational Researcher, 37*(1), 5–14.

South Carolina Department of Education. (2017). *Expanded program for assisting, developing, and evaluating principal performance.* Retrieved from https://ed.sc.gov/educators/school-and-district-administrators/collective-leadership-initiative/expanded-program-for-assisting-developing-and-evaluating-principal-performance-guidelines/

Switzer, D. & Green, R. P. (2016). *Education.* University of South Carolina. Institute for Southern Studies. http://www.scencyclopedia.org/sce/entries/education/

Tran, H., Aziz, M., & Reinhardt, S. F. (2020). Rage against the Machine: The Legacy of Education Leaders' Valiant Struggle for Social Justice in Abbeville v. South Carolina. *Journal of School Leadership.* https://doi.org/10.1177/1052684619899612

U.S. News. (2020). *U.S. news and world report education rankings*. Retrieved from https://www. usnews.com/news/best-states/rankings/education

Wenglinsky, H. (2000). *How teaching matters: Bringing the classroom back into discussions of teacher quality*. Educational Testing Service.

Wiseman, A. W. (2010). The uses of evidence for educational policymaking: Global contexts and international trends. *Review of Research in Education, 34*(1), 1–24.

Ylimaki, R., & Jacobson, S. (2013). Comparative perspectives on leadership preparation for organizational learning, instructional leadership, and culturally responsive practice. *Journal of Educational Administration, 51*(1), 6–23.

Ylimaki, R. Brunderman, L. & Moyi, P. (2019) Balancing evidence-based and humanistic education in school development for underperforming Arizona and South Carolina schools. *Leadership and Policy in Schools*. Retrieved from https://doi.org/10.1080/15700763.2019.1695850.

Chapter 9
The Swedish Context Bringing Support Structures to Scale: The Role of the State and School Districts

Olof Johansson and Helene Ärlestig

Abstract This chapter explores the "theory of action" underlying the Swedish government's national school improvement program called Cooperation for Better Schools. We discuss particularly the assumptions about the roles and responsibilities of key stakeholders, including schools, school districts, and universities. Our analysis focuses on the issue of institutional capacity for sustained system improvement. In this regard, our approach draws on the perspectives associated with contemporary policy analysis, which includes greater attention to qualitative and interpretive methods to understand the complexity of policy-induced change in contemporary society. We start by describing the project structure and our method. Thereafter, we analyze the government's understanding and arguments for why it is important to help underperforming schools, before we give examples about how involved actors define problems and solutions in project documents. In the conclusion, we highlight strengths and deficits in the improvement process.

Keywords Underpreforming schools · Restructing · External support · Goverment initiatives · Quality assurance · Self improvement

Introduction: Cooperation for Better Schools

The purpose of a Swedish government project that started in 2015, Cooperation for Better Schools (CBS), is to improve academic results and increase equality of those results within and between schools. The participating schools are those that have poor academic results and too many students who do not complete the Swedish

O. Johansson (✉) · H. Ärlestig
Centre for Principal Development, Umeå University, Umeå, Sweden
e-mail: olof.ca.johansson@umu.se; Helene.arlestig@umu.se

R. M. Ylimaki, L. A. Brunderman (eds.), *Evidence-Based School Development in Changing Demographic Contexts*, Studies in Educational Leadership 24, https://doi.org/10.1007/978-3-030-76837-9_9

basic education program. This paper explores the "theory of action" underlying the CBS program, particularly the assumptions about the roles and responsibilities of key stakeholders, including the schools, school districts and universities. Our analysis focuses, in particular, on the issue of institutional capacity for sustained system improvement. In this regard, our approach draws on the perspectives associated with contemporary policy analysis, which includes greater attention to qualitative and interpretive methods to understand the complexity of policy-induced change in contemporary society (Hajer et al., 2003; Stevenson, 2016; Roberts, 2004).

The CBS project is ongoing, but there are good reasons to map, analyze and learn from the work and initiatives that have occurred. We examine the efforts that are being made to help them, and how the efforts are described and justified. Finally, it is also important to make an initial estimate of the extent to which the initiatives are adequate given the aspirations of the Swedish government's remit. Our contribution will, thus, shed light on the difficulties to bring interventions to scale in an accurate manner. In this paper, we will examine information from 78 CBS schools with a full program of basic education (through 9th grade), along with information from the 44 municipal school districts responsible for those schools.

We begin by addressing the motivation underlying the policy problem and the government resolution concerning CBS. The first part of the analysis is based in part on written documents from the Swedish Schools Inspectorate, regarding the processes between the schools, the school districts, the Swedish National Agency for Education, and the universities. These documents comprise the Inspectorate's school reports and subsequent decisions about the schools, action plans from most of the schools, as well as descriptions in those cases where they are not included in the action plans. It also includes any associated appendices, as well as the subsequent contracts between the Swedish National Agency for Education and the participating universities with regard to their efforts within CBS.

Rather than driving our analysis of the documents with a pre-existing theoretical framework, our approach was to engage with the emerging narrative suggested by the documents. That is, we approach the documents as if they held a story of how the complex (but weakly articulated) process of stakeholder engagement envisioned by the National Agency for Education would tell us which voices were reflected, how they framed the interventions, and the degree to which the collaborative ideal was achieved (Riessman, 2005).

The study concludes with summarizing reflections.

The Policy Problem – According to the Government

The Swedish Education Act (2010:800) contains provisions that are intended to guarantee equal access to education for all children and students. Efforts must be made to weigh differences in the conditions and assumptions surrounding children and students in assimilating their education (Chapters 1 § 4), and to ensure equal access to education in the school system regardless of geographic place of residence or social and economic conditions (Chapters 1 § 8). The Act also outlines that the instruction provided in the school system must be equivalent within each type of school and after-school center regardless of its location in the country (Chapters 1 § 9).

The introduction to the Act makes it clear that the term "equivalent" does not mean that instruction is identical, but rather that the quality of the education must be sufficiently high that the established national goals can be achieved regardless of where the education is being provided (Government Bill, 2009/10:165 p. 638). Thus, the equivalent education requirement does not require conformity in practices or that the school resources must be distributed in the same way. Instead, consideration must be given to the differing circumstances and needs of the students, and the school has a special responsibility for those students who, for various reasons, are having difficulty in achieving their educational goals (Government Bill, 2013/14:160 p. 20). The Act further outlines that municipalities must distribute resources for education within the school system based on the differing circumstances and needs of the children and students (Chapters 2 § 8a).

Despite the requirements of the Swedish Education Act, national and international reports and metrics indicate that equality within the school system is not being maintained. In particular, the Swedish Schools Inspectorate's inspections and reviews indicate that such is the case. Many school districts and schools are seeking support for their continued development in accordance with the reports of the Inspectorate. The issue of inequitable school experiences and outcomes was also noted by the Organization for Economic Cooperation and Development (OECD) in its report, Improving schools in Sweden: An OECD perspective (2015).

According to a study by the International Association for the Evaluation of Educational Achievement (IEA), Trends in International Mathematics and Science Study (TIMSS) 2011, socioeconomic background still plays a major role in academic performance in mathematics and science. The results of OECD's Programme for International Student Assessment (PISA) 2012 study show that Swedish 15-year-olds' skills in mathematics, reading comprehension and science continue to deteriorate. The decline in mathematics is of equal magnitude among both low- and high-performing students, but in reading comprehension and science, it is mainly the low-performing students who have lost the most. IEA's Progress in International Reading Literacy Study (PIRLS) 2011 notes that Swedish students with well-educated parents outperform those whose parents have less education.

National studies reinforce the results from international tests. According to the Swedish National Agency for Education's 2012 status assessment (Report, 2013:387), there continues to be a strong correlation between socioeconomic background and scholastic success. According to the Agency, the discrepancies in the average results for elementary schools have doubled over the last 20 years, albeit from what was previously a low level from an international perspective. In earlier reports, such as Resource Allocation based on Circumstances and Needs? (Report, 2009:330); Resource Allocation to the Elementary School – Principals' Perspectives (Report, 2011: 365) and Municipal Resource Allocation to Elementary Schools (Report, 2013:391). The Swedish National Agency for Education has also shown that the compensatory element in resource allocation by school districts is relatively weak, and that the municipalities do not always allocate based on need. In its status assessment, the Agency noted that the increased differences in scholastic results require robust remedial measures at the national and municipal levels if equality in the school system is to be maintained.

Upon completing elementary school or corresponding types of schooling, nearly all young people in Sweden (99%) embark on a gymnasium (upper secondary school) education. At the same time, only some 70% of those who began such a program in 2011 received their diploma or school completion certificate after 3 years. The proportion receiving a final report card increased by roughly 5% after a fourth year. The Schools Inspectorate's quality review One in Two to the Finish Line (2009:1) reviewed the ability of the gymnasium schools to get all students to complete their education. The review indicates in part that schools lack goal-based initiatives to get all their students to complete their education, have weak oversight over their results and the quality of instruction, and that major differences exist between the reviewed schools in terms of adapting instruction to the individual student.

The Schools Inspectorate conducted a quality review of the instruction provided in the introductory programs vocational introduction and individual options, which is programs for students with low academic results who are in need of extra support. The Instruction in Gymnasium School Introductory Programs (2013:6) report states in part that the instruction being given is planned based on the needs of the school rather than the needs of the students, that teacher treatment of students has a major impact on their learning, and that inadequate support in the form of, for example, scholastic or vocational guidance or student health, limits the opportunities available to the students. The Inspectorate's Instruction in Vocational Programs (2014a:5) report indicates that, at just over half of the schools reviewed, students in need of special support were not the targets of measures that were customized based on their particular needs. The Inspectorate also found that the expectations of the students were too low.

Of particular relevance to this paper is the Inspectorate's recent focus on the role of municipalities (and districts).[1] In its Municipal Resource Allocation and Work Against the Negative Effects of Segregation in the School System (2014b:01) report, the Schools Inspectorate states that most of the municipalities reviewed could improve their strategies for counteracting the negative effects of segregation. The review encompassed 30 municipal school districts, which means that it is not possible to draw general conclusions at the national level from the report. However, the review offers examples of schools that improved their results dramatically when the municipality provided significant resources in combination with the schools having converted those resources into a long-term and quality-based development initiative founded on research results. The review also offers examples of municipalities in which a deliberate and long-term development initiative was carried out at the school district level, resulting in improved goal fulfillment for the municipality as a whole. This report sets the stage for the development of the government's approach to the design of the CBS initiative.

The Government's CBS Resolution as a Response

In Government Resolution (2015/3357/S), the government tasks the Swedish National Agency for Education with undertaking initiatives, in dialogue with school districts, to improve skills results and increase equality within and between schools. These initiatives are intended to target schools with low skills results or high proportions of students who do not complete their studies, and which have otherwise found it difficult to improve their results on their own. The Agency's assessment as to which schools are to be prioritized for participation and the identification of relevant areas for development must be based on documentation from the Schools Inspectorate.

The purpose of the CBS remit is to improve skills results and increase equality within and between schools. The wording chosen by the government is interesting, as it indicates that increased equality should be achieved both within the relevant schools and between schools in the municipality, and that this is to take place in dialogue with the school districts. This perspective and the requirement of collaboration among schools and between schools and districts is new within the Swedish context. Because of its novelty, it raises the question of whether the school districts (or for private school the responsible school owners) have the capacity to independently improve the results at other schools within the municipality if the selected school(s) receive support via the Swedish National Agency for Education together with input from the universities. The question is particularly relevant since, in larger municipalities, only a few schools might be selected as program targets. More specifically, the initiatives are to target:

1. Schools with low skills results or
2. with a high proportion of students who do not complete their studies and
3. that have faced or are deemed to be facing difficult conditions in terms of improving their results on their own.

This means that the schools that are to be supported via these initiatives have low merit ratings or grades, as well as many students who are not meeting the goal fulfillment requirements in the year in which they are chosen to participate in the CBS project, and that the degree of equality between different classes at the school is low. In addition, the schools must be considered to be facing difficulties in improving their results on their own.

The Government's "Theory of Action":
A Deliberative Response

The aforementioned policy problem description consists largely of reports and interpretations of the government remit. This problem description (see Fig. 9.1) constitutes the government's perception of reality, in other words how the problem

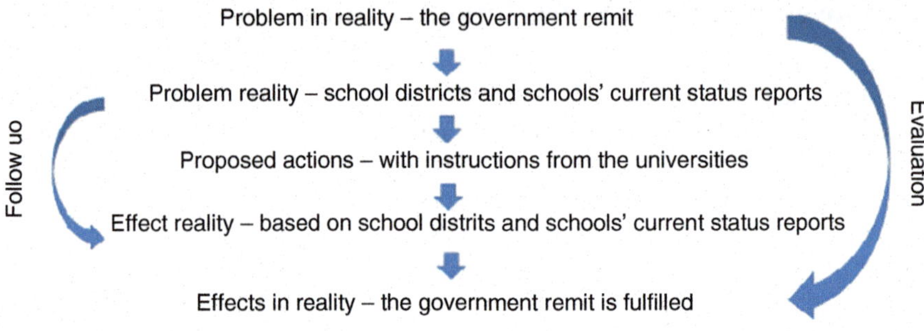

Source: Inspired by Hans Esping (1980) [Social programs on developing and dismantling public commitments]

Fig. 9.1 Theory of action model in the government remit

is perceived. The government also says that the selection of schools should be based in part on the Schools Inspectorate's inspection reports prepared for those schools, which identify specific problems. Based on these reports, the Swedish National Agency for Education must then prepare a proposal as to which schools should be offered initiatives to improve their scholastic results. The invitation to participate in the project is then sent to the school district where the school is located. The school districts will then, working with the schools, decide whether they view participating in the CBS project as a means to improve their results and increase equality within and between the schools in the municipality. In other words, there was no mandate or requirement for school participation. But during the CBS project period from 2015 very few schools and school districts have declined to participate.

Part of the government's approach was to develop a collaborative relationship from the beginning. If districts and schools decide to participate in the CBS project, they have the opportunity to reshape the government's perception of what the "real problems" are to conform to the school's own problem reality. This response is reported in a document known as a Current Status Analysis.[2] The schools' reports on their current status follow a set structure developed by the Agency, and the document is to be viewed as a support, and is called a Support for Current Status Analysis. The Current Status Analysis includes the following headings:

1. Current Status Analysis based on collected data – Results and documentation at the individual level, process level and structural level
2. Identifying and specifying problems associated with the school's ability to achieve curriculum goals
3. Making assumptions with regard to the causes of each prioritized problem
4. Identifying areas for development, with proposed initiatives

This analysis leads to an additional dialogue with participating universities: Proposed actions and initiatives from the university. We can thus examine the correspondence between the report from the Schools Inspectorate (which was the reason a school was selected) and any feedback reports to the Inspectorate that identify problems, proposed actions and initiatives for school improvement. The recommendations for particular initiatives that derive from these can then become a dialogue between the Swedish National Agency for Education and the school, while the scope of the resources allocated is determined in dialogue between the Agency and the universities.

According to the government theory of action, these university-supported initiatives must be focused on improving skills (test results), increasing the proportion of students who meet the goal fulfillment requirements (i.e., complete their studies with passing results), and enhancing the school's ability to continue to improve its results following the conclusion of supportive initiatives from the university. In other words, the government set out a classical vision of a goal-driven improvement initiative. However, the assumption that the school and school district goals might be different from the government's goals and would need to be part of any locally designed initiative introduced a very new aspect, leading to an "effect reality" based on the "problem reality" that the school district and school outlined in their Current Status Analysis. The introduction of this variable and uncertain understanding of desired outcomes also altered the timeframe associated with the measurement of CBS outcomes. Almost all CBS university supported initiative will continue over at least 2 years and if we take in the pre-planning, they will last almost 3 years. The broader effect reality could be measured no sooner than 1 year after the conclusion of the project, although tendencies in terms of merit ratings and goal fulfillment may be discernible during the course of the project. If the initiatives and the collaboration and support given by the universities the district leadership are successful in the long term, the degree of equality between and within schools should increase, and the results at the municipality level should improve.

The model assumes a feedback/follow-up that examines the relationship of the effect reality to the school's formulated problem reality. Thus, the model is collaborative in the sense that the government's desired effects can be augmented by including the degree to which the school believes that its problems have been ameliorated. Finally, the model offers a means of studying whether any visible effects arise in the reality that could be evaluated in relation to the government remit and the resources and initiatives to which the organization of the remit assigned to the Swedish National Agency for Education have led.

In the Beginning: The Results of the Document Analyses

The schools included have low skills results and have had them over a long period of time. They also have a high proportion of students who are not completing their studies, which has again been the case for a long time. We excluded students for whom information as to place of residence, for example, is lacking, with the result that newly arrived students are not included in the statistics. This means that the schools have underperformed with a completely stable student population. Our purpose is to analyse the processes and created documents in the CBS initiative to boost these schools' performance. That is, we approach the documents as if they held a story of how the complex (but weakly articulated) process of stakeholder engagement envisioned by the National Agency for Education would tell us which voices were reflected, how they framed the interventions, and the degree to which the collaborative ideal was achieved (Riessman, 2005).

The documents we use in the policy analysis are the Schools Inspectorate's comments and its follow-up decisions, the schools' proposed action plans, Agreement 2 between the Swedish National Agency for Education and the school and the school district, and the agreement between the Agency and the universities. Our purpose with the analysis was to examine the patterns that reflect the timelines and experiences of the majority of the different stakeholders and the language they use in the 'narratives'.

The Swedish Schools Inspectorate's Oversight of the Schools

The Swedish National Agency for Education's selection of schools for inclusion in the CBS project is based in part on inspection reports from the Schools Inspectorate. These reports are documented on the Inspectorate's website, from which they were obtained. Any follow-up reports that were accessible have been analyzed as well.

We coded the Inspectorate's comments on the schools and present these in Table 9.1. The table shows that the first eight items received the most comments. These also have clear ties to the quality of the instruction and the learning environment of the school, and offer proposals as to what improvements should be made. Items 9–15 are more generally focused on various processes that are tied to the principal's administrative leadership, while items 1–8 pertain more to the principal's pedagogical leadership and responsibility for ensuring that the students receive the quality of education they are entitled to. It is also interesting that all of the first eight items have connections to equitable treatment of students and support for low-performing students.

We also examined the Inspectorate's responses to the schools' reports on how they have addressed the Inspectorate's comments. It is evident here that all of the 78 schools were able to show that their work has improved and have thereby been approved by the Inspectorate. Most were approved directly after the reporting of remedial measures, but in a small number of cases after the Inspectorate failed to approve the initial report, they issued an order imposing a fine. All of these fines have since been eliminated from the critical schools, indicating that they had incorporated the Inspectorate's required changes into their activities. However, it says nothing about whether their activities have actually changed and whether their approved plans are being followed.

The Schools Inspectorate's oversight of the schools' districts. The Inspectorate also provides feedback to the municipalities/districts that outline areas for improvement. The 78 schools included in the study are located in 44 municipal school districts throughout the country. The comments directed at these school districts focus on the need for expanded organizational support for the students, while comments pertaining to systematic quality assurance were directed at 27 of the 44 school districts. [3] This suggests that quality assurance was a systemic problem since nearly 100% of schools involved in the CBS project in these municipalities also drew criticism for their systematic quality assurance (Table 9.2).

Table 9.1 Compilation of the main qualities that are comments directed by the Schools Inspectorate to the schools included in the CBS project between 2015 and 2017

1.	Systematic quality assurance	39 comments
2.	Formulation, follow-up and evaluation of actions for students in need of special support	39 comments
3.	Abusive treatment	38 comments
4.	Safe and good learning environment	31 comments
5.	Prompt support in the form of extra adaptations outside the framework of the regular instruction	30 comments
6.	Student health	22 comments
7.	Prompt support in the form of extra adaptations within the framework of the regular instruction	19 comments
8.	Student influence	17 comments
9.	Grading, grade structure and documentation	15 comments
10.	Cooperation between teachers and to improve collegial and stimulating instruction	12 comments
11.	Information for students and guardians	10 comments
12.	Scholastic guidance and student counseling	10 comments
13.	Active teacher support	9 comments
14.	School library	9 comments
15.	Internal organization and leadership	7 comments

Table 9.2 Compilation of the main quality comments by the Schools Inspectorate to the municipal school districts who had schools that participated in the CBS project between 2015 and 2017

1.	Systematic quality assurance	27 comments
2.	Student health	20 comments
3.	Student counseling in native language	16 comments
4.	School library	13 comments
5.	Abusive treatment	11 comments
6.	Internal organization and principal's role	11 comments
7.	Study and vocational guidance	8 comments

The study has, in the same way as for the schools, analyzed the Schools Inspectorate's reports of all the school districts' responses to its comments. The analysis here shows that a majority addressed all the comments, although the comments also led to the imposition of fines in six cases, and in three additional cases the Inspectorate stated that the deficiency was still present, while declining to impose a fine.

Linking the Inspectorate's comments and university interventions. Table 9.3 shows a generalized model and timeline of the relationship between the various

Table 9.3 The chain between the Schools Inspectorate's comments, the schools action plans, agreement with the National Board of education and tasks given to the universities at the model school

Schools Inspectorate's report (school unit level)	The Schools Inspectorate's follow-up (school unit level)	Action plans from the school	Agreement 2: Between the National Agency for Education and the school	Supplemental Agreement between the national Agency and the school	Task as per agreement between the National Agency for Education and the universities
June 25, 2015	May 26, 2016	April 12, 2016	May 11, 2016	November 28, 2017	December 9, 2016
1) Active teacher support 2) Individualized instruction 3) Prompt assessment of the students' need for special support 4) Formulation, follow-up and evaluation of action programs for students in need of special support 5) Safe and quiet environment for studies 6) Abusive treatment 7) Systematic quality assurance 8) Student health	The report from the school concerning the School inspections critic Is accepted by the school inspection And the school inspections critic is not considered a problem any more	Designation of process manager as support in processes for building the improvement organization. Process manager must have training in analytical skills Counselor/coach with extensive knowledge of the school's policy documents. Purpose: observe, coach, develop quality instruction Counselor training. to create conditions for planning, organizing, collegial teaching based on prior areas; exhibit consensus on instruction and assessments Literacy boost Lectures/workshops Consensus on basic values and democratic mission. Competence assessment of teachers' ethical learning processes to enhance students' sense of self and	Initiatives Pedagogic leadership, training and counseling. Systematic quality assurance: focus on analysis of skills results. Counseling: strengthen pedagogic leadership. Initiatives throughout the entire chain of command Initiatives with regard to quality of instruction: professional counseling for teachers, literacy boost, locally adapted education impacts' assessments and grading	Extend professional counseling for teachers	Administrative management/ principals/advanced skills teachers/teachers in the municipality given locally adapted support in the form of training and counseling. Content is mainly pedagogic leadership and systematic quality assurance: 1) Process management and counseling targeting children and education manager/principals: Build up sustainable school assessment organization and support municipality in its own efforts to build its model for assessment work 2) Training and counseling in analysis of skills results as basis for school development Administrative management/ principals/advanced skills teachers 3) Counselor training to advance teacher skills 4) counseling of teachers provided to teachers in subject groups based on teacher's pedagogic plan. Also individual counseling through

documents and analysis produced by the stakeholders in response to the identification of the 78 schools in 44 districts. The documents comprise the Schools Inspectorate's comments and its follow-up decisions, the schools' proposed action plans, Agreement 2 between the Swedish National Agency for Education and the school, and the agreement between the Agency and the universities. The model was derived by examining the patterns that reflect the timelines and experiences of the majority of the schools are intended to hypothetically illustrate the exchanges and experiences of the key stakeholders.

The first agreement with our test municipality was prepared on November 4, 2015. The decision emphasized that the school and the municipality had had low academic results for a number of years, as well as deficiencies in terms of systematic quality assurance. Forceful and broad criticisms of deficiencies with regard to systematic quality assurance were directed at grades 7–9, which serve students from roughly ages 14–16.

The table shows that, on June 25, 2015, the school received numerous comments from the Schools Inspectorate, of which the first six concerned the work being done with the students, particularly those in need of support. The comments clearly point out that there are deficiencies in the management of the school and in compliance with rules, plus a school culture that lacks safe and good learning environment for studies and have problems in terms of abusive treatment. Some of the deficiencies cited in the other items also have clear connections to deficiencies in the work and school culture.

It is noteworthy that an agreement was entered on November 4, 2016 between the school and the Swedish National Agency for Education for the school to take part in the CBS project. The school was then tasked with preparing a current status plan and developing action plans to improve conditions at the school. That document is dated April 12, 2016. It reflects only hints of the criticisms from the Schools Inspectorate. The school presumably failed to take the criticisms seriously since they believed that they were already dealt with when the school submitted its response to the Inspectorate's comments, a response that the Inspectorate then approved, saying that the deficiencies had been rectified. However, that approval did not occur until May 26, 2016, after the school had presented its action plans. Systematic quality assurance, which is the basis for the school development assumptions laid out by the Government and reflected in the Inspectorate's comments, is not mentioned in the school's action plans.

Systematic quality assurance is reintroduced in the next phase of the CBS process that engages the Swedish National Agency for Education and the school, including a focus on results development. This is followed by a number of initiatives pertaining to the quality of the instruction, a literacy boost, formative assessment training, and professional counseling for teachers.

It is worth noting that the professional counseling support is directed toward school improvement and building a personalized/individualized model for growth and development. This also includes training and counseling in analyzing academic results as a basis for school development. On the other hand, the last two items — counseling of advanced skilled teachers and counseling of teachers— were included as a result of initial conversations with the supporting university staff. However, these can easily be seen as responsive to the school's self-analysis and report. In other words, the university's proposed response sought to meet both the self-analysis and the Inspectorate's analysis.

Our table attempts to summarize the items in the document pertaining to the school's proposed action plans that is Agreement 2 between the Swedish National Agency for Education and the school. One issue that arose is the difficulty of coherent interpretation of meaning of the Agreement, as there is no common language that clearly delineates the precise meaning of each of the terms, nor the relationship between stakeholders, objectives, functions and desirable results (Ball et al., 2012). This brings to mind the often-noted lack of a common language for describing school processes and, with the exception of standardized test results, the characteristics of an effectively functioning school (Lindensjö & Lundgren, 2000). One other aspect connected to the language can be that we are scrutinizing a hierarchical chain from the government though their agencies down to the local municipalities and the school district and the schools. Is this chain characterized by authority or thrust? There is in Sweden a growing criticism of the traditional top down governing chain and its structure and functions (SOU, 2018:47). There is a drift towards a governing system based on trust and capacity. When trust is given, the assumption is that the lower level has the capacity to act in relation to the organizational goals. This can also be an explanation for the lack of coherent language between the municipal and state levels. Is there a chain of thrust or is it broken? (Johansson et al., 2016).

However, although the language and meaning of educational terms is imprecise, there are clear connections between Agreement 2 and the agreement with the universities. But those agreements between the National Agency of Education and the seats of higher learning are formulated between two state agencies. They exhibit a number of recurring categories (Table 9.4).

Different initiatives are of course concealed under each heading. The question that arises is whether, despite everything, the will to change will be created through these school development-oriented initiatives, along with a transformation of the work and school culture that will lead to improved skills results for all students. The Schools Inspectorate's primary criticism pertains to the school's work with its low-performing students, and nothing specific is found in the texts. We reviewed all the comments directed by the Inspectorate to the schools that managed initiatives

Table 9.4 Recurring categories in agreements between the Swedish National Agency for Education and the universities

Counseling	34 instances
Instruction-related	33 instances
Pedagogic leadership	33 instances
Systematic quality assurance	32 instances
Collegial processes	17 instances
Student health issues	13 instances
Formative working methods	8 instances
Language-developing working methods	7 instances

targeting students who required support or special adaptation. We then supplemented the list with student health, which often affects such students, and found 100 comments directed at the schools. This is discussed further in the Summarizing Reflections section.

Summarizing Reflections

The reading through these documents trying to find their improvement narrative bolsters the impression that, despite low skills results and low goal fulfillment, the participants in the processes failed to note the connection between the quality of their activities and the instruction provided and the need to develop the schools in order to better address students who require extra support and adaptations. What remains as the strongest impression is the nearly total absence of any connection to the Inspectorate's comments with regard to deficiencies in the schools' work with low-performing students, safe and good learning environment for studies and abusive treatment.

With regard to the Governments third policy objective — targeting schools that face or are considered to be facing difficult conditions in terms of improving their results on their own — the analyses indicate that this will remain and can be a major problem.

These schools have been underperforming for the last 20 years, albeit without being aware of the fact. This is apparent in their action plans, which contain mainly general initiatives, and why we see so few traces of the Schools Inspectorate's comments in the schools' action plans. Furthermore, there are not many comments concerning the work with students in need of support and extra adaptations in the tasks assigned to the universities at the end of the process.

Another major problem with meeting the government's third policy objective is that the school districts responsible for these schools are underperforming in relation to the national levels in terms of both merit ratings and goal fulfillment. The ability of these school districts to help their schools improve their results and goal fulfillment may be highly questionable. In terms of the chain of command, we can see that, in the schools included in the CBS project, the school district level is too weak to provide support at the school level.

The challenge for the CBS project is to determine how the school district level and the entire local organization can be strengthened. Is it by counseling the chief administrator and their employees at the school office, or also by training the school districts with regard to their responsibilities? The analysis indicates that the entire local organization must be the object of targeted initiatives, in other words, the school district's policy and administrative levels and all the underperforming schools for which the school district is responsible.

Our analysis also shows that the results point to problems in the work and school culture. Part of this pertains to the view of the students outlined in the Schools Inspectorate's comments about the ways the schools are managed and governed with respect to students who need support and extra adaptations. The following documents do not address how the schools are succeeding with such adaptations and the compensatory support outlined in the government description of the policy problem. This could be attributed to a lack of understanding, but also to an unwillingness to work together.

It is problematic that there is no major overlap or common language in the documents concerning the problems and initiatives at the same school, as there are many actors and activities that must function as support for the individual school. These differing interpretations make it difficult to monitor, assess and analyze what is successful and important in moving the process forward.

This lack of coherence between the documents does also affect the way the universities are interpreting their task according to the agreement with the National Agency of Education. But through the money spent on the different CBS projects and the involvement of many universities we can conclude that the state has managed to bring support structures to scale, but the process can be improved to give more coherent narratives and better goal fulfillment in relation to the Governments CBS policy.

[1] Most municipalities in Sweden are responsible for a single school district.
[2] Unfortunately, these are viewed by the Swedish National Agency for Education as municipality documents, and consequently are not documented in the Agency's database and could not be included in the analyses for this paper. This has of course affected our understanding of how school districts and schools analyze their problems, and how the connections between selection criteria such as the Inspectorate's comments, the school's action plans and the initiatives undertaken by the seats of higher learning are to function.
[3] There were also a few comments directed at just a single school organizer, usually a private school, which were administrative in nature.

References

Ball, S., Maguire, M., & Braun, A. (2012). *How schools do policy – Policy enactment in secondary schools*. Routledge.

Esping, H. (1980). *Sociala program: Om att utveckla och avveckla offentliga åtaganden/Social programs – on developing and dismantling public commitment* (Delrapport, 605). Liber.

Hajer, M., Hajer, M. A., & Wagenaar, H. (Eds.). (2003). *Deliberative policy analysis: Understanding governance in the network society*. Cambridge University Press.

IEA's Progress in International Reading Literace Study (PIRLS) 2011.

Johansson, O., Nihlfors, E., Jervik Steen, L., & Karlsson, S. (2016). *Superintendents in Sweden: Structures, cultural relations and leadership*. Springer.

Lindensjö, B., & Lundgern, U. P. (2000). *Utbildningsreformer och politisk styrning/Education reforms and political governess*. HLS Förlag.

OECD's Programme for International Student Assessment (PISA) 2012.

OECD report, Improving schools in Sweden: An OECD perspective (2015).

Riessman, C. K. (2005). *Narrative analysis. Qualitative research methods* (Vol. 30). Sage.

Roberts, N. (2004). Public deliberation in an age of direct citizen participation. *The American Review of Public Administration, 34*(4), 315–353.

SOU/Swedish Public Investigations. (2018:47) *Med tillit växer handlingsutrymmet/With thrust the liberty of actions grow.* Nordsteds Juridik.

Stevenson, H. (2016). Deliberative policy analysis. In P. H. Pattberg & F. Zelli (Eds.), *Encyclopedia for global environmental governance and politics* (pp. 96–103). Edward Elgar.

Swedish Government Bill Den nya skollagen – för kunskap, valfrihet och trygghet [The New Education Act – for Knowledge, Freedom of Choice, and Safety] (2009/10:165 p. 638).

Swedish Government Bill Tid för undervisning – lärares arbete med stöd, särskilt stöd och åtgärdsprogram [Time to Teach – Teacher's Work with Support, Special Support and Action Plans] 2013/14:160 p. 20.

Swedish Government Resolution Uppdrag om samverkan för bästa skola [Mission for Cooperation for Better Schools] (2015/3357/S).

The Schools Inspectorate Utbildningen på introduktionsprogrammen i gymnasieskolan [Instruction in Gymnasium School Introductory Programs] (2013:6).

The Schools Inspectorate's quality review Kommunernas resursfördelning och arbete mot segregationens negativa effekter i skolväsendet [Municipal Resource Allocation and Work Against the Negative Effects of Segregation in the School System] (2014a:01).

The Schools Inspectorate's quality review Varannan i mål [One in two to the finish line] (2009:1).

The Schools Inspectorate's quality review Undervisning på yrkesprogram [Instruction in Vocational Programs] (2014b:5).

The Swedish Education Act Skollag 1. kap. Inledande bestämmelser [The Swedish Education Act. Chapter 1 Initial Regulations] (2010:800, chapter 1).

The Swedish National Agency of Education; Resursfördelning utifrån förutsättningar och behov? (rapport 2009:330) [Resource Allocation based on Circumstances and Needs? (Report 2009:330)].

The Swedish National Agency of Education; Resursfördelning till grundskolan – rektorers perspektiv (rapport 2011: 365) [Resource Allocation to the Elementary School – Principals' Perspectives (Report 2011: 365)]; and.

The Swedish National Agency of Education; Kommunernas resursfördelning till grundskolor (rapport 2013:391) [Municipal Resource Allocation to Elementary Schools (Report 2013:391)].

Chapter 10
The Australian Context: National, State and School-Level Efforts to Improve Schools in Australia

David Gurr, Daniela Acquaro, and Lawrie Drysdale

Abstract Australia, like many countries, has a history of colonisation and extensive controlled and humanitarian immigration, with this shifting from an Anglo-Celtic emphasis to include, in succession, an emphasis on migrants from Europe, Asia and Africa. This chapter provides several perspectives on evidence-based school development in this changing context. The first focus is on national school-wide improvement initiatives: IDEAS (Innovative Designs for Enhancing Achievements in Schools), which utilises professional learning communities to improve student outcomes; and PALL (Principals as Literacy Leaders) which provides principals with literacy and leadership knowledge to support teachers to improve student reading performance. The second perspective explores the state level through considering work at the Melbourne Graduate School of Education in terms of evidence-based teacher training through the development of a clinical teaching model, and evidence-based school improvement through the Science of Learning Schools Partnership. The final perspective is at the school level, where the development of two schools in challenging contexts are described: the first a school formed from the closure of three failing schools; the second a school that was at the point of closure when the current principal was appointed to turn-it-around.

Keywords School development · School improvement · School effectiveness · Success schools · Principal leadership · School leadership · Initial teacher training · Evidence-based improvement

---

D. Gurr (✉) · D. Acquaro · L. Drysdale
The University of Melbourne, Melbourne, Australia
e-mail: d.gurr@unimelb.edu.au; d.acquaro@unimelb.edu.au; drysdale@unimelb.edu.au

© The Author(s) 2022
R. M. Ylimaki, L. A. Brunderman (eds.), *Evidence-Based School Development in Changing Demographic Contexts*, Studies in Educational Leadership 24,
https://doi.org/10.1007/978-3-030-76837-9_10

Introduction

Australia, like many countries, has a history of colonisation and extensive controlled and humanitarian immigration, with country prosperity partly tied to continued population growth. The last 70 years has seen migration move from an Anglo-Celtic emphasis to include, in succession, an emphasis on migrants from Europe, Asia and Africa. Historically, since the colonial occupation of Australia, schooling has undergone major periods of change (see Campbell & Proctor, 2014). Initially, governments were little involved in schools and the provision of schooling was left to church schools (Anglican, Catholic and Protestant) or private schools (small schools owned and run by person or family). The private schools did not survive the domination of the church schools and, in the 1870s, the church schools were faced with competition from government schools as the states and territories that existed then all instituted education acts that provided free and secular education (initially for the primary years in the main). Some private schools went on to become larger independent schools, and whilst church schools were challenged by the arrival of widespread government school provision, they survived. This meant that for the first half of the twentieth Century, school education was a mixture of the dominant government school system which charged no or very low fees and provided a secular education, and the many church and non-church independent schools, with the largest number being parochial Catholic schools, often small and attached to a local parish.

In the 1960s, with the number of religious teachers declining, the cost of providing Catholic school education increased dramatically to the point that these schools sought government support. Whilst governments were reluctant to provide this, a pivotal moment occurred when the Catholic schools threatened to close and the Commonwealth Government came to rescue and provided substantial funding; the funding provided to non-government schools has increased considerably over the years to the point now that an independent school serving a socio-educational community with low advantage can get up to 80% of its operating costs funded by the government. This was also the stimulus for the Commonwealth Government to exert more influence on schools, with this trend continuing through to current times as is explained further in the next paragraph.

The central Commonwealth Government (also called the federal government), oversees regional governments comprised of six states and two territories, with the federation having formed in 1901 from the six states that existed then. Each of these has a department of education, variously named. Education in Australia is a complex interplay between these different levels of government involving nine education departments, and between government and non-government schools. Whilst the responsibility for the provision of government schooling constitutionally rests with the state and territory governments, increasingly there has been federal government influence especially in terms of significant financial grants to both government and non-government schools, the development of a national curriculum, the creation of a national accountability system through the development of a national assessment program in literacy and numeracy and public reporting of these results, and other matters. The federal government provides funding for all schools, but does so in a complicated way, with the bulk of the funding distributed by the state and territory governments. Whilst the state and territory governments provide the main funding for government schools and supplementary funding for non-government schools, much of the income for these governments comes from taxation fees collected and distributed by the federal government (e.g. income tax, and the goods and services tax are only collected by the federal government). This federal funding seems to be one of the major areas of contention in the community with government school champions decrying the lack of funds and the amount going to non-government schools, and non-government school champions arguing it is fair that all tax-payers receive some level of financial support for schooling from the government. Mostly these arguments ignore the full complexity of school funding and the significant role that states and territories have for government school funding.

The governance of schools is also complex. Within the multiple external contexts, imposed or otherwise, local school governance arrangements vary greatly (Anderson, 2006; Gurr et al., 2012). Victorian government schools have had compulsory school councils since 1975 and these include school and parent elected members, and typically also have student and community members (elected or co-opted). School councils have a role in school accountability and improvement processes with specific responsibilities for finance, strategic planning, policy development and review and principal selection. Whilst government schools in South Australia and the Australian Capital Territory also have similarly long histories of school councils, Australia's largest state, New South Wales, still does not have compulsory school councils. Catholic schools in Australia have a variety of governance arrangements depending on whether they are parochial (under the authority of the parish priest with or without an advisory school board), systemic (under canonical authority and advisory in nature), or congregational (depending on their legal status there are a variety of delegated responsibilities and authorities). Most independent schools in Australia will have a board or council, and most are incorporated (i.e. companies limited by guarantee), regulated by government acts, and expected to adopt the principles of corporate governance. Parent, teacher and student voice is often non-existent or limited in the Catholic and independent governance arrangements.

In this chapter we provide several perspectives on evidence-based school development in this complex and changing context. The first focus is on national school-wide improvement initiatives and two programs are described. IDEAS (Innovative Designs for Enhancing Achievements in Schools) is an extensive and on-going school improvement project that has developed a framework for establishing professional learning communities to improve school outcomes (e.g. Crowther et al., 2009; Lewis & Andrews, 2007). PALL (Principals as Literacy Leaders) is an on-going research, school improvement and professional learning program focussed on improving literacy in schools through providing principals with literacy and leadership knowledge to support teachers to improve student reading performance (Dempster et al., 2017). The second perspective explores the state level through considering work at the Melbourne Graduate School of Education in terms of evidence-based teacher training through the development of a clinical teaching model, and evidence-based school improvement through the Science of Learning Schools Partnership Initiative which utilises a cycle of inquiry approach to develop an important learning focus; in 2019 the focus is on using student voice to inform school improvement (solcnetwork.com/solnos2019). The final perspective is at the school level, where the development of two schools in challenging contexts are described; the first a school formed from the closure of three failing schools (Gurr et al., 2018, 2019; Huerta Villalobos, 2013); the second a school that was at the point of closure when the current principal was appointed to turn-it-around.

National Level School Improvement – The IDEAS and PALL Projects

Gurr (2019) described two major school improvement initiatives. One was a response from a team of researchers at the University of Southern Queensland, led initially by Crowther, to devise a school-wide improvement program that could be used in any school. The other was a collaboration that was instigated by a principal association with federal government support, and involving three universities and school systems from three Australian states and one territory.

IDEAS (Innovative Designs for Enhancing Achievements in Schools)

IDEAS is an extensive and on-going school improvement project that has developed a framework for establishing professional learning communities to improve school outcomes (e.g. Crowther et al., 2009; Lewis & Andrews, 2007). From its beginnings in 1997, it was designed to explore how school-based management could be constructed to ensure it had a positive effect on classrooms (Andrews et al., 2004; Crowther et al., 2012; Crowther et al., 2009; Crowther et al., 2002; Lewis & Andrews, 2007). In particular, the research was concerned with establishing professional learning communities to improve school outcomes. IDEAS involved three components: a research-based framework for enhancing school outcomes that includes development of strategic foundations, cohesive community, appropriate infrastructure, schoolwide pedagogy, and professional learning; a five-phase school-based implementation strategy — initiating, discovering, envisioning, actioning and sustaining (this is a process version of the IDEAS acronym; Crowther et al., 2012); and, parallel leadership in which the principal and teachers engage in mutualism (mutual trust and respect), a sense of shared purpose and an allowance of individual expression.

IDEAS promoted teacher leadership (these are generally middle leaders who are teachers with a leadership position) and defined the core roles of the principal to include: facilitating the development of a shared vision, creating cultural meaning through identity generation, supporting organisational alignment, distributing power and leadership and developing networks and external alliances. IDEAS is a process that is designed to help schools embark on major schoolwide change to teaching and learning. It works through the parallel leadership of teachers (focus on pedagogical development) and principals (focus on strategic development) combining to activate and integrate culture-building, organisation wide professional learning, and development of schoolwide pedagogy, which leads to school alignment and an enhanced school community capacity to improve school outcomes. IDEAS has been shown to lead to improved school outcomes, often concerned with changes associated with teachers and teaching practice such as increased teacher confidence, self-reflection and review, and the development of a professional learning community (Lewis & Andrews, 2007). Whilst there was less focus on reporting student outcomes in the early stages of the program and less surety about the impact of IDEAS on students (e.g. Andrews et al., 2004; Lewis, 2006), in more recent years there has been clear evidence for improved student learning and behavioural outcomes (Crowther et al., 2012). More substantial evidence of success of the program, with a focus on the sustainability of success, and more research from those outside the project would be useful to confirm the importance of IDEAS (see Wildy & Faulkner, 2008, and Gurr & Drysdale, 2016, for discussion of these points). In terms of understanding successful school leadership, its main contribution is to highlight the importance of principals in direction setting (as meta-strategists), in supporting change and the work of teachers, and promoting a distributed view of leadership through the concept of teacher and parallel leadership to support principal efforts in driving school improvement (Crowther et al., 2009; Lewis & Andrews, 2007).

Principals as Literacy Leaders (PALL)

This project formed as a response by a principal association, the Australian Primary Principals Association (APPA), to a federal government call for projects to address educational disadvantage. The APPA saw an opportunity to develop primary principals as literacy leaders, and in 2009 a collaboration was born that involved association with the federal education department and a state education department, three universities (Griffith, Edith Cowan and the Australian Catholic University), and the government, Catholic and independent school jurisdictions from the Northern Territory, Queensland, South Australia and Western Australia. PALL was a professional learning opportunity, a school improvement program and a leadership for learning research project. Dempster et al. (2017) described how the project expanded to three further research projects and programs in all six states and two territories – it was a vibrant, impactful learning and research program designed to 'provide principals with both the literacy knowledge and leadership support they need to assist their teachers to improve reading performance in their schools' (Dempster et al., 2017, p. 150). It was a project that clearly linked leadership with learning and did so in the important area of reading development.

An initial review of relevant literature established a program framework, the leadership for literacy learning blueprint that had five components (shared leadership, professional development participation, enhancing the physical, social and emotional conditions for learning, planning and coordinating the curriculum and teaching across the school, and connecting with parent and community support) surrounding a core that had developing shared moral purpose around improving student learning and performance, disciplined dialogue and a strong evidence base to inform practice (Dempster et al., 2012). Schools participated in a two-year program that included completion of five modules (leadership for learning, learning to read, gathering and using reading achievement data, designing and implementing literacy interventions, and intervention evaluation) and the construction of a literacy improvement plan in the first year, and implementation of the plan in the second year. It was a program that focused on what was called The Big Six: oral language, vocabulary, phonological awareness, letter-sound knowledge, comprehension and fluency. Principals were supported by a literacy achievement advisor (usually a system-based peer mentor), and this role was considered to be very important (the importance of having critical friends to support school improvement is well known: Butler et al., 2011; Huerta Villalobos, 2013; Swaffield, 2004; Swaffield & MacBeath, 2005).

The program was clearly focused on principals, provided considerable support and opportunities for principals to be literacy leaders, and there was evidence that with support they could become better at doing this (Dempster et al., 2017). Importantly, from the beginning the project adopted an inclusive view of leadership, and the development of teachers in leadership roles, such as literacy leaders, or class teachers that became more widely influential, were features of many of the case study schools (Dempster et al., 2017). Teacher leadership (positional and non-positional) was seen to be 'central to school-wide action' (Dempster et al., 2017, p. 94).

Dempster et al. (2017, p. 150) reported on findings from six PALL studies and concluded that in terms of impact on student achievement, and despite some methodological difficulties in the studies (such as the relatively short nature of the program and problems in getting principals to complete program evaluations), that 'there is certainly considerable evidence of increases in student achievement in reading – at the individual, class, and school level…' However, as with IDEAS, the core focus of the program was not student outcomes per se, but rather changes in what happened in schools. In the case of PALL, changes in how principals led their schools were demonstrated, with flow-on effects to how other staff worked across curriculum, pedagogy, assessment and reporting. In many cases this led to improved student learning outcomes in a short time, with the project hopeful that as time progresses more substantial and sustainable evidence of learning gain will be shown. In some cases, there was evidence of impact on families, although family engagement was an area identified as needing more development and one that is being explored in further studies. As for IDEAS, what is now needed is more substantial evidence of success of the program (especially in relation to student outcomes), with a focus on sustainability of success, and more research from those outside of the project.

State/Regional Level School Improvement – MGSE Teacher Training and School Improvement Initiatives

This section provides an example of university programs that impact on schools in one state. It reports on two programs from the University of Melbourne in the state of Victoria: a leading initial teacher education program, and a school improvement initiative. Each program utilises an evidence-based approach to improve student outcomes and development.

Melbourne Graduate School of Education's Master of Teaching

In an effort to advance schools and systems, the federal government introduced National reforms through its Student's First (TEMAG, 2014a April) approach which identified four key areas necessary in the improvement of student outcomes: teacher quality, school autonomy, engaging parents in education and strengthening the curriculum. With recognition that, of school-controlled factors, teachers have the most impact on student learning (e.g. Barber & Mourshed, 2007; Hattie, 2003), the Teacher Education Ministerial Advisory Group (TEMAG) was established to provide advice on how to improve the quality of teachers through a national reform of initial teacher education programs. The enhancement of teacher education was seen to be central in the federal government's plans to 'lift the quality of and respect for the teaching profession' (TEMAG, 2014a April). The advisory group, comprised of leading education tertiary academics and school leaders, identified divergent practices amongst initial teacher education providers and a need for structural and cultural change to improve and align practice. Six key directions and 38 recommendations were outlined in the *Action Now-Classroom Ready Teachers* (TEMAG, December 2014b) report, with a call for national accreditation, transparent selection processes, evidence-based program design and delivery, greater integration between schools and higher education providers, and evidence of classroom readiness. The report signalled a wave of change in Australia's initial teacher education and by 2017 all initial teacher education programs at the graduate level were required to become 200 point, two-year equivalent Masters programs, accredited against a set of national standards. This meant that a one-year graduate diploma in teaching was no longer able to be offered as a teaching qualification at the graduate level. Aspiring teachers could select between an undergraduate Bachelor of Teaching or a postgraduate pathway through the Master of Teaching. Improving the quality of teaching by greater regulation of initial teacher education programs was seen to be fundamental in improving the profession, schools and education outcomes (TEMAG, 2014b December).

The Melbourne Graduate School of Education's (MGSE) Master of Teaching Program was first developed in 2008 when the University of Melbourne moved to the *Melbourne Model* which emphasised broad areas of undergraduate education, with professional specialisation occurring at the graduate level. As part of this, the then Faculty of Education stopped its undergraduate initial teacher education program and shifted entirely to become a graduate school, with a two-year Master of Teaching program. The design of the program drew heavily from the Stanford Teacher Education Programme (STEP) from Stanford University in California and from the University of Virginia and Bank Street Teachers' College, New York (Kameniar et al., 2017) which adopt an evidence-based clinical approach. The Master of Teaching was the first of its kind in Australia and a paradigm shift in initial teacher education, promising to deliver not only high-quality initial teacher education but also equipping teacher graduates with knowledge in areas such as wellbeing, curriculum or leadership through a carefully constructed Masters level elective offering.

The creation of the Master of Teaching at MGSE pre-dated the TEMAG recommendations, and its success was an influence on TEMAG's recommendation that all graduate initial teacher education courses become two-year Masters programs. The program is evidence-based and designed around a clinical teaching framework (Burn & Mutton, 2013; Conroy et al., 2013; McLean Davies et al., 2013; Darling-Hammond & Bransford, 2005), the focus of which is to develop teachers who are interventionist practitioners able to assess, diagnose and support the individual learning needs of all students, as well as work with students with mixed abilities. The program teaches its pre-service teachers how to utilise evidence and data about learners to target their teaching in order to improve student learning and development (Dinham, 2013). A central tenet of the clinical model is the centrality of the clients (Alter & Coggshall, 2009), interdependency of theory and practice and the importance placed on clinical practice in the school context, whereby pre-service teachers are supported to develop their ability to make evidence informed judgements (Kriewaldt et al., 2017). Three core components characterised teaching as a clinical practice profession: (1) a focus on student learning and development; (2) evidence-informed practice; and (3) processes of reasoning that lead to decision-making (Kriewaldt et al., 2017). The six tenets underpinning these three components are (Kriewaldt et al., 2017, pp. 154–155):

- *The student and their learning needs are pivotal to all decision-making about what, when and how to teach;*
- *The teacher uses evidence about the student, what they already know and what they are ready to learn to make decisions about subsequent teaching;*
- *The teacher draws on current research evidence about effective practice in making decisions about how to work with a student or group of students;*
- *The teacher integrates knowledge about who the student is, including knowledge of their characteristics, circumstances and prior experiences, into decision-making about the student and their own teaching;*

- *The teacher evaluates their own impact on student learning on a regular basis; and The teacher exercises professional judgement involving all these elements.*
- *The teacher exercises professional judgement involving all these elements.*

Through a clinical model, the effectiveness of the teaching and learning cycle is heightened as pre-service teachers are explicitly taught the skills necessary to meet the individual needs of students through a process of reasoning and decision making. Pre-service teachers are taught to integrate various forms of evidence about what the student knows or can do, in order to develop their pedagogical thinking (Sahlberg, 2012). The focus of their training is 'on the importance of data, evidence and research in order to determine the next stage or step to advance student's learning' (Kriewaldt et al., 2017, p. 157). A key component of the program has been the development of an assessment and curriculum innovation- the Clinical Praxis Exam (CPE). The task first piloted in 2010, was designed to integrate learning amongst academic subjects and the professional practice component of the program by assessing student's clinical reasoning. 'The CPE is an oral assessment task that involves a cyclical process of analysis and reflection, integrating theory, evidence, practice and evaluation' (Kameniar et al., 2017, p. 58). Research (Kameniar et al., 2017) into the impact of the CPE suggest that students considered it to be the most valuable learning in their studies. Students felt that the task helped them bridge the gap between theory and practice and assisted them in developing greater understanding of 'the complex intellectual, diagnostic, planning, intervention, and evaluative aspects of teaching practice' (Kameniar et al., 2017, p. 62).

The size and scope of the Master of Teaching program expanded with five courses offered in 2019 including secondary, primary, primary and early childhood, early childhood and a secondary internship program which combines study and paid work in a teaching role. Compared to other universities, it was ranked number one for student satisfaction, skills attained in the degree, and 90.7% of graduates were successful in attaining full time employment, which again was well above the national average of 83.8% (QILT, 2018). A small scale study completed by the Australian Council for Educational Research (ACER) in 2010 found that 90% of MGSE Master of Teaching graduates claimed that they were 'well' of 'very well prepared' and they claimed that they had entered the profession with knowledge of best practice, emphasis on deep reflection and reflective practice and an ability to integrate theory and practice in an evidence-based approach (Scott et al., 2010, p. 4).

'While the impact of university programmes on teachers has proved difficult to measure' (Kameniar et al., 2017, p. 54) to date, as part of the National reforms introduced, all initial teacher education providers will be required to submit evidence of student learning impact of programs to their state level accreditation body within 5 years of their initial program accreditation. For most providers, the next couple of years will serve to generate data to better understand what works and why and by 2022, we should begin to see impact data on the effectiveness of Australian teaching programs since the introduction of the recent National reforms. As one of the first programs to be accredited, MGSE's Master of Teaching will be amongst the first to complete Stage 2 of the accreditation process and will utilise teaching performance assessments, graduate outcomes data, graduate and school principal survey data and case studies to evaluate graduate and program performance. This data will be useful in confirming the importance of the program in preparing the next generation of teachers.

Science of Learning Partnership Schools Initiative

Motivated by a desire to improve learning outcomes in Australian schools and funded as an Australian Research Council Special Research Initiative, The Science of Learning Research Centre (SLRC) was established in 2012 by Professor John Hattie at MGSE.

As part of the work of the SLRC, a Science of Learning Partnership Schools Initiative (SLPSI) was created in 2017, offering schools an opportunity to improve learning outcomes in their schools. The initiative teaches school leaders and educators to implement an evidence-based cycle of inquiry to identify school needs, use high impact teaching and learning interventions and evaluate the effectiveness of the interventions. Through the program, schools work with leading education researchers over the course of 1 year. The partnership requires the commitment of the school principal to engage in the program which includes intensive professional development programs, forums, school professional development sessions and ongoing personalised support to achieve school improvement goals. The school is taught to use evidence-based approaches to improve student educational and wellbeing outcomes. In order to do this, the principal and teachers must establish a deep understanding of how to diagnose the school's needs, implement evidence-based interventions, and evaluate their impact. The fundamental goal of the program is to connect research with practice for the purpose of translation and impact on student outcomes. In its first 2 years, the program allowed schools to focus on an area of inquiry unique to their school, whereas the program in 2019 has trialed a new approach delineating a focus on *Using Student Voice to Drive Improvement* which is described at (https://solcnetwork.com/sol-nos2019/). The program has four main stages:

Stage 1: Diagnose- Pre-test diagnostic tools utlilising student voice are used to identify areas for improvement within the school.
Stage 2: Intervention- Professional learning and online modules are provided to support teacher improvement using evidence-based interventions.
Stage 3: Implementation: Leadership coaching supports school leaders to understand the science of effective implementation.
Stage 4: Evaluation: Post-intervention measures are provided to support teachers and school leader to evaluate impact and plan for next steps.

Within the program, schools are offered a series of intensive professional development programs at the University of Melbourne for several members of their staff delivered by MGSE academics. In addition, staff participate in several forums, including participating in online learning activities. Whole school professional learning is also offered to all school staff with ongoing personalised support and access to a suite of online professional learning resources. The program, albeit still in its infancy, has attracted strong numbers with 16 schools enrolled in the 2019 program. The rationale for the initiative derives from Hattie's (2015) work on collaborative expertise where he sees the importance of school leaders coming together to work and learn from one another. The premise of the SLPSI is to create a culture of collaborative expertise in which 'highly expert, inspired and passionate teachers and school leaders working together to maximize the effect of their teaching on all students in their care' (Hattie, 2015: p. 2). Hattie (2012, 2015) encourages school leaders and staff to focus on measuring impact on student learning; work together to evaluate their impact; to move from what students know to explicit success criteria; to build trust and welcome errors and opportunities to learn; to attain maximum feedback from others about their effect; understand the difference between surface and deep learning; and knowing when to and how to challenge students. Anecdotal evidence suggests that the program of learning has made an impact on participating schools, however the program in 2019 will commence a more formal stage of evaluation. Whilst internal satisfaction data rate the program highly with testimonials from participants outlining the impact on their development as educators and on their school more broadly, more substantial evidence of the effectiveness of the initiative is needed to know how this program of learning is making a sustained impact on student and school outcomes.

School Level Improvement: Evidence-Based Improvement in Two Schools

Schools in all educational systems in Australia are moving to evidence-based school development. This section of the chapter provides an example of two government schools in challenging circumstances that have developed their own individual school improvement strategy based on several sources including evidence-based research, school data and effective decision-making processes.

Hume Central Secondary College

Hume Central Secondary College is a school we have previously written about as part of our contribution to the International Successful School Principalship Project and International School Leadership Development Network (Gurr & Drysdale, 2018, 2019; Gurr et al., 2018, 2019; Huerta Villalobos, 2013; McCrohan, 2021). This school demonstrates how a school at the local level can autonomously construct its own evidence-based improvement goals and strategies using several sources to improve student outcomes. Drysdale and Gurr were involved with the principal for many years and with the school at various levels. For example, Drysdale was a critical friend, professional development facilitator in the school's 'emerging leaders' program', a participant observer in regular leadership meetings, and member of the research team that investigated the school. The major formal research methodologies used have been that of in-depth, multiple perspective case studies based on ISSPP protocols: Huerta Villalobos (2013) conducted masters level research about the role of critical friends at the school and McCrohan explored the leadership of the principal (Gurr et al., 2018, 2019; McCrohan, 2021). This provided a unique and valuable in-depth insight into the school's strategies, practices and leadership. The studies took place between 2009 and 2016.

Hume Central Secondary College was established as a new school in 2009 because of a government school improvement project in the Northern Region of Melbourne. The project was aimed at transforming the educational opportunities and achievement levels of students in one of the most disadvantaged communities in Australia. The school was born out of the ashes of three failing schools that were closed and re-opened as one school occupying three new campus sites – two Year 7 to 9 campuses and one Year 10 to 12 campus. The school appointed Glenn Proctor as an executive principal overseeing the three campuses. Whilst each campus site had its own campus principal, our research findings demonstrated that Glenn was the driving force for change through setting-up the early initiatives and interventions.

What was interesting in this case study was that while the government system central and regional education administrations offered programs and professional development opportunities for the school, Glenn Proctor was confident that the school could forge its own pathway to success by exploring multiple sources of authoritative expertise and research-based studies to establish its own direction and develop its own targets and strategy. At the same time, Glenn was responsible for initiating a rigorous process for collecting and analysing school and student data.

Glenn and his team developed an integrated plan for change. The strategy was to set a new vision for the school; establish targets for students and staff; develop strategies to improve teaching and learning; build leadership and staff capacity; improve student behaviour, attendance and achievement levels; develop a new viable and relevant curriculum that engaged students; and develop a new school culture. Each strategy was evidence-based. The strategy was largely based on the four practices of successful leaders championed by Leithwood and colleagues (e.g. Leithwood & Riehl, 2005; Leithwood et al., 2010): setting direction, developing people, redesigning the organisation, and focusing on student learning. Following is our analysis of the school focussing on building leadership capacity, redesigning the organisation, building teacher capacity to improve teaching, support from external experts and agencies and establishing a performance and development culture.

Building Leadership Capacity

Glenn focused on developing the capacity of the campus administrators and the 16 leading teachers from the three campuses. The school invested in several leadership programs and opened opportunities for professional learning. Two of the programs conducted by a local Technical and Further Education institute (TAFE) – Coaching for Success' and 'Coaching for Improvement' – were highly intensive workshop programs conducted over several days. These formed the basis for ongoing leadership training for the next 6 years.

The focus of leadership team meetings was professional learning. Activities included professional reading, presentations by leadership team members, guest speakers, data analysis and review, strategic planning, and setting targets for improvement. Key topics for team meetings included managing change, team building, instructional leadership, instructional models of learning, peer coaching and review, professional conversations, and differentiation of lessons according to student needs.

Glenn regularly set professional reading for the school leaders. Each year Glenn distributed and set a leadership book that included: *Our Iceberg Is Melting* (Kotter & Rathgeber, 2006); Leadership on the Line (Heifetz & Linsky, 2002); *The Practice of Adaptive Leadership* (Heifetz et al., 2009); and *Leading School Turnaround* (Leithwood et al., 2010). Chapters, topics and ideas were discussed during leadership team meetings.

The professional learning was aimed at changing leader behaviour which was seen by Glenn to be central to organisational change and improvement. The emphasis on leadership development was re-enforced in the opening of the School Review Report (2009: 3) conducted in the first year of the school:

"(T)he emphasis has been rightly on building leadership capacity to drive overall change. This has been progressed through a focus on changing leadership behaviours using a range of targeted and sophisticated strategies and provides an excellent foundation for the major challenge of improving student outcomes through quality teaching and learning."

Glenn placed high expectations on leaders. Whilst there was significant support for leaders, those who did not meet expectations were replaced. This was reflected the school policy, *Leading Teacher Renewal of Tenure Policy*, which outlined the expectations of the leadership roles and criteria for application and appointment. Every 2 years all leadership positions were opened for renewal. In the 2013 round of appointments, one third of the 16 positions were awarded to teachers external to the school. Glenn believed that getting the right people in place was critical and more effective than training the wrong people and he stated, 'If you want an excellent leadership team you must have excellent people.'

To support leadership development, the school conducted an *emerging leaders' program* for teachers and staff who aspired to more senior leadership positions. This was conducted by Lawrie Drysdale for 1.5 h, eight times a year.

Redesigning the Organisation

Glenn introduced a distributive leadership structure based on the work of Harris (2009). Glenn believed that to secure the best from teachers and staff, they had to be 'empowered' and the distributed leadership model was best able to support this. In 2012 Glenn created 98 leadership positions (positions with responsibility) for 120 teaching staff – 80% of teachers had leadership responsibilities compared with 30% previously.

Another example of using research to restructure the school, Glenn used a paper called *Schools that achieve extraordinary success: How some disadvantaged Victorian schools 'punch over their weight'* (Zbar et al., 2009). This paper outlined the findings of research on Victorian schools in challenging circumstances that achieved beyond expectations. The paper noted four pre-conditions - strong leadership that is shared, high levels of expectations and teacher efficacy, ensuring an orderly learning environment as a precondition, and a focus on what matters. The school used this as a reference and basis for its improvement strategy.

Team orientation was an important aspect. Glenn established common team meeting procedures and protocols. There was a focus on team development and collaborative decision making within teams. Team leaders across the disciplines and numerous functions met regularly to discuss common issues and challenges. External experts supported team development.

Building Teacher Capacity to Improve Teaching

To improve teaching and learning, Glenn sought to focus on professional practice and purposeful teaching. A key strategy was to develop a common instructional model of teaching. Glenn and the leadership team investigated the research of John Hattie (2009) and adopted his approach by developing what was entitled 'The Hume Central SC Explicit Instructional Model'. This became the default model of teaching in the school and staff were trained in how it operated.

Establishing an orderly learning environment was a high priority in the first year of operation. The student management policy was ineffective, student behaviour was extremely poor, absences were high and engagement very low. Glenn set about developing a common approach to student management by adopting a student management program offered by the regional office and based on the work of Ramon Lewis (2008). The program proved to be important in reducing student absence and promoting engagement.

Another key initiative to improve student engagement was to change the curriculum and its delivery. Glenn initiated *Curriculum Design Teams* that brought discipline teams of teachers together from the three campuses to develop the curriculum to better meet student needs by building teacher capacity for differentiating teaching and achieve the aim of *2 years of learning in 1*. Common assessment tasks were also set so that teachers had a common understanding of standards and satisfactory completion and were consistent in their assessment of student progress.

Another key strategy for improving teaching and learning was to focus on classroom practice. A process for monitoring and improving teacher professional practice was established that required teachers to reflect on their practice and plan for improvement. To support this approach the annual review system was evaluated and enhanced; teachers were encouraged to participate in peer observation of classroom practice; and a coaching culture was established starting with literacy and numeracy coaches and then introducing triads of teachers who would take turns to observe each other in the classroom. The triad coaching process was modelled by all members of the leadership team before it was introduced throughout the school.

Support from External Experts and Agencies

Glenn was also highly successful in drawing on external agencies for support. These played a significant role in positively influencing the school's performance. Welfare agencies, partnerships with other schools in other education systems (independent schools), and programs and facilities from the local TAFE institute were examples.

A key influence on improvement was engaging two critical friends who were expert in leadership and school improvement. The two critical friends were instrumental in guiding and supporting the improvement strategy and supporting the leadership team (Huerta Villalobos, 2013). Educational consultant Vic Zbar was engaged to work with the leadership team to implement a framework of school improvement based on his research in successful schools in disadvantaged areas (Zbar, 2013). Vic also guided an extensive school review and supported the capacity building of leadership team. As noted previously, Lawrie Drysdale, was engaged (voluntary) as a critical friend from 2009 to 2015. He regularly attended senior leadership meetings and conducted a program for emerging leaders for 6 years. Huerta Villalobos (2013) found that the critical friends had a direct impact on the work of senior and middle level leaders, and through this, an indirect impact on the work of teachers and student outcomes. They were not only able to provide professional support, advice, reflection, but also showed a willingness to question and challenge.

Establishing a Performance and Development Culture

Finally, the strategy to establish a performance and development culture in the school was based on setting high expectations and new benchmarks. Glenn set high expectations of students, teachers and the community; however, he recognised that culture building takes time. He constantly questioned the behaviour, norms, beliefs, attitudes and assumptions of teachers. Glenn acknowledged that changing low expectations into high expectations was an ongoing education for the whole school community. But he was resolute to succeed. As one campus principal said, 'He does not take his foot off the pedal.'

School Performance

After 6 years there emerged evidence that Glenn's strategy was successful. Whilst student achievement was still a work in progress, other targets were highly successful. Evidence from survey and recorded data show that engagement, student wellbeing and attendance had improved. For example, within 5 years, student attendance increased from 60% to 90%; entry to tertiary education went from 80% to 97%; student and parent attitudes to school improved to be above state medians; enrollments increased against the trend in other local schools; and there were good signs of improved student learning with results on the national literacy and numeracy testing program at the level of similar schools. Whilst final year results remained low between 2010 and 2017, in 2018 these results improved significantly to be just below the state average for government schools.

With this improvement, the school is better able to meet community expectations for quality school. Families that would have once upon a time driven past the school are now enrolling their children. It appears that the challenge is not in turning the school around but sustaining the change and continuing to improve.

Scoresby Secondary College

Scoresby College is another example of a school in challenging circumstances that under the leadership of a new principal used evidence-based methodology to drive school improvement. As with the previous case, Drysdale and Gurr have a long association with the principal, and the research evidence is from a multiple perspective case study conducted by McCrohan (2021) based on the ISSPP research protocol and supported by Drysdale and Gurr. Drysdale was a challenge partner in the school's review conducted in 2018.

The school was established in 1975 and is a Year 7–12 coeducational government school situated in the south eastern suburbs of Melbourne, approximately 40 kilometres from the Melbourne CBD. In 2018 the enrollment was 253 students. There were 30 staff and 10 non-teaching staff. Gail Major was appointed as an executive principal with the challenge to save the school from closure (Major, 2018). When she took over in 2015 the school's results were declining, its reputation poor, and it was perceived to have a dysfunctional culture and poor student management. The school, led by Gail, is an example of a school that has developed its own improvement strategy using evidence from several sources. Following is our analysis of the school's improvement strategy: setting new direction, teaching and learning, leadership for professional capacity building, and focus on student needs.

School Improvement Strategy

From our research it was clear that Gail had carefully diagnosed the situation and developed a plan based on her observation and findings. Like Hume Central, the plan reflected the four practices of Leithwood and Riehl (2005). Gail set about establishing a new direction, transforming teaching and learning, building staff leadership and professional capacity, re-organising the school, developing a positive high expectations culture, and focusing on student learning. Gail's and the school's journey were clearly identified in school documents and case study research. The School Self-evaluation Report 2018 (Scoresby Secondary College, 2018a) shows the school's key strategies from 2015 to 2018. Gail also documented every initiative and activity completed by the school from 2014 to the present (Scoresby Secondary College, 2018b). The following points do not include all the evidence-based approaches but provides a valuable insight to the improvement strategy.

Setting New Direction

After strong community consultation, a clear vision and values statement for the College was developed. The new vision identified what the college stood for, the beliefs and guiding principles that underpinned everything that the school community did, and it articulated the quality of education that was expected. In 2015, the college launched its vision to become the *College of Choice*. The values of integrity, nurture, success, pride, innovation, respect and excellence were expressively outlined in detail. This was supported by creating a new school brand, new uniform, and the establishment of a safe and orderly environment. The new motto was *inspiring brilliance.*

Teaching and Learning

Curriculum and pedagogy were reformed through five major strategies:

1. Gail developed an instructional core. She was influenced by City et al. (2009) who outlined three key ways to improve student learning at scale: raise the level of content that students are taught; increase the skills and knowledge teachers bring to teaching that content; and increase the level of students' active learning (engagement) of the content.
2. A guaranteed and viable curriculum was developed as this is the most important factor in Marzano's (2003) view of what works in schools. In 2015, she introduced teaching practices to support this initiative. Each student was now guaranteed to be taught in the time available what was imperative to teach, irrespective of the class they were in.
3. An evidence-based instructional framework, known as the Scoresby Instructional Model, was developed and agreed to by all staff. The framework was developed to ensure the adoption of a consistent approach to building teacher practice from Year 7 to 12. The model was fully implemented in 2017 requiring teachers to deliver all the components of the instructional model and have a goal in their performance and development plan related to peer observation and feedback.
4. The school introduced a 'blended learning' model of instruction. Teachers in each lesson were required to identify learning intentions. Each class lesson was required to rotate three pedagogical components – direct instruction, group work

and individual activities on their laptops. Gail had introduced this model successfully in her previous school and had presented the model at various conferences and network meetings. The school imbedded the model during 2018.

5. Structural changes were made to support these initiatives. For example, teachers were reallocated to faculty-based areas to support professional dialogue, curriculum teams were created with renewed accountability, and teachers were expected to share their practice. Gail appointed a head of curriculum and pedagogy and teaching and learning leaders. Improvement teams were established that met weekly. The college prioritised collaboration. Teachers were expected to work together to plan learning programs. Team meeting times were timetabled into the program.

Leadership and Professional Capacity Building

One of the first strategies she embarked on was to establish a strategic leadership team with a clear purpose, moving away from operational to strategic leadership, so all decisions and resourcing (human, physical and financial) were consistent with meeting teaching and learning goals. In 2017 an emerging leaders' program was introduced. An external coach was engaged for emerging leaders to take on *authentic leadership* through the school review and to actively be engaged in directions for the new strategic plan for the next 4 years (2019–2023).

Initiatives such as a shared leadership model, professional learning communities and growth coaching for performance and development processes, demonstrated programs designed to build capacity. Meeting schedules were designed to provide the opportunity for teachers to develop extensive professional learning plans and professional learning teams that work on a common unit planner and build in collaborative practices. In addition to scheduled meetings times, the college created purposeful learning spaces. The college addressed a major curriculum imbalance by enabling teachers to teach in their own areas of expertise with skills and knowledge to raise achievement.

The college established collaborative partnership with networks, tertiary providers and educational consultants. Sustained professional learning, including peer observation, observations in high performing schools, professional readings, data literacy training for members of the numeracy, and staff exposure to quality presentations and visits by experts were all identified as enablers for improvement.

Focus on Student Needs

The focus on student needs was central to the school's strategy. Goals were established to develop strong relations between student and teachers, student voice and student leadership. Personalised learning was introduced as a school wide approach to target the needs of each student and monitor performance. The school invited

Professor Brian Caldwell (Former Dean of Education, The University of Melbourne) to provide a workshop on the indicators of personalised learning (Scoresby Secondary College, 2018b). The school adopted this approach. Using this model teachers were able to know the progress of each student on a continuing basis and were able to deliver appropriate teaching methods to maximise the skill set of each student.

Student voice was a major focus and was promoted to a core group of students although the avenue to develop this with all students was not clear. Students were encouraged to provide feedback to teachers on learning and teaching materials with the aim to give student greater voice in how they learn rather than what they learn.

Findings

As part of the school review conducted in 2018, the school identified four major achievements from 2015 to 2018 (Scoresby Secondary College, 2018a): college partnerships; raising achievement; student leadership; and respectful relationships education in schools. These were verified by the external reviewers who identified that the school now had a visible positive learning climate, pride demonstrated by students and staff, high expectations, student voice and advocacy, and effective professional collaboration. Student, staff attitudes, and parent opinion had increased to be above state averages. Most significantly was the student growth in final year results and on year 7 and 9 results on the national literacy and numeracy testing program. Results were either at or above that of schools with similar levels of educational advantage.

Scoresby Secondary College is an example of a school that has been transformed over the past 3 years with a high performing culture, improved curriculum and many new staff. Student achievement has been publicly recognised. Melbourne's largest circulation newspaper, the Herald Sun newspaper, published an article regarding the great improvement that has occurred at Scoresby Secondary College (Argoon, 2018). It noted that in 2015 the school data showed that the school was declining in the national literacy and numeracy testing program for years 7 and 9. The article confirmed our own analysis that the school showed the characteristics of a turn-around school and was recognised as one of the most improved schools for final year results in the state. Results on the national literacy and numeracy testing program confirmed the improvement and valued added for students in Year 9. Scoresby Secondary College is an example of a school that has been transformed over the past 3 years with a high performing culture, curriculum and many new staff. Student achievement has been publicly recognised, and the school has successfully demonstrated the link between evidence-based methodology and positive school performance.

Discussion

The programs described are symptomatic of an educational climate focussed on school choice, quality and equity (the following arguments are taken from (Gurr, 2020). Major issues that are at play in Australia include federal versus state/territory government control of education, disputes about the amount of school funding going to government, Catholic and independent schools, increased emphasis on parental choice, the influence of student testing programs, and school equity and quality concerns. The core role of federal and state/territory governments has not changed substantially since the turn of the century (and indeed, over the previous century). However, as was mentioned previously, the trend since the 1960s of a greater federal role has continued through aspects such as increased federal school funding to both government and non-government schools, the introduction of national curriculum, increased testing and accountability, substantial grants programs for building and digital infrastructure, and the importance of international testing programs for policy and practice changes.

Funding issues and parental choice are major sources of angst as the right to school choice is somewhat limited by the funds parents have to spend on schools, and despite all schools getting some government funding (ranging from approximately 90% for a government school to 10% for a high-fee independent school), family school costs range from a few hundred dollars (government schools) to over $35,000 (high-fee independent schools), which is nearly half of the average Australian wage. There is now a quasi-market for schools that has created 'an uneven playing field that benefits a portion of the community more than it does the remainder' (Bonner & Shepherd, 2016, p. 7), and the neo-liberal stance of successive federal and state governments, whilst valuing parental choice, has had the unintended consequence of enhancing inequity. However, these issues combined with a focus on school performance caused by concerns about performance on national and international testing programs (Bentley, 2018; Hattie, 2016), have, fortunately, resulted in a focus on equity and quality. Whilst there are justifiable concerns about the intended and unintended consequences of national and international tests (see the papers in the special issue of *Educational Philosophy and Theory*, *47*(2), 2015, for several critical perspectives on national testing and reporting in Australia), these tests have highlighted performance concerns related to overall performance and disparity in performance, and once these are exposed there is an imperative, taken up by governments, to address them.

It is this focus on equity and quality that has driven all of the six programs we have described - from the nationally focussed and research-driven IDEAS (school improvement) and PALL (instructional leadership) projects, through to state/regional initiatives to improve initial teacher education and to help schools create data-driven improvement, to the two examples of schools in challenging contexts that have used knowledge and data to improve student and school outcomes. These programs also align with Caldwell's call for greater structural and professional autonomy to enable schools to be in control of what they do (Caldwell, 2016, 2018).

Caldwell (2016) argued that school autonomy seems to have a premium or advantage for those systems that can provide this, provided that schools have the capacity to utilise this autonomy and that professional forms of accountability are in place to guide judgement on what to do. Caldwell made a distinction between structural autonomy through policies, regulations and procedures, and professional autonomy in which teachers have the 'capacity to make decisions that are likely to make a difference to outcomes for students, and this capacity is exercised in a significant, systemic and sustained fashion' (Caldwell, 2016, p. 4). For school autonomy to make a difference to students, professional autonomy is required, and there needs to be alignment between the various systems that surround schools (such as the state/territory/federal layers of government in Australia) (Caldwell, 2018).

At the state/regional level, two programs from a leading university were described, but the evidence of their impact was weak relying mostly on anecdotal perceptions of worth, with some evidence of attitudinal change, but no trustworthy evidence as yet of impact on students. At the school level, however, the two described schools both had improvement agendas that utilised trustworthy evidence sources, and both were able to demonstrate significant changes in structure, processes, leadership development, and teaching and learning, that ultimately was impacting on student learning. What seems to be evident with the two schools was that they had: a clear sense of what was needed; evidence to support their changes; mandates and will to stay true to the improvement course; control over key variables; a focus on developing the capabilities in staff to implement the changes; use of data to inform school and classroom changes; and a concern to produce evidence to show success. The other programs have some of these elements, but not all, and their true success can only be measured through the improved outcomes of schools and students.

Amidst international testing and benchmarking, schools have been placed under extreme scrutiny to offer more, and to guarantee improved student outcomes. It is school leaders who are facing the brunt of criticism around declining literacy and numeracy and their impact in student success is being scrutinised more than ever before (Bentley, 2018; Bonner & Shepherd, 2016; Hattie, 2016; Savage, 2017). Timperley (2010) advocates that school leaders need to have sufficient understanding of evidence informed practice in order to evaluate their own effectiveness and support teachers in their work. She goes on to suggest that "when teachers are provided with opportunities to use and interpret a range of evidence in order to become more responsive to their students' learning needs, the impact is substantial" (Timperley, 2010:10). Whilst each school has differing needs and operates within a distinct context, it is widely understood that a common approach to teaching and learning can have a positive impact on student outcomes and an important role for school leaders is to ensure quality and consistency of practice. Leaders with high expectations for learning and an understanding of their role in leading teaching and learning can improve student outcomes, and the two case schools described in this chapter highlight examples of how this happens. Our Victorian school examples support Caldwell's (2016, 2018) call for greater structural and professional autonomy to promote school success, and suggest that a shift towards school autonomy can provide an impetus for schools at the local level to set their own improvement pathway and introduce processes to measure, not only key elements that contribute to school success, but those that will guarantee student achievement. Importantly, we have shown elsewhere (Gurr & Drysdale, 2019), how schools in Victoria are supported by central and regional system leadership, and how this system leadership, combined with schools with a high degree of autonomy, can lead to exceptional school and student performance.

When we began this chapter, we intended to describe evidence-based practice at the national, state and school level through examples of programs and practice. What is noticeable across each of the examples is a commitment to education and a fundamental desire to improve schools and student outcomes. Whilst the programs are quite distinct, each focuses on best practice utilising an evidence base to underpin the various approaches to improve teaching and learning. The continued implementation of evidence-based programs like these, inevitably makes an impact on the quality of teaching and learning in Australian schools, and may, in time, even impact on international test performance.

References

Alter, J., & Coggshall, J. (2009). *Teaching as a clinical practice profession: Implications for teacher preparation and state policy*. National Comprehensive Center for Teacher Quality.

Anderson, M. (2006). *Being a school councillor in a government secondary college in Victoria: Constructions of role and meaning*. Doctor of Education thesis, The University of Melbourne.

Andrews, D., Conway, J., Dawson, M., Lewis, M., McMaster, J., Morgan, A., & Starr, H. (2004). *School revitalisation the IDEAS way* (Monograph, 34). Australian Council for Educational Leaders.

Argoon, A (2018). Students put the score into Scoresby, *Herald Sun Newspaper* 20 November.

Barber, M., & Mourshed, M. (2007). *How the world's best performing school systems come out on top*. McKinsey & Company.

Bentley, T. (2018). *The responsibility to lead: Education at a global crossroads* (Monograph, 57). Australian Council for Educational Leaders.

Bonner, C., & Shepherd, B. (2016). *Uneven playing field: The state of Australia's schools*. Centre for Policy Development.

Burn, K., & Mutton, T. (2013). *Review of research informed clinical practice in initial teacher education*. British Education Research Association and RSA Action and Research Centre.

Butler, H., Krelle, A., Seal, I., Trafford, L., Drew, S., Hargreaves, J., Walter, R., & Bond, L. (2011). *The critical friend: Facilitating positive change in school communities*. ACER Press.

Caldwell, B. J. (2016). *The autonomy premium: Professional autonomy and student achievement in the 21st century*. ACER Press.

Caldwell, B. J. (2018). *The alignment premium: Benchmarking Australia's student achievement, professional autonomy and system adaptivity*. ACER Press.

Campbell, C., & Proctor, H. (2014). *A history of Australian schooling*. Allen & Unwin.

City, E. A., Elmore, R. F., Fiarman, S. E., & Teitel, L. (2009). *Instructional rounds in education: A network approach to improving teaching and learning*. Harvard Education Press.

Conroy, J., Hulme, M., & Menter, I. (2013). Developing a 'clinical' model for teacher education. *Journal of Education for Teaching: International Research and Pedagogy, 39*(5), 557–573.

Crowther, F., Andrews, D., Morgan, A., & O'Neill, S. (2012). Hitting the Bullseye of school improvement: The IDEAS project at work in a successful system. *Leading and Managing, 18*(2), 1–33.

Crowther, F., Ferguson, M., & Hann, L. (2009). *Developing teacher leaders* (2nd ed.). Corwin Press.

Crowther, F., Kaagan, S., Ferguson, M., & Hann, L. (2002). *Developing teacher leaders*. Corwin Press.

Darling-Hammond, L., & Bransford, J. (Eds.). (2005). *Preparing teachers for a changing world: What teachers should learn and be able to do*. Jossey Boss.

Dempster, N., Konza, D., Robson, G., Gaffney, M., Lock, G., & McKennariey, K. (2012). *Principals as literacy leaders: Confident, credible and connected*. Australian Primary Prinicpals Association.

Dempster, N., Townsend, T., Johnson, G., Bayetto, A., Lovett, S., & Stevens, E. (2017). *Leadership and literacy: Principals, partnerships and pathways to improvement*. Springer.

Dinham, S. (2013). Connecting clinical teaching practice with instructional leadership. *Australian Journal of Education, 57*(3), 225–236.

Gurr, D. (2019). Australian considerations in relation to instructional leadership and leadership for learning. In T. Townsend (Ed.) *Instructional leadership and leadership for learning in schools: Understanding theories of leading* (pp. 77–104). Heidelberg, Germany: Palgrave Macmillan.

Gurr, D. (2020). Australia: The Australian education system. In H. Ärlestig & O. Johansson (Eds) *Educational authorities and the schools - organization and impact in 20 states* (pp. 311–331). Dordrecht, Netherlands: Springer.

Gurr, D., & Drysdale, L. (2016). Successful and effective school leadership: Insights from Australasia. In P. Pashiardis & O. Johansson (Eds.), *Successful school leadership: International perspectives* (pp. 139–154). Bloomsbury.

Gurr, D., & Drysdale, L. (2018). Leading high need schools: Findings from the international school leadership development network. *International Studies in Educational Administration, 46*(1), 147–156.

Gurr, D., & Drysdale, L. (2019). Improving schools in Victoria, Australia: System, region and school perspectives. In H. Shaked, C. Schechter, & A. Daly (Eds.), *Leading holistically: How states, districts, and schools improve systemically* (pp. 217–235). Routledge.

Gurr, D., Drysdale, L., Longmuir, F., & McCrohan, K. (2018). Leading the improvement of schools in challenging circumstances. *International Studies in Educational Administration, 46*(1), 22–44.

Gurr, D., Drysdale, L., Longmuir, F., & McCrohan, K. (2019). Successful school leadership that is culturally sensitive but not context constrained. In E. Murakami, D. Gurr, & R. Notman (Eds.), *Educational leadership, culture, and success in high-need schools* (pp. 25–44). Information Age Publishing.

Gurr, D., Drysdale, L., & Walkley, D. (2012). School-parent relations in Victorian schools. *Journal of School Public Relations, 33*(3), 172–198.

Harris, A. (Ed.). (2009). *Distributed leadership: Different perspectives*. Springer.

Hattie, J. (2003). Teachers make a difference: What is the research evidence? Paper presented at the *Building Teacher Quality: What does the research tell us?*, ACER Research Conference, Octover, Melbourne, Australia.

Hattie, J. (2009). *Visible learning: A synthesis of over 800 Meta analyses relating to achievement*. Routledge.

Hattie, J. (2012). *Visible learning for teachers: Maximizing impact on learning*. Routledge.

Hattie, J. (2015). *What works best in education: The politics of collaborative expertise*. Pearson.

Hattie, J. (2016). *Shifting away from distractions to improve Australia's schools: Time for a reboot* (Monograph, 54). Australian Council for Educational Leaders.

Heifetz, R. A., Grashow, A., & Linsky, M. (2009). *The practice of adaptive leadership*. Harvard Business School Press.

Heifetz, R. A., & Linsky, M. (2002). *Leadership on the line: Staying alive through the dangers of leading*. Boston, MA: Harvard Business School Press.

Huerta Villalobos, M. (2013). *The role of the critical friend in leadership and school improvement*. Master of Education thesis, The University of Melbourne.

Kameniar, B., McLean Davies, L., Kinsman, J., Reid, C., Tyler, D., & Acquaro, D. (2017). Clinical praxis exams: Linking academic study with professional practice knowledge. In M. A. Peters, B. Cowie, & I. Menter (Eds.), *A companion to research in teacher education* (pp. 53–67). Springer.

Kotter, J., & Rathgeber, H. (2006). *Our Iceberg is melting*. St Martin's Press.

Kriewaldt, J., McLean Davies, L., Rice, S., Rickards, F., & Acquaro, D. (2017). Clinical practice in education: Towards a conceptual framework. In M. A. Peters, B. Cowie, & I. Menter (Eds.), *A companion to research in teacher education* (pp. 153–166). Springer.

Leithwood, K., Harris, A., & Strauss. (2010). *Leading school turnaround*. Jossey-Bass.

Leithwood, K., & Riehl, C. (2005). What we know about successful school leadership. In W. Firestone & C. Riehl (Eds.), *A new agenda: Directions for research on educational leadership* (pp. 22–47). Teachers College Press.

Lewis, M. (2006). It's a different place now: Teacher leadership and pedagogical change at Newlyn Public School. *Leading and Managing, 12*(1), 107–121.

Lewis, M., & Andrews, D. (2007). The dance of influence: Professional relationships evolve as teachers and administrators engage in whole school renewal. *Leading and Managing, 13*(1), 91–107.

Lewis, R. (2008). *The developmental management approach to classroom behaviour*. Australian Council for Educational Research.

Major, G. (2018). *A centre for continuous learning, Scoresby Secondary College*. Scoresby Secondary College.

Marzano, R. J. (2003). *What works in schools: Translating research into action*. ASCD.

McCrohan, K. M. (2021). *Practices and characteristics of principals in low educational advantage, improving Victorian secondary schools; contextually aware leadership*. Doctor of Education Thesis, The University of Melbourne.

McLean Davies, L., Anderson, M., Deans, J., Dinham, S., Griffin, P., Kameniar, B., Page, J., Reid, C., Rickards, F., Tayler, C., & Tyler, D. (2013). Masterly preparation: Embedding clinical practice in a graduate pre-service teacher education programme. *Journal of Education for Teaching: International Research and Pedagogy, 39*(1), 93–106.

Quality Indicators for Learning and Teaching. (2018). *Graduate employment*. [Online]. Available at: https://www.qilt.edu.au/about-this-site/graduate-employment. Accessed 13 Apr 2018.

Sahlberg, P. (2012). The most wanted: Teachers and teacher education in Finland. In L. Darling-Hammond & A. Lieberman (Eds.), *Teacher education around the world: Changing policies and practices* (pp. 1–21). Routledge.

Savage, G. C. (2017). Improving national policy processes in Australian schooling. In T. Bentley, & G. C. Savage (Eds) *Educational Australia: Challenges for the decade ahead* (pp. 348–366). Carlton, Victoria: Melbourne University Press.

Scoresby Secondary College. (2018a). *Pre-review Self-evaluation Report Strategic Plan 2015–2018 19/4/2018*. Scoresby Secondary College.

Scoresby Secondary College. (2018b). *2018 annual report to the school community*. Victorian Department of Education and Training.

Scott, C., Kleinhenz, E., Weldon, P., Reid, K., & Dinham, S. (2010). *Master of teaching MGSE: Evaluation report*. Australian Council for Educational Research.

Swaffield, S. (2004). Critical friends: Supporting leadership, improving learning. *Improving Schools, 7*(3), 267–278.

Swaffield, S., & MacBeath, J. (2005). School self-evaluation and the role of a critical friend. *Cambridge Journal of Education, 35*(2), 239–252.

Teacher Education Ministerial Advisory Group (2014a, April). Issues Paper, Department of Education and Training, Canberra, https://docs.education.gov.au/documents/teacher-education-ministerial-advisory-group-issues-paper

Teacher Education Ministerial Advisory Group (2014b, December). Action now: *Classroom Ready Teachers*, Department of Education and Training, Canberra, https://docs.education.gov.au/system/files/doc/other/action_now_classroom_ready_teachers_accessible.pdf

Timperley, H. (2010). *Using evidence in the classroom for professional learning.* Paper presented to the Ontario Research Symposium.

Wildy, H., & Faulkner, J. (2008). Whole school improvement Australian-style: What do IDEAS and RAISe offer? *Leading and Managing, 14*(2), 83–96.

Zbar, V., Kimber, R., & Marshall, G. (2009). *Schools that achieve extraordinary success: How some disadvantaged Victorian schools 'punch over their weight* (Occasional Paper 109). Incorporated Association of Registered Teachers of Victoria.

Zbar, V. (2013). *Generating whole-school improvement: The stages of sustained success* (Occasional Paper 132). Incorporated Association of Registered Teachers of Victoria.

Chapter 11
The German Context: School Turnaround in Ten Schools in Difficult Circumstances: The Need for Adaptive and Contextualized Approaches to Development and Change

Guri Skedsmo and Stephan Huber

Abstract In this chapter, we report on the research findings from a school development project which took place in a large city in Germany over a period of 5 years. In 2013, the central educational authorities formed a public-private partnership with a foundation to start a development project that was inspired by school turnaround models in the US and included various interventions and efforts to support change in ten schools that were identified as 'schools in difficult circumstances'. As such, the adapted school turnaround model serves as an example of introducing policies or models in school systems that have proven to be successful elsewhere. In this chapter, we present findings from our analysis of the changes taking place in the schools related to efforts and interventions to support the schools. Moreover, we discuss challenges regarding measurement of success according to the school turnaround logic and the need for more adaptive approaches for changing and developing schools in difficult circumstances - at least a long-term perspective on school development.

Keywords School Turnaround · School development and change · School leadership · Datafication · Quality indicators · Participation

G. Skedsmo (✉)
Schwyz University of Teacher Education/University of Oslo, Oslo, Norway
e-mail: guri.skedsmo@phsz.ch

S. Huber
University of Teacher Education Zug, Zug, Switzerland
e-mail: stephan.huber@phzg.ch

Introduction

During the last two decades, increasing attention has been paid towards schools defined as 'failing,' 'low-achieving', 'underperforming,' or 'declining', a categorisation which, first of all, follows low student performance on standardised tests and consecutive years of failure in meeting targeted levels of achievement (Murphy & Meyers, 2008; Meyer et al., 2021). The labeling of schools has emerged with increased datafication as a core element in education governance. Datafication is often used to characterise how different aspects of education are transformed into digital data, which makes it possible to connect these aspects and perform calculations on them (Williamson, 2017). As such, data represents a key to identify low-achieving schools, a basis to make decisions on strategies to improve, and to measure the progress and impact of interventions (Racherbäumer et al., 2013). This trend has given rise to policies and school development models that have proven to be successful in certain country contexts and promoted as 'evidence-based' (Bryk et al., 2015).

'School turnaround' is an example of a model proven to be effective in the United States (US) context. In the US, accountability policies have developed since the 1990s that aim to boost school performance in low-achieving schools. The idea of turning around such schools began to take form when it became clear that using rewards and consequences, in terms of sanctions on schools, proved to be a difficult strategy (Meyers, 2013). School turnaround is often described in terms of a specific strategy or model targeted at schools in difficult circumstances (Murphy, 2008). The following is an often-used definition:

> Turnaround is a dramatic and comprehensive intervention in a low-performing school that:
> a) produces significant gains in achievement within two years; and b) readies the school for
> the longer process of transformation into a high-performing organization. (Kutash et al.,
> 2010, p. 4)

Such models generally aim towards rapid improvement of student achievements combined with federal models for organisational change within school terms. More concretely, the local education agency (LEA) replaces the principals, evaluates the staff and rehires half of them, stresses the use of data-informed instruction and provides job-embedded professional development to build staff capacity (ibid.). Other federal models for organisational change in the US include various combinations of school closure, reopening or transformation of schools. Generally, such models are accompanied by transparency about results for important stakeholders, and accountability measures to create pressure that is intended to drive improvement and push key actors in schools to work harder (Webb, 2006; Mintrop, 2004).

In this chapter we report on research findings from a school development project, which took place in a large city in Germany over a period of 5 years. In 2013, the central educational authorities formed a public-private partnership with a foundation to start a development project involving ten schools. The project was inspired by school turnaround models in the US and included various interventions and efforts to support the schools. In the context of this project, turnaround was defined more broadly to include local and central authorities. Due to their complex problems as well as local governing contexts, schools were expected to improve with important stakeholders supporting them. The research question guiding our analysis is as follows: What characterises the 'turnaround process' in the ten participating schools and what kind of indicators are needed to identify and understand the changes?

The chapter is structured as follows: We start by presenting a short overview of previous research in the area of school development for schools in difficult circumstances. Second, we describe school turnaround policies in the US and similar attempts to improve schools in Germany, including this particular project. Furthermore, we also present some key characteristics of the German educational contexts and the structures of school systems. Third, we describe our methodological approach before presenting key findings of the project. Finally, we discuss these findings on changes in schools related to support efforts and interventions, the challenges regarding measurement of success according to the school turnaround logic and the need for more adaptive approaches for changing and developing schools in difficult circumstances.

International Research on Key Characteristics and Initiatives to Improve Schools in Difficult Circumstances

In addition to low student performance on standardised tests, key characteristics of low-achieving schools also often include school communities with a high number of families with low social economic status (SES), high degrees of migration etc., in combination with the school's dysfunctional organisation (e.g., Baumert et al., 2006). With respect to datafication and specific attempts to calculate the contribution of schools (value-added models), and even teachers, to student outcomes, these methods often control for SES and migration to produce 'fair' scores but lack other types of information to provide a comprehensive picture (Levy, 2019). It can be argued that these schools cannot be blamed for their surroundings, which, in many countries, are a consequence of the housing market and government policies, such as student enrollment and funding for educational materials.

Since the 1970s, international research into the effectiveness of schools has produced a fairly comprehensive level of knowledge that distinguishes successful schools. However, knowledge about the characteristics of dysfunctional school settings is still lacking. From an efficiency perspective, failing schools are sometimes described in terms of psychological dysfunction. Studies on ineffective schools show specific characteristics at the student level, the class level, and the school level, or they identify external causes (location) as well as internal causes (school). In summary, the following risk factors, which may lead schools into a spiral of decline, are identified in international scholarship (Altrichter et al., 2008; Altrichter

& Moosbrugger, 2011; Clarke, 2004; Harris & Chapman, 2002; Hochbein, 2012; Murphy & Meyers, 2008; Potter et al., 2002; Datnow & Stringfield, 2000):

- Difficult conditions at home
- Student behavioural problems
- Strong student turnover
- Low student achievement levels
- Low teacher qualification levels
- Low degree of collegial cooperation among teachers
- High faculty turnover
- Lack of school management and leadership

More extensive experiences and findings on school development strategies for schools in difficult circumstance have been found in the US and England over the last few decades (Huber & Mujis, 2012; Murphy & Meyers, 2008; Muijs et al., 2004; Murphy, 2008; Ainscow et al., 2004). In general, differentiated measures tailored to each individual school are needed and not a panacea strategy. Moreover, schools need time to go through the following stages of development: a mission statement or audit; a school programme as well as the initiation, implementation and institutionalisation of suitable improvements; and an evaluation of the implementation and beginning of a new quality cycle (Huber et al., 2014; Meyers & Hitt, 2017). However, there are some strategies that, according to the literature, are generally considered helpful for many schools (Huber, 2013):

- Rapid intervention with directly perceptible success
- Strengthening of the school administration
- Ensuring transparent objectives
- Initiating intensive continuous professional development
- Revising the curriculum
- Structuring teaching and learning processes
- Focusing on developing the school programme
- Defining clearer goals
- Strengthening cooperation and external support
- Inspection and accountability
- 'Reconstitution'- school closure and reopening after redesign

One limitation related to the aforementioned overview of international research is that most of these studies have been conducted in the US and England, two countries that have longer traditions of performance management systems with tools for measuring students' performance as well as policies and practices in place for holding key actors accountable for achieved results (Gunter et al., 2016). Therefore, further research is necessary in other countries to explore strategies for developing and supporting schools in difficult circumstances that meet challenges in specific contexts.

The German Education Context

Over the last decade, strategies on how to improve schools in difficult circumstances have appeared on agendas in German-speaking countries with increasing frequency, along with the introduction of standardised testing and other indicators of school performance as part of evidence-based school governance. Some German federal states, such as the city-states of Hamburg, Bremen, and Berlin, have already addressed this issue by initiating projects where schools have been identified by quality indicators or early warning systems and followed up with interventions and support to 'turn around a circle of decline.' These projects have clearly been inspired by policies and strategies from the US, but attempts have been made to select and adapt ideas to fit German educational contexts.

As in the US, Germany has a federal structure where the responsibility for education lies basically with the 16 states and the federal government plays only a minor role. Kindergarten is optional and provided for all children between 1 and 6 years old. From the age of six, school attendance is compulsory. Primary education generally lasts 4 years (ages 6–9). After that, secondary education includes five school types, and students are normally streamed according to their achievements at the age of 10. *Gymnasium* prepares students for higher education and finishes with a final examination, *Abitur*, when students are 18 years old. *Realschule* prepares students to attend a professional or general education *Gymnasium*, vocational training or apprenticeship, after grade 10. *Hauptschule* prepares students for vocational education after grade 9. In some states, *Realschule* and *Hauptschule* have been merged and replaced by integrated secondary schools. *Gesamtschule* represents another integrated school type by combining *Gymnasium*, *Realschule* and *Hauptschule*. Even though inclusion policies have been promoted over the last decade, there are still various types of schools for special needs education and students with disabilities.

A federal structure and education, which is mainly a task for the states, are common characteristics of the American and German systems. Other system features vary, and one main reason may lie in the different curriculum traditions. In contrast to the American curriculum, the state's curriculum in Germany has not been seen as something that could or should explicitly direct teachers' work (Westbury et al., 2000). The curriculum (*Lehrplan*) lays out prescribed content and aims, and as such, it provides a framework for autonomous professional teachers to develop their own approach to teaching. In this work, the teachers are guided by a normative concept, *Bildung,* which refers to overall ideas of educating and bringing up children to engage productively and critically in democratic societies. To support them in this work, teachers apply *Didaktik*, which can be viewed as a system for thinking about and reflecting on problems of the curriculum related to teaching; therefore, it represents a larger rationale that teachers incorporate into their classroom work (Reid, 1998).

Recently, schools have been encouraged to develop local educational programmes congruent with the state curriculum (Huber et al., 2017). They do so by school-based curriculum renewal (often in intuitive ways). The state-run organisation, *Landesinstitute*, which exists in each of the 16 states, is expected to support the schools in their local curriculum development by means of consulting, providing materials, creating joint projects, qualifying teachers for new tasks and establishing school networks.

Along with the development of evidence-based approaches to school governing, Germany introduced standardised testing in seven states in 2004, and in the 2009–2010 school year, the VERA (VERgleichsArbeiten in der Schule) tests were expanded to all German states. Many scholars have noted the shock that was felt as the first results of the Programme for International Student Assessment (PISA) were published in 2001, one of the main drivers for introducing the tests to monitor student achievements over time (Hopmann, 2008). In addition, school inspections were established in several states, combined with school-based evaluations and work on school programmes to develop school quality (Böttcher & Kotthoff, 2007; Altrichter & Merki, 2010). Along with systems for monitoring student performance, new systems of control and accountability developed as well as national education standards (*Bildungsstandards*) and monitoring agencies (*Quliatätsagenturen*), which are run by each of the majority of the 16 states.

Projects in the city-states of Berlin, Hamburg and Bremen have resulted in approximately 15 years of experience in identifying and working with particularly low-performing schools (Huber, 2018). In Bremen, the action programme 'Schule macht sich stark' (SMS; literally 'School is getting strong') was implemented from 2004 to 2009 and marked the first nationwide school development project for schools in difficult circumstances, which was intended to strengthen and support the entire school development process. This project ran in parallel with a quality development campaign, which included the obligation to create annual work plans and school programmes and included external evaluations of all general education schools. The objectives of the project were to ensure mastering basic competencies (mathematics and German) and to increase student independence and responsibility for their own learning. The programme's activities included strengthening school leadership through coaching and counselling, staff development and teacher training, and diagnosing learning progress. The external coaching of the school administration and a network of the involved school management teams, which extend beyond the actual duration of the project, are considered to be particularly successful. In 2006, a process consulting method called 'proSchul' was established in Berlin, with the goal of providing schools in need of development with a seamless consultation process immediately after school inspections (Huber, 2018). The voluntary process consultation takes place in a triangular relationship between the school, proSchul, and the school inspectorate. In principle, this systematic approach to school development, characterised by goal orientation, transparency, strengthening collegial cooperation and communication by involving as many participants as possible, evaluation as a tool of process monitoring and systemic consideration of the organisation, teaching, and staffing, can be considered effective.

In Hamburg, the State Institute for Teacher Education and School Development carried out the project 'Unterstützung von Schulen in schwieriger Lage' (Supporting

Schools in Difficult Circumstances) in 2007–2010. Focus was on support services in the developmental areas of teaching and teaching skills, teaching-related cooperation of the faculty and management and control of the development process (Huber, 2018). KESS-7 data and initial learning surveys in grade levels 5 and 7 of the participating schools were evaluated, and qualitative surveys with school administrators and faculty members were conducted. The project's coherence can be highlighted as successful because of the support provided for teaching, cooperation, management and control, each of which had a high level of adaptability for the individual school situation.

Adapting a School Turnaround Approach in the German Context

This chapter reports findings from a school turnaround approach, which was a collaboration between school authorities in a larger city in Germany and a private foundation (the Foundation). The project was inspired by school turnaround strategies applied in the US context. Due to regulations in the German education system, several of the organisational changes applied to turn around low-performing schools in the US are not possible in the German context. Thus, the organisational changes Meyers (2013) describes as central school turnaround strategies, in terms of replacing the principal and staff, would be illegal because the rights of employees are regulated by law in the German system. Key school turnaround strategies included several interventions, paid for by the Foundation, which mainly aimed to strengthen the capacity of schools to manage a turnaround process.

Four improvement areas were targeted by the project partners: (1) school leadership, (2) cooperation, (3) school culture and environment ('Schule als Lebensraum' which means 'school as living space'), (4) quality of teaching and learning processes and student outcomes.

The most important intervention was to provide each of the participating schools with a *school development coach*. The responsibility of the coach was to support the principal and the school towards change. Further interventions included:

- School leadership training
- Professional development for teachers
- Establishing networks between the project schools
- Internships or visits to other schools (e.g., visits to prize-winning schools which have developed concepts for teaching across age groups or have experience with adapted teaching)
- Development funds for each school in the sum of €3000
- School-based initiatives

Agreements with the schools, which included project specific aims, were signed by the principal and local authorities to commit the latter to prioritising support for the project schools, especially during the project period. These agreements were renewed for the second phase of the project.

The 10 project schools were selected by the central and local school authorities informed by the early warning system, an online system that put together different indicators of school quality, such as the number of students applying for school enrollment, teaching capacity, percentage of students with low SES, percentage of students with migrant backgrounds, VERA-results, and students' completion rate. This early warning system was also used by the school inspectorates. The project schools included three primary schools and seven lower secondary schools, which were located in five different areas of the city and, accordingly, five different local authorities.

In the initial project phase, an important task for the schools was to define project aims as part of a collective decision-making process, and they were asked to define areas where they could achieve 'quick wins,' similar to the rapid improvement strategy in the US context.

Theoretical and Methodological Approaches

For the overall research project, a theoretical model based on Cronbach et al. (1972) (cited in Ditton, 2002, p. 776) was adapted and applied. The model takes into account that for schools to successfully turn themselves around, concentrated efforts and actions had to be made in parallel on various levels: *Input factors* would need to improve, such as personnel and material resources, characteristics of the student population, finances, and the various conditions under which the schools operate. A major problem in all schools was that they did not have sufficient teaching personnel, and when teachers became ill, the situation worsened, and many lessons had to be cancelled. Material resources, for example, the school building and, in particular, the sanitation equipment for students in some schools, were in bad shape. Over half of the student population in each of the schools were exempted from paying for books and materials due to the SES of their families. Regarding improving these input factors, the schools needed extra support from both the LEA and Central Educational Authorities (CEA), and also needed to enhance their network in the local community.

The *throughput factors* included work on organisational structures, establishing a leadership team and middle-management and improving communication, coordination and cooperation throughout the school organisation.

Considering the aims of the project and previous research on developing schools in difficult circumstances, two types of *output* were defined: first, output on the school level, such as the perceptions of key actors (school leaders, teachers, support teams, students and parents) of the overall quality of the school, including teaching and learning environments. For school staff, a particular focus was directed towards perceptions of their work conditions. The second type of output includes student outcomes (e.g., the results of VERA tests and student completion rates) (Fig. 11.1).

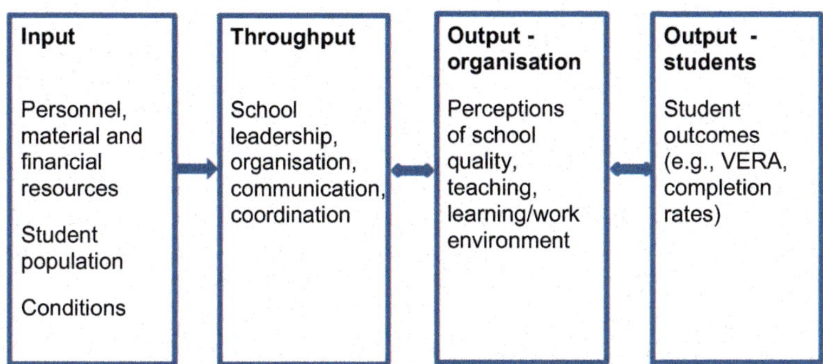

Fig. 11.1 Theoretical approach: input, throughput and output factors (Huber et al., 2017)

The logic of the model implies that coordinated support and interventions targeted towards input and throughput factors would lead to school improvements on organisational and student levels, but also that the interplay between throughput and output factors are important. This model differs from prevailing school turnaround models due to its focus on throughput factors rather than factors such as exchanging school staff and student output.

The research project draws on a mixed methods and longitudinal design, which included three rounds of semi-structured interviews with actors in the participating schools (3 × 80 interviews from the first, third and fifth year with school leaders, teachers, support staff, students and parents in the project schools), and interviews from the first and final years with project stakeholders and system actors (2 × 27 interviews with the project leaders, the reference group, coaches, local authorities, representatives from the state authority, and the Foundation).

Three surveys were conducted among school staff: teachers and school leaders in the project schools and in the 15 comparison schools in the first, third, and final years of the project (response rates: 44–48%).

For the quantitative analysis, we examined changes in results on different scales over time, as measured by Cohen's d. We looked at the partial correlation network with the Least Absolute Shrinkage and Selection Operator (LASSO) between different scales to identify stable correlation patterns. Moreover, we analysed differences in the correlation patterns between different scales over time and conducted a path analysis.

For the qualitative analysis in this chapter, we have focused on interview data from principals, teachers, school development coaches and representatives from the LEA. As such, the analysis focused on creating meanings and structures of organisational realities and change seen from multiple perspectives in the school system (cf. Connelly et al., 1999). The data selected for the analysis serve as examples to deepen and understand the key findings from the quantitative analysis.

Presentation of Findings

In the following, we concentrate on describing some of the main identified changes in the schools that demonstrate the importance of using various indicators on organisational and student levels and that recognise the importance of various factors in the development of schools in difficult circumstances. After this, we discuss the indicators used to evaluate the success of the overall project, as well as improvement logic in prevailing school turnaround approaches in the US.

An important finding in this project is the strengthened position of the principals and mid-level leaders as perceived over time by the school staff. The figure below is based on the quantitative analysis of survey data among teachers and leaders in the 10 schools. The model shows that school leadership has positively influenced how staff perceive their work conditions, which has enhanced the capacity for innovation and cooperation among teachers and support personnel, which in turn has positively impacted how the staff evaluate their overall work environment (Fig. 11.2).

Based on the qualitative study, we will describe in the following sections factors contributing to this chain of positive development in more detail, such as school leadership, time, support and important indicators of organisational change in the participating schools.

Leadership as a Key to Improvement

Findings from both the qualitative and quantitative studies showed that a well-functioning school leadership was key to improvement. The quantitative study showed that the strategic school leadership was generally strengthened during the project time – the contributions of mid-level leaders were especially considered by staff as increasingly important for motivating and initiating change. These results align with the focus of interventions in the project, and project schools developed significantly more in these areas than the comparison schools. In addition, staff reported improved information flow and transparency as related to distribution of tasks and responsibilities.

In 9 out of 10 schools, a change of principal took place either before the project started or during the lifetime of the project. The reasons for the changes before the

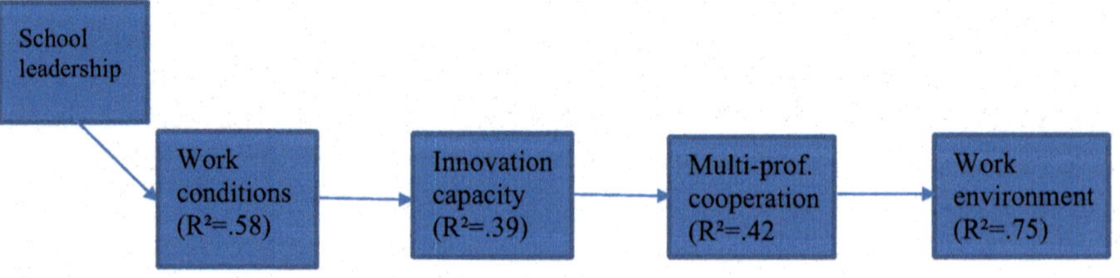

Fig. 11.2 Positive changes identified in the project schools (Huber et al., 2017)

start of the project were that principals were retiring. In three schools, a second leadership change took place during the project due to highly problematic situations in the schools. Before the change, the principals received coaching from the school development coach and additional support from LEA, but eventually the principals' contracts were terminated, and new principals were hired.

For two schools in particular, the principal was described as the 'engine' of the development process. On the one hand, this is described positively. One the other hand, the teachers find it difficult to keep up with the speed of the principal. In three schools, there were challenges with the school leadership team during the first 2–3 years of the project, and it proved difficult for the principal to start the change process when he or she was legitimised formally (due to their preliminary position as principal or having had a position as a deputy principal) to lead the change. In one of the schools, the teachers described that 'innovations were passively tolerated.' However, as the school attained a new principal, they experienced that 'she brought with her necessary drive and structures to really start the process – and we are now in the middle of a change process' (Interview 3, 2017, Teacher, School A).

In several schools, the teachers describe the importance of principals in concentrating on building relationships with them. This seems to be an important factor for developing a basis for change. The process is often described by teachers in terms of managing to align various leadership tasks and concerns; for instance, to give clear direction and secure staff commitment, or to make unpopular decisions, and at the same time, take time to listen to their concerns and provide support. In one school, this was described by teachers as the principal promoting a welcoming culture just by keeping her door open: 'By this, she showed clearly that "I am here". If you went inside, she always listened – it was not only an open door' (Interview 1, 2013, Teacher, School C).

The teachers in this school describe the strength of the principal in her collective focus when initiating and driving development projects. It was important for her that the staff agreed to move collectively in a certain direction, and joint discussions were an important strategy to manage this:

> I think she worked intensively to initiate discussions around key ideas. Mrs. X was one of the first leaders – she has not worked in our school that long – who, from the beginning, understood the importance of a joint discussion, and then decided in what direction we move (Interview 2, 2015, Teacher, School C).

The second interview round especially revealed that all the schools, independent of their project aims and with the support of the development coaches, had spent the first 2 years of the project improving the school's organisation. In particular, the principals focused on setting up the leadership team, consisting of the principals and mid-level leaders, and using these new structures to improve communication with staff. According to interviews with the development coaches as well as their written logs, they supported the schools mainly in these areas.

Development Requires Time

Originally, the project period was planned for 3 years. Parallel to improving their structure and coordination, the schools worked on the programme to establish a common ground for their work. However, the project was prolonged by a second project phase of one and half years, it was important for the schools to move their focus to improving the quality of the teaching and learning processes.

The time factor was emphasised by all the school development coaches, due to the fact that most of the schools also experienced a phase of stagnation, or that their development work was put on hold due to other pressing priorities, for instance, the large number of refugees arriving to Germany in 2015. In some of the schools the sports hall was used for housing purposes, and they had to reorganise and prepare to start up "welcome classes". All the schools developed new school programmes and started to work on innovative teaching concepts and strategies to meet the needs of heterogenous student groups. However, the initiated changes did not reach the classrooms of all schools during the project period. One of the school development coaches stated the following:

> [...] the teachers have stated: 'Yes, we want to do this, and we plan this...", in other words there is a shift in attitudes among staff, it was even noticed by the school inspectors. However, so far, this did not impact the teaching and this will take time. But the teachers are willing to change – this is clear (Interview, 2017).

This quote illustrates that there is a need to develop and improve organisational aspects as well as to work on a collective change of attitudes among staff before teachers are ready to take concrete steps to change their practice.

Development Requires Support

The school development coaches were regarded as important partners by the principals in initiating and implementing changes, and continuous and open conversations were highly valued. One of the principals particularly emphasised the role of the school development coach in backing her and the school up:

> She always encouraged me to move on by reinforcing that this is the right direction and that we must continue. Personally, I perceived that she followed us through the process by her way of positive reinforcement (Interview, Principal, 2017)

The frequency of contact and meetings varied according to the needs of the principals and many of the school development coaches invested in the project,

> We always had an open conversation and we usually talked a lot on the phone and on the weekends. It was intensive and productive, and we went through everything critically. In this school I did not have to deal with resistance from the principal. I coached her throughout the process, and we had at least weekly contact, either over the phone or we met in the school. I also had contact with the school staff (Interview, School Development Coach, 2017).

The quote above also indicates possible problems in some schools. The degree of fit between the principal and the school development coach was crucial for their collaborative work. In some schools, the school development coach was replaced after a while. It was emphasised that the school development coaches needed work experience from the school system to understand the conditions and not just the school context.

Generally, the school development coaches viewed their roles as keeping the schools on track by reminding them what they previously had agreed on in meetings, by establishing new routines and by reflecting, together with the principals, the best way to make difficult decisions:

> In the coaching sessions we had the opportunity to talk about issues that were not so easy to talk about in bigger groups, such as how to deal with staff who do not manage their tasks because of lack of competency (Interview, School Development Coach, 2017).

The support of LEA was particularly important with respect to hiring staff, where the responsibility of finding a suitable work environment for each teacher to identify and contribute to necessary change processes, such as key pedagogical concepts, was vital. As one representative stated:

> You can only change a school through the people who work there. You would need to accept them as they are and start the process of convincing them. It is, however, a difficult and slow process [...] (Interview, 2017).

An important factor to succeed in improving these schools was described as the collective spirit and willingness to change, and some representatives expressed the wish to have more authority to reallocate teachers who were not willing to commit themselves to invest in necessary collective efforts.

Improvement of the School's Organisation and Student Outcomes

As previously described, the results of focusing on improving the school's organisation has led to better work environments and is demonstrated by strengthening school leadership, improving work conditions, increasing innovation capacity and intensifying cooperation among staff. These improvements were additionally demonstrated by several key figures in the new system of indicators, which was established by CEA during the project. For instance, in all the schools, the number of sick days and the number of cancelled lessons for staff decreased, as did the number of absence days for students (Huber et al., 2017). Moreover, the number of violent incidents decreased in schools where this was previously a problem. Finally, completion rates increase slightly and the number of students signing up for the lower secondary schools increased. The quantitative survey results of the ten project schools, as well as the indicator results reported above, showed a significant difference in improvement compared to schools that were selected for the comparison group. Even though some improvements with respect to the VERA-data can be observed, it is hard to relate this effect to the interventions and development work conducted by the schools. There is also a clear limitation of using such data, since the tests are conducted in 8th grade when students have completed 1 year in the integrated secondary schools. While the other types of data are longitudinal, these are cross-sectional, and it is questionable whether these data can be used to evaluate schools' success using a turnaround approach.

Discussion and Conclusion

The findings demonstrate how a model of school turnaround is influenced by school governing approaches, traditions and culture in a specific country. The results may contradict prevailing evidence-based logic of school turnaround approaches from the US, where the main indicator of change is the improvement of student performance as measured by standardised tests. Instead, the findings reflect the importance of project organisation, planning, timeline and involvement of stakeholders for the implementation process and project results.

Essential outcomes become clear: While the United States turnaround models are designed to be relatively radical with regard to school closures and staff layoffs, the project in Germany relies heavily on supporting the schools, empowering and increasing the competence of the school/internal stakeholders, and promoting various forms of cooperation with school/internal stakeholders. School leadership seems to be an important key factor in all projects. School leaders, who are able to restore the ability to act by establishing an appropriate leadership organisation and focus their work on pedagogical issues, play a special role. In England, there is a strong reliance on school networks, where schools in difficult situations collaborate, network, or even merge institutionally with successful schools in the area. Due to cultural and legal differences, solutions from the international context have to be examined closely, but within the framework of the melioristic function of international comparative educational research and educational planning, they represent an extremely interesting potential for simulation.

All of the strategies outlined in the above cases are part of school turnaround, but they are not a quick-fix recipe for success. To be successful in the long run, different approaches are needed that are tailored exactly to the unique circumstances of the individual school and contextualised to the respective school system. This paper reports various interventions integrated in a development process as a promising way to provide support to principals and schools according to their contextual challenges and individual needs. In our perspective, a 'turnaround process' needs to be viewed as a long-term process requiring concerted efforts with professional, profound and persistent action by all of the involved stakeholders. In addition to the intervention architecture, the school authorities and school leadership team are part of the first successful steps, followed by a gradual involvement of the entire staff. However, it should also be kept in mind that all school interventions are limited.

Assuming that schools in difficult circumstances are often found in low SES catchment areas, and that the effect on a school explains about 10–40% of the variance in student achievement, it becomes clear that much more complex interventions are needed that go beyond the reach of the school and include the school environment. Schools cannot compensate for all the weaknesses and shortcomings of a community or a society, and no matter how well-intended and professional school development is, it cannot absorb the difficult social circumstances in which students live outside of school. Ultimately, the key to school improvement lies in political action and measures that focus not only on the individual school or the school system but also on community development in terms of poverty, unemployment, health deficits, deficient housing, educational difficulties and lack of life-management strategies of parents, to name but a few.

In the following we will summarise some important lessons learnt from the school turnaround project in Germany:

- School leadership is key to initiating and driving change, which are collectively supported
- School turnaround is a complex process and principals need support to lead the necessary change
- From top-down to participatory approaches, mid-level leaders can improve communication and transparency and ensure commitment
- Improved innovation capacity and cooperation are important factors for change and development
- Interventions are needed that are adaptive to the individual school's needs

Schools in difficult situations need targeted help in deriving school-specific goals from the programme objectives in conjunction with the organisational diagnosis. It is important to ensure coherence by focusing on improving the school's organisation first, by strengthening the leadership team and middle-management, focusing on staff work conditions and then building the innovation capacity through strengthening the cooperation between school actors. An overall improved school organisation provides a good basis to change and renew classroom practices along with agreed concepts and the school programme.

In addition, the overall intervention measures need to be managed well, and systematically coordinated measures must have clearly defined objectives. This may be easier in smaller organisational units. Overall, it is mainly about the work on structures and processes, the behaviour of staff members, and the other, undoubtedly complex, aspects that make up school culture.

Finally, suitable indicators of success need to be carefully selected by taking the interventions and development work of the schools into account as part of an adaptive and coherent evaluation. We argue that further research on development in schools in difficult circumstances is needed to further explore the contextual challenges of schools and what kind of interventions can contribute to improvement of the whole school's organisation, classroom practices and student outcomes in a broader sense. In further research, it is necessary to question what is counted as 'evidence' and the use and abuse of the term 'evidence-based' in school development processes that require highly contextualised knowledge and skills to initiate and drive change processes. According to the Norwegian philosopher Kvernbekk, 'based' in 'evidence-based' creates a misunderstanding (2011). She emphasizes that what makes something evidence is that it stands in a certain relation to a hypothesis, namely confirmation or disconfirmation. Her point is that 'facts are not made to support a hypothesis, but they can be recognized as supportive or not supportive' (2011, p. 532). Evidence-based practice suggests that we choose – in this case – an approach to school development which is well supported.

References

Ainscow, M., West, M., & Nicolaidou, M. (2004). Putting our heads together: A study of head-teacher collaboration as a strategy for school improvement. In P. Clarke (Ed.), *Improving schools in difficulty* (pp. 117–136). Continuum.

Altrichter, H., Gußner, N., & Maderthaner, P. (2008). Failing schools—Auf der Suche nach der, schlechten Schule. Ein Literaturüberblick [In search of the "bad school". A literature review]. *Journal für Schulentwicklung, 1*, 43–55.

Altrichter, H., & Merki, K. M. (2010). *Handbuch Neue Steuerung im Schulsystem*. Springer.

Altrichter, H., & Moosbrugger, R. (2011). Schulen in Schwierigkeiten. Was sagt die Schulforschung über Anzeichen, Ursachen und Lösungen? [Schools in Difficulties. What does research say about characteristics, reasons and solutions]. *Lernende Schule, 14*(56), 8–11.

Baumert, J., Stanat, P., & Watermann, R. (2006). *Herkunftsbedingte Disparitäten im Bildungswesen. Vertiefende Analysen im Rahmen von PISA 2000*. VS Verlag für Sozialwissenschaften.

Böttcher, W., & Kotthoff, H.-G. (2007). *Schulinspktion: Evaluation, Rechenschaftslegung und Qualitätsentwicklung*. Waxmann.

Bryk, A. S., Gomez, L. M., Grunow, A., & LeMehieu, P. G. (2015). *Learning to improve. How America's schools can get better at getting better*. Harward Education Press.

Clarke, P. (2004). Endpiece: Legitimacy and action. In P. Clarke (Ed.), *Improving schools in difficulty* (pp. 172–181). Continuum.

Connelly, F. M., Clandinin, D. J., & Applebaum, S. D. (Eds.). (1999). *Shaping a professional identity: Stories of educational practice*. Teachers College Press.

Cronbach, L., Gleser, G. C., Nanda, H., & Nageswari R. (1972). *The dependability of behavioral measurements. Theory of generalizability for scores and profiles*. Wiley.

Datnow, A., & Stringfield, S. (2000). Working together for reliable school reform. *Journal of Education for Students Placed at Risk (JESPAR), 5*(1–2), 183–204.

Gunter, H., Hall, D., Serpieri, R., & Grimaldi, E. (2016). *New public management and the reform of education: European lessons for policy and practice*. Routledge.

Harris, A., & Chapman, C. (2002). Leadership in schools facing challenging circumstances. *Management in Education, 16*(1), 10–13.

Hochbein, C. (2012). Relegation and reversion: Longitudinal analysis of school turnaround and decline. *Journal of Education for Students Placed at Risk, 17*(1–2), 92–107.

Hopmann, S. T. (2008). No child, no school, no state left behind: Schooling in the age of accountability. *Journal of Curriculum Studies, 40*(4), 417–456.

Huber, S. G. (2013). Perspektiven für Schulen in kritischer Lage. Expertise zum Projekt „School Turnaround: Berliner Schulen starten durch". Robert Bosch Stiftung.

Huber, S. G. (2018). No simple fixes for schools in challenging circumstances. Contextualisation for Germany. In C. Meyers (Ed.), *International perspectives on leading low-performing schools* (pp. 243–266). Information Age Publishing.

Huber, S. G., Hader-Popp, S., & Schneider, N. (2014). *Qualität und Entwicklung von Schule: Basiswissen Schulmanagement*. Beltz.

Huber, S. G., & Muijs, R. (2012). Schulentwicklung bei besonders belasteten Schulen. *Schulverwaltung spezial, 14*(2), 9–13.

Huber, S. G., Skedsmo, G., Pham, G. H., Koszuta, A., Karwat, K., Schwander, M., Kots, S., & Luig, C. (2017). Schlussbericht der wissenschaftlichen Begleitung zum Projekt *School Turnaround*. *Report*.

Kutash, J., Nico, E., Gorin, E., Rahmatullah, S., & Tallant, K. (2010). *The school turnaround field guide. Social impact advisors*. New York: FSG Social Impact Advisors. Abgerufen von http://www.wallacefoundation.org/knowledge-center/Documents/The-School-Turnaround-Field-Guide.pdf

Kvernbekk, T. (2011). The concept of evidence in evidence-based practice. *Educational Theory, 61*(5), 515–532.

Levy, J. (2019). Methodological issues in value-added modeling: An international review from 26 countries. *Educational Assessment, Evaluation and Accountability, 31*(3), 257–287.

Meyers, C. V. (2013). School turnaround as National Policy in the United States: Considerations from three studies conducted in the Midwest. *Journal of International and Comparative Education, 2*(2), 98–11.

Meyers, C. V., & Hitt, D. H. (2017). Planning for school turnaround in the United States: An analysis of the quality of principal-developed quick wins. *School Effectiveness and School Improvement, 29*(3), 362–382.

Meyer, C., Wronowski, M., & Van Groningen, B. (2021). Preparing for the worst: Identifying predictors of school decline as an improvement initiative. *Educational Assessment, Evaluation and Accountability, 33*(2), 255–290.

Mintrop, H. (2004). High-stakes accountability, state oversight, and educational equity. *Teachers College Record, 106*(11), 2128–2145.

Muijs, D., Harris, A., Chapman, C., Stoll, L., & Russ, J. (2004). Improving schools in socio-economically disadvantaged areas: An overview of research. *School Effectiveness and School Improvement, 15*(2), 149–176.

Murphy, J. (2008). The place of leadership in turnaround schools: Insights from organizational recovery in the public and private sectors. *Journal of Educational Administration, 46*(1), 74–98.

Murphy, & Meyers. (2008). *Turning around failing schools: Leadership lessons from the organizational sciences*. Corwin Press.

Potter, D., Reynolds, D., & Chapman, C. (2002). School improvement for schools facing challenging circumstances: A review of research and practice. *School Leadership & Management, 22*(3), 243–256.

Racherbäumer, K., Funke, C., van Ackeren, I., & Clausen, M. (2013). Datennutzung und Schulleitungshandeln an Schulen in weniger begünstigter Lage. Empirische Befunde zu ausgewählten Aspekten der Qualitätsentwicklung. In *Die Deutsche Schule 13, Beiheft 12, S* (pp. 226–254). Waxmann.

Reid, W. A. (1998). Systems and structures or myths and fables? A cross-cultural perspective on curriculum content. In B. B. Gundem & S. T. Hopmann (Eds.), *Didaktik and/or curriculum: An international dialogue*. Peter Lang.

Webb, P. T. (2006). The choreography of accountability. *Journal of Education Policy, 21*(2), 201–214.

Westbury, I., Hopmann, S., & Riquarts, K. (2000). *Teaching as a reflelctive practice. The German Didaktik Tradition*. Routledge.

Williamson, B. (2017). *Big Data in education: The digital future of learning, policy and practice*. Sage.

Part IV
Conclusions and Looking Ahead

Finally, in this part, we draw on lessons across the Arizona project and school development in South Carolina, Sweden, Australia, and Germany to offer conclusions and thoughts about next steps for contextually sensitive and multi-level school development as well as cross-national dialogue and research.

Chapter 12
Concluding Comments and Looking Ahead

Rose M. Ylimaki and Lynnette A. Brunderman

Abstract This chapter provides concluding reflections and implications for future work in school development amidst global trends toward evidence-based practice, tensions between centralization of curriculum and evaluation policy and the needs of particular, and increasingly diverse communities, schools, and students. We see the globalization of evidence-based school development policies and university-community partnerships, the use of generalizable models developed from experimental design, and increasingly diverse demographics in schools. Thus, we have argued that context matters; evidence does not necessarily mean that a model developed from an experimental design is appropriate for a problem of practice in particular school settings. At the same time, school and district leaders benefit from dialogue within levels and beyond as they work toward improvement in order to navigate the Zone of Uncertainty in their particular school and community context and in relation to particular problems of practice affecting schools in other communities, other states, or even other nation states.

Keywords Multi-level school development · Context · Process · International dialgoue

This chapter provides concluding reflections and implications for future work in school development amidst global trends toward evidence-based practice, tensions between centralization of curriculum and evaluation policy and the needs of particular and increasingly diverse communities, schools, and students. We can observe global borrowing and lending (Steiner-Khamsi, 2006) of evidence-based school development policies and university-community partnerships, the use of

R. M. Ylimaki (✉)
Northern Arizona University, Flagstaff, AZ, USA
e-mail: rose.ylimaki@nau.edu

L. A. Brunderman
University of Arizona, Tucson, AZ, USA
e-mail: lbrunder@arizona.com

© The Author(s) 2022

R. M. Ylimaki, L. A. Brunderman (eds.), *Evidence-Based School Development in Changing Demographic Contexts*, Studies in Educational Leadership 24, https://doi.org/10.1007/978-3-030-76837-9_12

generalizable models developed from experimental design, and increasingly diverse demographics in schools. Thus, as we review in Chap. 1, many scholars and educators have argued that context matters; evidence does not necessarily mean that a model developed from an experimental design is appropriate for a problem of practice in particular school settings. At the same time, school and district leaders benefit from dialogue within levels and beyond as part of a network of improvement (Bryk et al., 2015) in order to navigate the zone of uncertainty in their particular school and community context and in relation to particular problems of practice affecting schools in other communities, other states, or even other nation states.

In this volume, then, we propose school development amidst what we call the zone of uncertainty, including an evolution of policies aimed at school development or improvement and equity as well as changing demographics. Chapters in this volume review popular approaches to school development designed to provide evidence-based generalizable models aimed at measurable and sustainable improvements as well as recent critiques about the exclusive use of such approaches in all school contexts and for all problems. Critiques of these models also feature reliance on organizational systems change and improvement without explicit attention to education traditions and values or the broader culture and needs of communities (e.g. health, poverty) and the needs of increasingly diverse students within communities. Moreover, critiques feature the lack of attention to schools or even districts in relation to states, nation states, and the globe. The approach featured in the Arizona process as well as in school development processes in Sweden, Germany, Australia and another U.S. state, South Carolina, extends the literature on school improvement models with explicit attention to the cultural, historical, and policy context and to multi-levels of development needed for sustainable, long-term change. More specifically, we propose that school development is a multi-level process grounded in education and sensitive to the cultural and historical situation as well as the needs of the contemporary situation in particular schools, districts, states, nation states, and communities within them.

We describe in detail a school development project whereby university faculty partnered with the state (ABOR) and districts to provide professional development for leadership teams in persistently underperforming Arizona schools. The Arizona project served over 70 persistently underperforming schools over a five-year period. Essentially, the model was designed to build team leadership capacity for sustainable school development in schools that were persistently underperforming but not yet designated for turnaround status. Importantly, the project was developed across the state of Arizona in relation to state-administered curriculum and evaluation policies as these state policies related to national policies and global trends toward curriculum and evaluation centralization (e.g. Common Core and related externalized evaluation policy pressures). Prior to our initial application of school development in the Arizona Institute for Leadership Development and Research (AZiLDR), we had conducted research on principals in successful schools as part of the International Successful School Principalship Project (ISSPP) and related leadership studies. The ISSPP is a network of researchers from 27 different countries, including Sweden, Australia, and the United States. In addition, as the project evolved in relation to our own findings, we drew upon literature on leadership capacity (Bennett, 2012; Mitchell & Sackney, 2009) and culturally responsive leadership (e.g. Johnson, 2007; Scanlan & López, 2014) as well as theories guiding education amidst changing demographics (Dewey, 1887, 1916; Uljens & Ylimaki, 2017). Further, the project was grounded in a research-based delivery system (Desimone, 2009) and evaluation results and lessons from our work over a five-year period. Over time, results were positive and indicated the need for attention to process and use of common elements (i.e. the school culture, leadership capacity, curriculum and pedagogical traditions, evidence as a source of reflection, and culturally responsive practices) in relation to particular problems of practice more than an aim toward the development of a generalizable model.

Results of the Arizona project were analyzed using quantitative (a pre- and post-survey measuring leadership and school capacity; school letter grades based on student outcomes) and qualitative (interviews and observations) methods. Research results and lessons from that project implementation indicated the importance of key elements in the school development process, including values and culture, leadership capacity, direction and goals, use of data for reflection and feedback, curriculum and pedagogical activity, and strengths-based approaches for diverse populations. Each element required attention to communication with levels beyond the school, including particularly the district and state department of education officials. Moreover, each element required a readiness for change and a culture of trust and positive relationships as well as explicit attention to the other elements. With the ultimate goal of diffusing the learning throughout the school as part of a microcosm of democratic education within individual schools, this was imperative. The district representative was chosen in consultation with the superintendent; this individual was an integral part of the school team, offering insight and buffering them from competing district initiatives that could derail their progress. Additionally, regional coaches provided expertise to school teams, participating in all phases of the project. State representatives were also included in order to facilitate leadership team teaching or pedagogical activity and mediation with district and state policy. In other words, the elements and processes were designed to work together to support leadership capacity for education in continuous school development. Chapters in Part II further describe these elements, applications, and lessons from case studies.

In Part III, chapters feature school development in another U.S. state of South Carolina as well as contributions from Sweden, Australia, and Germany, especially focusing on the policies, underlying conceptions of education and leadership, and pointing at the need for a long-term, community-based approach with a common language to communicate about school development within and between levels (district or municipality, state, nation state and increasingly transnationally). Lessons from the Arizona project along with learning from the Carnegie ILead network informed school development projects in South Carolina; however, the South Carolina project was also developed for the particular and somewhat different cultural and historical context of schools in that state. In South Carolina, many schools are situated in rural areas and serve many students whose families are part of an historical legacy of slavery and black-white racism as well as subsequent civil rights movements and more recent demographic shifts to include refugees and a growing number of LatinX from internal demographic shifts. Rural schools with increasingly diverse students also suffer from reduced state and local tax base funding (the so-called I-95 Corridor of Shame). In the South Carolina school development chapter (Moyi, Hardie & Cunningham, this volume), we see a South Carolina school development project from the same nation state (USA) informed by a common leadership research base as well as practical lessons from the Arizona project and yet contextualized for particular state policies, culture, and needs of schools and students.

Similarly, in Australia, Gurr, Acquaro, and Drysdale (this volume) provide several examples of distinct evidence-based school development at multi-levels (national, state, local school) amidst the complex and changing context of policies, an increasing scrutiny of testing, and demographic shifts. The first example features national school-wide improvement initiatives and two programs are described. IDEAS (Innovative Designs for Enhancing Achievements in Schools), is an extensive and on-going school improvement project that has developed a framework for establishing professional learning communities to improve school literacy outcomes. The second example explores the state level through considering work at the Melbourne Graduate School of Education in terms of evidence-based teacher training through the development of a clinical teaching model, and evidence-based school improvement through the Science of Learning Schools Partnership Initiative which utilizes a cycle of inquiry approach to develop an important learning focus. Finally, the Australian chapter provides an example of two government schools in challenging circumstances that have developed their own individual school improvement strategy based on several sources including evidence-based research, school data and effective decision-making processes. Here we see positive results from both the centrally developed model and the bottom-up, school-developed approaches, with both improvement processes explicitly responsive to the contexts of schools and surrounding communities as well as the demands of policies. Although specific terminology varies among the centralized and school-based approaches, the potential for broad-based school development is evident. Moreover, as Gurr et al. (this volume) clearly illustrate, for school autonomy to make a difference for students, professional autonomy and strong leadership is required.

In Sweden, school development is initiated at the national level with policy documents and inspection reports as well as university support in dialogue at that level. However, as Johansson and Ärlestig (this volume) also point out, despite a system of inspections and a clear national policy, there is often a lack of a common language for articulating problems and theories of actions, and for describing school processes and change (Lindensjö & Lundgern, 2000). Johansson and Ärlestig examine a hierarchical chain from the government though their agencies down to the local municipalities and the school district and the schools, questioning the extent to which this chain of communication is characterized by authority or trust. Moreover, there is a lack of coherent language across and between levels, and this lack of coherence affects the ways in which leaders at different levels (national to school) approach the problem. Likewise, school development approaches in other contexts note similar challenges and the need for a common language of communication, one that features a language of education.

Germany is experiencing similar policy trends toward evidence-based school development as well as demographic shifts due to a recent influx of refugees and other global population migrations. In recent years, Germany has implemented externalized evaluation policies and borrowed from turnaround models from the U.S. and the U.K. In this chapter, Huber and Skedsmo (this volume) report on research findings from a school development project in a large city in Germany over a five-year period. In this project, school turnaround is defined more broadly to include local and central authorities in order that the school's stakeholders would provide contextual knowledge and ownership for school improvement efforts. Results from the project were promising in terms of improved student outcomes, the importance of leadership, time for sustained effort, and a school development coach but also point toward the need for an adaptive approach that is more aligned with the country's educational traditions and governance context.

Drawing on findings from all school development work in this volume, we argue two points: (1) school development must be considered as a multi-level education and mediational process, one that would benefit from coherent mechanisms for reflection and communication within and between levels around key elements (e.g. leadership capacity, autonomy, culture, education traditions, including curriculum and pedagogical activity, use of data or evidence, culturally responsive practices) and evaluations (qualitative data as in policy and inspection reports/document analysis as well as quantitative data from student testing) from schools and districts or municipalities to states (if appropriate), national levels and increasingly at transnational levels; and (2) school development must be considered as a contextual process, one that is explicitly sensitive to the culture and needs of students as well as to the time and support necessary for improvements to be developed and sustained. We see this volume as a beginning attempt toward a multi-level, contextually based school development process, one that features a cross-national dialogue for exchange and support.

To begin, the review and comparison of school development approaches and examples in various national and local contexts helps us to better see connections among global trends, national policies, state policies, district policies and school approaches as well as the need for contextually-based and educationally relevant work on problems of practice. Like Australia, Germany, and the U.S., the Swedish chapter criticizes traditional top-down policy requirements for school development that promote the use of evidence-based models tested with randomized controlled trials or experiments and that assume the same capacity for implementation at lower levels and the same contextual problems of practice. A research-based mechanism, coherent language and structure for pedagogical activity, and coherent language for other communication about the school development processes among university, policy, and practitioner levels may serve as a point of departure to understand school development amidst the contemporary situation. Further, this common language for school development and evaluation thereof may support efforts toward comparative research on how school development and educational leadership is implemented between policy documents and leadership at different levels and in different cultural and historical contexts.

This volume features university faculty working in partnership with educational leaders on problems of practice, developing culturally relevant solutions to particular problems. Some of these solutions actually utilize externally developed solutions to educational problems of practice but contextualize them to fit particular situations and the needs of students. In other instances, solutions are developed on-site from the ground up. While these school development processes vary to a degree across national contexts, all of these processes include some attention to elements like school culture, leadership capacity and cooperation, curriculum work, pedagogical leadership and effectiveness in classrooms, use of data or evidence as a source of reflection, and cultural sensitivity and responsiveness.

Going forward, we plan to draw on the strengths of the different approaches in Sweden, Australia, Germany, the US, and perhaps elsewhere to develop a contextually sensitive school development process, including a structure for mediation and communication with a common language about school development that extends beyond the school level to include districts, policy leaders (state and national) as well as translational organizations. In all of the chapters, communication between schools and districts supports coherence but does not always leave room for exploration of alternative ways to approach the same problem of practice. Further, school development work and communication between schools and districts does not necessarily extend to policy levels nor do policy language and expectations necessarily reach schools and districts/municipalities. Development with national policy leaders is more explicit in the Swedish case and with state and national policy leaders in the case of Australia, Germany, and the U.S. In other words, we see an advantage to combine the strengths of communication and school development processes and elements across all of the cases to develop a culturally sensitive and multi-level approach to school development.

We also see opportunities for cross-national research and leadership development as well as cross-institutional courses or programs that give explicit attention to education traditions and interculturality. With technology and existing international co-operations (e.g. ISSPP, ISLDN), there will be opportunities to work across institutional and national boundaries in ways that may benefit increasingly pluralistic student needs within these and other national states. Other scholars have provided a foundation for understanding mutual influences among levels from schools to various policy levels, including Louis et al.'s (2010) project funded by the Wallace Foundation on leadership influences on student learning whereby school leadership, from formal and informal sources, helps to shape school conditions (including goals, culture, and structures) and classroom conditions (including curriculum, the size of classrooms, and the pedagogy used by teachers). Here many factors within and outside schools and classrooms help to shape teachers' sense of professional community. School and classroom conditions, teachers' professional communities, and student/family background conditions are directly responsible for the learning of students. Drawing on another stream of literature, we support a strengths-based approach to education as essential for successful school development in culturally diverse schools, communities, and nation states. As noted in Chap. 6 and throughout the chapters from Sweden, Australia and Germany, education in school development lies in the pedagogical relations and provocations into the self-realizations and growth of increasingly diverse young people. Thus, we consider Moll et al.'s (2006) research on teachers' connections with children's cultural background strengths or funds of knowledge (Moll et al., 2006) and leadership scholars' (e.g., Johnson, 2006; Scanlan & López, 2014) applications of culturally responsive pedagogy and *funds of knowledge* to leadership practice. Johnson (2006) define culturally responsive leadership as leadership that involves philosophies, practices, and policies that create inclusive schooling environments for students and families from ethnically and culturally diverse backgrounds. Scanlan and López draw on culturally responsive leadership practices that reduce marginalization and successfully educate what they term the new mainstream of students.

The school development processes in this volume extend and contribute lessons and examples beyond the mainstream turnaround literature from the U.S. and the U.K. Findings and lessons from the featured school development efforts in Germany, Australia, Sweden and the U.S. may support the development of a new international dialogue with a common, coherent, and intercultural language around *how* leadership capacity for education and school development can be supported and sustained within and between all levels that must be open to new uncertainties.

References

Bennett, J. V. (2012). "Democratic" collaboration for school turnaround in Southern Arizona. *International Journal of Educational Management, 26*(5), 442–451.

Bryk, A. S., Gomez, L. M., Grunow, A., & LeMahieu, P. G. (2015). *Learning to improve: How America's schools can get better at getting better*. Harvard Education Press.

Desimone, L. M. (2009). Improving impact studies of teachers' professional development: Toward better conceptualizations and measures. *Educational Researcher, 38*(3), 181–199.

Dewey, J. (1887). My pedagogic creed. In M. S. Dworkin (Ed.), *Dewey on education*.

Dewey, J. (1916). *Democracy in education*. The Free Press.

Johnson, L. (2006). "Making her community a better place to live": Culturally responsive urban school leadership in historical context. *Leadership and Policy in Schools, 5*(1), 19–36.

Johnson, L. (2007). Rethinking successful school leadership in challenging US schools: Culturally responsive practices in school-community relationships. *International Studies in Educational Administration (Commonwealth Council for Educational Administration & Management (CCEAM)), 35*(3).

Lindensjö, B., & Lundgern, U. P. (2000). *Utbildningsreformer och politisk styrning/Education reforms and political governess*. HLS Förlag.

Louis, K. S., Leithwood, K., Wahlstrom, K. L., & Anderson, S. E. (2010). *Investigating the links to improved student learning: Final report of research findings*. University of Minnesota.

Mitchell, C., & Sackney, L. (2009). Sustainable improvement. *Building learning communities that endure*.

Moll, L., Amanti, C., Neff, D., & Gonzalez, N. (2006). Funds of knowledge for teaching: Using a qualitative approach to connect homes and classrooms. In *Funds of knowledge* (pp. 83–100). Routledge.

Scanlan, M., & López, F. A. (2014). *Leadership for culturally and linguistically responsive schools*. Routledge.
Steiner-Khamsi, G. (2006). The economics of policy borrowing and lending: A study of late adopters. *Oxford Review of Education, 32*(5), 665–678.
Uljens, M., & Ylimaki, R. M. (2017). Chapter 1: Non-affirmative theory of education and foundation of curriculum studies, Didaktik, and educational leadership. In M. Uljens & R. M. Ylimaki (Eds.), *Bridging educational leadership, curriculum theory, and Didaktik: Non-affirmative theory of education* (pp. 3–145). Springer.

Printed by Printforce, United Kingdom